New Perspectives in Mormon Studies

New Perspectives in Mormon Studies
Creating and Crossing Boundaries

Edited by

QUINCY D. NEWELL and ERIC F. MASON

Foreword by

JAN SHIPPS

UNIVERSITY OF OKLAHOMA PRESS : NORMAN

Also by Quincy D. Newell

Constructing Lives at Mission San Francisco: Native Californians and Hispanic Colonists, 1776–1821 (Albuquerque, 2009)

Also by Eric F. Mason

'You Are a Priest Forever': Second Temple Jewish Messianism and the Priestly Christology of the Epistle to the Hebrews (Leiden, The Netherlands, 2008)

(co-ed.) *Theology in the Service of the Church: Essays Presented to Fisher H. Humphreys* (Macon, Ga., 2008)

(co-ed.) *Reading the Epistle to the Hebrews: A Resource for Students* (Atlanta, 2011)

(ed.) *A Teacher for All Generations: Essays in Honor of James C. VanderKam* (Leiden, The Netherlands, 2012)

Library of Congress Cataloging-in-Publication Data

National Endowment for the Humanities. Summer Seminar (2005 : Brigham Young University)

New perspectives in Mormon studies : creating and crossing boundaries / edited by Quincy D. Newell and Eric F. Mason ; foreword by Jan Shipps.

pages cm

Includes index.

ISBN 978-0-8061-4313-2 (pbk. : alk. paper) 1. Church of Jesus Christ of Latter-day Saints—History—Congresses. 2. Church of Jesus Christ of Latter-day Saints—Doctrines—Congresses. 3. Mormon Church—History—Congresses. 4. Mormon Church—Doctrines—Congresses. I. Newell, Quincy D., 1975– editor. II. Mason, Eric Farrel, editor. III. Title.

BX8611.N38 2005

289.3—dc23

2012022270

The paper in this book meets the guidelines for permanence and durability of the Committee on Production Guidelines for Book Longevity of the Council on Library Resources, Inc. ∞

In fond memory of Kenneth Hovey
October 17, 1945–May 25, 2006

Contents

Foreword

Jan Shipps

The interest and excitement surrounding the impending 2002 Winter Olympic Games in Salt Lake City led to the twenty-first century's initial "Mormon moment" when both the print and electronic media concentrated attention on the Latter-day Saints and the land where they lived. Many—perhaps even most—of the feature stories about the imminent sports event alerted readers and listeners to the reality that Mormons lived nearly everywhere around the globe. But since the Winter Games were held in Salt Lake City and the surrounding area, the public envisioned a bounded Mormon world with dazzling natural beauty and striking religious architecture, one inhabited by a polite and welcoming population living in what seemed, in those glorious days, to be truly a "promised land."

Three years later, yet another "moment" shaped a very different boundary around Mormonism as members of the Church of Jesus Christ of Latter-day Saints and members of other organizations whose genesis was the life of Joseph Smith celebrated the second centennial of their prophet's birth. Created from the inside rather than the outside, this was an institutional and cultural, rather than a geographical, boundary. Yet it had the same quality that a boundary always has: it made some people insiders and others outsiders. By this time, however, a number of intellectuals had become either "inside-outsiders" (people who were not and had never been Mormon, but who over the course of a career of study had become so much a part of the group that they appeared to themselves and others as essentially "insiders") or "outside-insiders" (people who were religiously and/or culturally Mormon but who had become so familiar with the study of other groups that, for all practical purposes, they functioned as outsiders). There were enough of these intellectuals—both inside-outsiders and outside-insiders—to make Joseph Smith's two hundredth birthday the occasion for two signal scholarly events that held boundary-crossing potential. The first was a two-day symposium on "The Worlds of Joseph Smith," cosponsored by and held at the Library of Congress in cooperation with Brigham Young University.[1] The other was a National Endowment for the Humanities seminar at BYU on "Joseph Smith and the Origins of Mormonism," papers from which are included in this volume. These were significant events, important because they pushed up against the boundaries of this particular Mormon moment by adding the boundaries of academic disciplines to the boundary set by being a part of a Mormon institution and/or Mormon culture.

Recognizing and describing the spatial boundaries around Mormonism created by the Olympic Games and the institutional and cultural boundaries created for the observance of the birth of the founder of the Mormon movement is far less difficult than identifying the nature of the boundaries surrounding Mormonism in two other Mormon moments in the twenty-first century: the 2007–2008 and 2011–2012 campaigns of Mormon Mitt Romney for the Republican nomination for president of the United States.[2] In these cases, those who viewed Mormonism as a legitimate religion were divided from those who did not. The boundaries in these instances did not necessarily include the members of every institution that developed from the initial Mormon movement, but they did include Latter-day Saints—both the Republicans and Democrats who opposed Romney's candidacy and those who supported it—as well as inside-outsiders, outside-insiders, and various scholars who were well acquainted with Mormon history, sociology, psychology, theology, or most anything else Mormon, whether or not they supported Governor Romney. The boundaries excluded many evangelical Protestants, even if some of them ultimately supported Romney's bid for the presidency despite his religious background (making Sara M. Patterson's essay in this collection of particular interest). Crossing these particular boundaries did not impose the cost that the crossing of boundaries usually entails. The obvious reason is that the boundaries did not effectively divide *them* and *us*. Such a large group of U.S. citizens stood between those who, willy-nilly, stood on one side of the boundary with the Mormon candidate and those who stood on the other side of the boundary, seeing Mormonism as a non-Christian "cult," that in these two instances the boundaries were extremely porous.

The creation of boundaries that accompanied these four "Mormon moments" of the twenty-first century is evidence that there is no *single* boundary in the world of Mormonism, if there ever was one in a religious tradition that came into being in the full light of historical time. Yet because Latter-day Saints occupied and settled the Great Basin west of the Wasatch Mountains and east of the Sierra Nevada in the middle of the nineteenth century, there were spatial boundaries that separated them from those who did not believe as they did. Such a spatial walling-off gave them time to become a people with a unique understanding of Zion, their homeland, as well as the nature of life on earth and life after death. Those understandings gave rise to a stark division between Mormons and "Gentiles," now better known as non-Mormons. The boundaries between the two kinds of people were so strongly maintained that the identities of those occupying the region made for two separate cultures and two separate histories.

After World War II, the maintenance of robust identities became more difficult as first radio and then television became a part of the everyday life of Mormons as well as virtually everyone else in the nation. In addition to the presence of the Gentile world in Mormondom, so many veterans of the recent conflict went to colleges, universities, and graduate schools outside Zion that writing the traditional church-approved history, sociology, or psychology became exceedingly difficult and eventually virtually impossible. (Writing anti-Mormon works, on the other hand, continued without difficulty.)

Instead, a new Mormon history appeared in books sold in Zion as well as outside the Mormon homeland. Additionally, new publishing opportunities not connected to, nor approved by, the Mormon Church appeared, attracting readers from among the general public as well as academics. Before too long, a new sort of Mormon intellectual developed, one able to allow academic disciplinary values and traditional Mormon values to coexist without setting one or the other aside. At the same time, Gentile scholars interested in things Mormon gradually became a part of what had once been the "brotherhood" of Mormon scholars. Almost in a trice, a loosely connected cluster of scholars was crossing the boundaries into what in the twenty-first century would become Mormon studies. Familiar with what Clifford Geertz called "blurred genres," very few disdained interdisciplinary studies; nearly all saw the virtue in comparative work and in insisting on placing whatever they studied in context.

For those in the field of Mormon studies in the twenty-first century, exploring the Mormon past, and perhaps the Mormon present, is in many ways easier than ever. The existence of the internet with all its information readily at hand allows even college students to broaden and deepen their research. Computers can do the searching that once took days, weeks, and sometimes months. Moreover, the coming into being of the LDS Church History Library and its well-indexed collection permits a scholar to use a greater range of source materials. It is true that using materials produced by General Authorities of the Church of Jesus Christ of Latter-day Saints remains *verboten*. Still, the church itself and the library at Brigham Young University are publishing so many documentary sources that serious scholars doing research on Mormonism have a reasonable chance of somehow finding what they need.

The key to crossing the boundaries into Mormon studies, then, may not be access. The key is an open mind and, if needed, a willingness to study the methods of more than a single discipline. Additionally, more important than is sometimes stated is the need for scholars to talk together, share information, compare notes, and just plain enjoy learning about the Mormon past and the Mormon present.

This volume is the fruit of just such a happy combination of individual work and mutual sharing. All the essays say something new, something not said before; they represent the work of fine scholars. Of even greater significance, they reveal how crossing disciplinary boundaries enriches Mormon studies.

NOTES

1. The papers from the symposium held at the Library of Congress were published in John W. Welch, ed., *The Worlds of Joseph Smith: A Bicentennial Conference at the Library of Congress* (Provo, Utah: Brigham Young University Press, 2006).

2. Jon Huntsman, the former governor of Utah, also sought the 2012 Republican nomination for president, but he received much less attention for his Mormonism.

Acknowledgments

This book is one happy result of the 2005 National Endowment for the Humanities Summer Seminar titled "Joseph Smith and the Origins of Mormonism: Bicentennial Perspectives," hosted by Brigham Young University and directed by Richard L. Bushman and Grant Underwood. The editors and contributors gratefully acknowledge the support of the NEH, which enabled the research for, and initial drafting of, most of the essays contained herein. Any views, findings, conclusions, or recommendations expressed in these essays do not necessarily reflect those of the National Endowment for the Humanities. In addition to the leadership of Professors Bushman and Underwood, we also benefited immensely from seminar presentations by (and conversations with) Claudia Bushman, Jan Shipps, Stephen J. Stein, and Sheree Underwood. While not all of the seminar participants also contributed to this book, their feedback during the seminar was invaluable. Melvyn Hammarberg, Cynthia Hendershot, Axel Ramirez, John Wise, and Serinity Young were wonderful conversation partners for the six weeks we all shared in Provo, Utah. Another participant, Kenneth Hovey, died suddenly less than a year after the seminar. His loss saddened all of us: Ken brought a wonderful sense of humor and an incisive mind to our discussions. We dedicate this book to his memory.

Throughout most of the editing process we were privileged to work with Robert A. Clark, publisher of the Arthur H. Clark Company, and we are grateful for his guidance on this project. It was Bob who suggested that our volume would best fit the publication program of Clark's parent press, the University of Oklahoma Press, where he also was assistant director, and we are delighted that this book appears under that imprint. We are much indebted to Emily Jerman for shepherding this project after Bob's departure to become editor-in-chief at the Washington State University Press and to Ursula Smith for her many editorial contributions to our manuscript. Likewise, we deeply appreciate the critiques we received from the scholars who reviewed the project—Spencer Fluhman, Susanna Morrill, and a third, anonymous reader. All of their comments helped improve the final product immensely. Finally, we are grateful for the assistance of John Hayes, who generously checked a quotation for us at the last minute from a rare volume. Of course, we take full responsibility for any errors or infelicities that remain.

Two of the essays included in this book have been published previously in somewhat different forms. John Matzko's "The Young Joseph Smith and Presbyterianism" originally appeared as "The Encounter of the Young Joseph Smith with Presbyterianism" in *Dialogue: A Journal of Mormon Thought* 40, no. 3 (Fall 2007): 68–84; and Sara Patterson's "The Ex Factor" was originally published as "'A P.O. Box and a Desire to Witness for Jesus': Identity and Mission in the Ex-Mormons for Jesus/Saints Alive in Jesus, 1975–90" in *Journal of Mormon History* 36, no. 3 (Summer 2010): 54–81. We thank *Dialogue* and *Journal of Mormon History* for their permission to reprint these essays.

Introduction

CREATING AND CROSSING BOUNDARIES IN MORMONISM AND MORMON STUDIES

Quincy D. Newell

My apple trees will never get across
And eat the cones under his pines, I tell him.
He only says, "Good fences make good neighbors."
Spring is the mischief in me, and I wonder
If I could put a notion in his head:
"Why do they make good neighbors? Isn't it
Where there are cows? But here there are no cows.
Before I built a wall I'd ask to know
What I was walling in or walling out,
And to whom I was like to give offence.
Something there is that doesn't love a wall,
That wants it down." . . .

—*Robert Frost, "Mending Wall"*[1]

In the summer of 2005, thirteen scholars from across the United States arrived in Provo, Utah, to spend six weeks in a seminar sponsored by the National Endowment for the Humanities (NEH). Some were senior scholars, others just out of graduate school. Some had attended many of these seminars on a wide range of topics. For others, this was their first experience with the NEH Summer Seminar program. The seminar, hosted by Brigham Young University (BYU), was entitled "Joseph Smith and the

Origins of Mormonism." It was led by Grant Underwood and Richard Bushman, both recognized scholars in the field of Mormon history. Seminar participants knew, going in, that it would be a grueling six weeks: we would meet for several hours most weekday mornings, and then adjourn in the afternoons to complete hefty reading assignments and work on original research using the resources at BYU and in Salt Lake City, a short drive to the north.

The seminar itself was an exercise in border crossing. Scholars coming from Catholic, Protestant, and secular institutions converged on Brigham Young University—in the minds of many, the bastion of orthodoxy for the Church of Jesus Christ of Latter-day Saints, also known as the LDS, or Mormon, Church. Some of the participants were people of faith, even ordained ministers, and some were not. All of us agreed implicitly to talk across that divide, to see if we could find a way to understand Joseph Smith and the origins of Mormonism that we could all agree on, Protestant, Catholic, Jew, Mormon, atheist, and agnostic.

In addition to an intellectual experience, the seminar was a cultural one. We attended dinners with church officials and the dress rehearsal for then-president Gordon B. Hinckley's ninety-fifth birthday celebration. We consumed prodigious quantities of ice cream at the BYU creamery and downed pitcher after pitcher of root beer at the local pizzeria. We went out for dinners together, watched movies, and talked. These shared experiences helped create the trust necessary to talk across the lines that divided us.

Insiders and outsiders both crossed, or at least talked over, borders during the six weeks of the seminar. As we read one another's work and digested that of other scholars, the boundary that might once have seemed to be marked with a concrete wall, razor wire, and armed guards diminished to a more humble fence—one like the wall in Robert Frost's poem "Mending Wall." Frost's narrator accepts only grudgingly the necessity of annually fixing the wall that separates him from his neighbor "beyond the hill," but recognizes at the same time the fellowship he enjoys with that neighbor as they walk the fence line, each on his own property, repairing the wall after the winter snows. In the same way, the camaraderie of the seminar nurtured friendship and respect across the various walls that divided us, but the walls did not disappear.

Boundaries are necessary. They include and exclude, demarcating "my apple trees" from "his pines." Humans draw boundaries in all sorts of concrete and abstract places, in all sorts of ways. These distinctions, beginning with *in/out* and advancing to *we/they* and *human/not-human,* are the most basic forms of comparison.[2] It is this sort of comparison that gave rise to the field of religious studies, one discipline that contributes to the burgeoning area of inquiry we know as Mormon studies.[3] As teachers, we encourage our students to get "distance" on their subjects—yet what is distance, if not a boundary, a demilitarized zone, a no-man's-land? For scholars, it is the demarcation of a border that allows the analysis of the object of study. Borders both contain and exclude, focusing our attention and allowing us to ignore that which we believe to be irrelevant.

In academia, then, the breakdown of boundaries can be both dangerous and generative. As scholars, we often zealously protect the boundaries of our disciplines—but we also recognize and celebrate the fertility of interdisciplinary work. And even as we encourage our students to get "distance" on their subjects, we urge them to bridge that distance, to enter imaginatively into the life and thought of someone different from themselves. That is the religious studies ideal, so often expressed in the mandate to "make the strange familiar, and make the familiar strange."[4]

Some of these boundaries are more easily crossed than others. In the NEH seminar, daily contact and plenty of opportunity for conversation, along with an abundance of scholarly respect for one another, quickly allowed participants to overcome any initial suspicions we may have held about each other. In the academy more generally, however, these suspicions remain strong. For many years, members of the LDS Church have dominated Mormon studies.[5] Concerned that these scholars were more interested in advancing the institutional and faith-promoting interests of the LDS Church than in hewing to the intellectual standards of the academy, many non-Mormon scholars have tended to view LDS scholars' work with suspicion, alert to any sign of pro-Mormon bias.[6] This perception that the LDS Church and the academy have divergent, even opposed, interests, and the suspicion that LDS scholars' loyalties are at the very least divided, if they do not lie with the church, have led many non-LDS academics to view scholarship on Mormonism with skepticism, creating an academic "ghetto" of sorts.[7] This skepticism, in turn, has made Mormon studies a risky field for junior scholars, encouraging the further marginalization of Mormon studies. "Be careful about working on a Mormon topic, and don't present yourself as a scholar of Mormonism," graduate students are told if they hope to land a job outside the LDS Church and its related organizations.[8] These well-meaning counsels from senior scholars, generally framed as advice to cultivate a field broader than, or in addition to, Mormon studies, function as warning signs posted around the perimeter of the Mormon studies enclave: DIFFICULT TERRAIN AHEAD; PROCEED WITH CAUTION.

The wall around Mormon studies shows signs of crumbling, though: this book, which brings together both Mormon and non-Mormon scholars from many different career stages and disciplinary perspectives, is one such indication. Other signs that the wall may be shrinking include increasing attention in academic societies like the American Academy of Religion, the creation of endowed chairs in Mormon studies at Claremont Graduate University and Utah State University (neither affiliated with the LDS Church), and the growing number of non-Mormon scholars who are making homes and names for themselves in Mormon studies, despite the warning signs advising extreme caution.

Breaking down the wall around Mormon studies is easier to the degree that scholars have access to information about the church—a signal that the wall, like Frost's, may never fully disappear. Like many religious bodies, the LDS Church protects sensitive information. At the Church History Library (CHL), the main archive of the church, this imperative means restricting access to documents deemed "sacred, confidential, [or] private."[9] These categories include documents pertaining to church finances, disciplinary actions, and temple ceremonies, placing this information off-limits for many, if not all, scholars.[10] As Morris Thurston points out, the results may be detrimental for the field of Mormon studies: "If folks feel that the Church is withholding material that might enlighten a subject," Thurston writes, "they are less likely to accept conclusions that are offered, even by 'objective' historians."[11]

While readers may become more skeptical, as Thurston points out, scholars themselves also become more wary, self-censoring according to their own calculations of how their publications may affect their access to information in the future. Tales of the excommunication of LDS academics imbue these calculations with an added sense of urgency, a sense (however mistaken or exaggerated) that the LDS Church really is paying attention, and really will respond to whatever one publishes.[12] Complicating everything is the fact that the openness of the church to scholarly inquiry shifts over time, and not always in a predictable manner.[13] Those of us beginning our research in the twenty-first century can only dream of the heady days known as the "Arrington spring" or, even more nostalgically, as "Camelot," when Leonard Arrington served as official church historian and a spirit of openness reigned in the LDS Church archives.[14] We watch changes in the LDS Church bureaucracy with care, trying to gauge the impact of this official's opinion or that apostle's statement on the access we might be granted, wondering what a change in administration might augur for the future of our research. In recent years, the church has appeared relatively open to intellectual inquiry, though it remains cautious about the potential for apostasy among its own intellectuals.[15] In addition to allowing the NEH seminar on Joseph Smith to be held on the BYU campus, the church has issued enthusiastic statements regarding the "cathartic powers of honest and accurate history"[16] and the academic investigation of Mormonism more generally, and it reacted positively to conferences and symposia held independently of the church on topics ranging from Joseph Smith to "Mormons and Politics."[17]

This openness is reminiscent of the spirit that held sway during Arrington's tenure as church historian, the period when a movement known as the "New Mormon History" came to dominate Mormon studies. When Moses Rischin originally named the movement, he described it as one that encompassed both LDS and non-LDS scholars. Kicked off by Thomas F. O'Dea (a sociologist of Roman Catholic background), the movement included scholars as diverse as Mormons Arrington and Klaus Hansen, Anglican P.A.M. Taylor, Catholic Mario De Pillis, and Robert Flanders, a member of the Reorganized Church of Jesus Christ of Latter Day Saints (now called the Community of Christ). Despite this denominational diversity among its practitioners, the New Mormon History's main audience was Mormonism's intellectual wing—those who read publications like *Dialogue: A Journal of Mormon Thought* and populated organizations like the Mormon History Association. Leonard Arrington described the supporters of *Dialogue* and the MHA—both founded in 1965, and both closely associated with the New Mormon History—as "practicing Latter-day Saints; they share[d] basic agreement that the Mormon religion and its history are subject to discussion, if not to argument, and that any particular feature of Mormon life is fair game for detached examination and clarification. They believe[d] that the details of Mormon history and culture can be studied in human or naturalistic terms—indeed, must be so studied—and without thus rejecting the divinity of the Church's origin and work."[18] These were Mormons, in other words, who believed that they could maintain a robust faith while simultaneously adhering to the intellectual standards of the modern academy.

With a primarily LDS audience, it is not surprising that the New Mormon History would be composed primarily of LDS scholars.[19] While many outsiders saw Mormon studies as an academic ghetto, many insiders experienced it as a refuge, a safe space where even the most arcane points would be taken up and dissected with interest and respect.[20] When D. Michael Quinn published a collection of essays representing the New Mormon History in 1992, only three of the seventeen authors whose work was included were not, and never had been, LDS—and one of those three was a member of the Reorganized Church of Jesus Christ of Latter Day Saints (RLDS).[21] Nevertheless, as Rischin remarked in his early article heralding the movement, the New Mormon History tentatively began bridging the divides between insiders and outsiders and, indeed, non-LDS scholars are generally welcomed into Mormon studies with open arms.[22] Historian Robert Flanders wrote that the interreligious dialogue taking place in venues such as the Mormon History Association was "a threat to sectarian boundaries," even as he recognized that this dialogue was "a religious experience of Christian fellowship in its own right" whose "ultimate purpose [was] to recover, to preserve, and to augment the faith of the fathers and the mothers."[23] The ambivalence in Flanders's statement illustrates the ways in which the New Mormon History both expanded boundaries, by allowing scholars to talk across religious lines, and reinforced them, by contributing to the preservation and augmentation of the faith.

For the past several years, scholars have been speculating that the New Mormon History may have spent itself—that the movement, having more or less achieved its goals, may be over.[24] Emerging in its place is an effort that has been dubbed, variously, "New-New Mormon History," "Newer Mormon History," "Post New Mormon History," and "Restorationist studies," among other things. Although the impulse itself is still inchoate, and may never become a coherent movement, the scholars who identify with it come from a variety of disciplines and emphasize the need for scholars of Mormonism to be in conversations broader than Mormon studies, the importance of situating Mormon history in its wider historical context, and the necessity of theoretical sophistication.[25] The successor movement to the New Mormon History, then, attempts to further erode the boundaries that divide scholars from one another religiously and disciplinarily.[26] We offer this volume as another possible model for scholarship in this new phase of Mormon studies. The scholars represented here come from a variety of religious and disciplinary backgrounds, and they link their scholarship on Mormonism to an array of scholarly conversations happening throughout the academy.

As the subtitle of this volume suggests, the essays herein all examine the creation or crossing of boundaries in Mormonism or Mormon studies, including the boundaries between insiders and outsiders in the scholarly community. At its core, each of these boundaries goes back to the distinction between *us* and *them*, or *in* and *out*—but in each case who constitutes "us" and "them," or where we find "in" and "out," varies widely. We have grouped the essays into three sections according to the nature of the boundaries under examination. Part 1 deals with internal boundaries, walls that divide some Mormons from other Mormons. Part 2 considers the boundaries that divide Mormons from others. In both of these sections, the essays are arranged roughly chronologically, according to their specific topics. Part 3 deals with a special case of the boundaries considered in part 2: Mormonism in the academy. The essays in this section trace the contours of, examine the breaches in, and experiment with crossing—or at least straddling—the wall that divides Mormonism from other areas of the academic world.

The academy, of course, is not the only place where boundary lines have been drawn around or through Mormonism. Like the larger American society from which its population was largely drawn, the LDS Church during Joseph Smith's time and afterward struggled with internal divisions of race and class, among others. Our first section considers internal boundaries Mormons both drew and erased within the LDS Church. In the first essay, David Charles Gore subjects Joseph Smith's sermons, revelations, and scripture to rhetorical analysis and finds a political economy that seeks to erase distinctions between families, economic classes, and even between matter and spirit.

Quincy D. Newell's essay on Jane James explores a different division within early Mormonism. While Gore argues that Smith's political economy tried to make traditional social distinctions irrelevant, James's life illustrates the ineradicable relevance of race in the structuring of nineteenth-century Mormon society. James used her access to Joseph Smith to argue against the salience of race in the LDS Church, but later church officials drew on common American beliefs about the origins of human races, as well as particularly Mormon beliefs, in order to justify separating James from her coreligionists when it came to access to temple ceremonies.

Mormons constructed these internal boundaries in part using the raw materials provided by American society, and boundaries dividing the Mormons from other Americans consisted of similar materials. Indeed, the LDS Church's history might be seen as an exercise in building and demolishing such boundaries: retreating to their mountain kingdom, the Saints left the United States behind, separating themselves geographically from their persecutors in the United States. A short time later they began petitioning Congress for statehood, seeking to erase the divide that distinguished Utah from the rest of the nation. In their beliefs and practices, Mormons have walked a similar line, sometimes building up the wall between themselves and other Americans and at other times breaking the wall down. R. Laurence Moore has argued that for Mormons, this symbolic boundary maintenance has been particularly important. "Mormons had to invent an identity for themselves and that required them to maintain certain fictions of cultural apartness," Moore writes, and Mormons accomplished this task by advancing claims of difference "frequently . . . in the most obnoxious way possible, prompt[ing] others to agree and treat them as such."[27]

In that light, our second section considers four exchanges between Mormons and others. First, John Matzko considers Joseph Smith's childhood experiences with Presbyterianism. Although the affinity between Mormonism and Methodism is often noted, Matzko argues that Presbyterianism had an even more formative, albeit negative, influence on Smith's thinking. In everything from theology to ritual to architecture, Matzko finds, Smith's history with the Presbyterians of upstate New York helped shape the religion he founded.

Exchange across Mormonism's symbolic boundary has gone both ways, and Mormonism has also helped shape other religions. D. William Faupel's essay on John Alexander Dowie shows the important ways in which Mormonism influenced the thinking of this powerful religious leader whose work was foundational to the later Pentecostal movement. Dowie's borrowings from Mormonism, Faupel argues, were based on a long history of encounter with Mormons, from missionaries in Australia to Brigham Young during a visit to Salt Lake City. Like Joseph Smith, Dowie folded the roles of prophet and city planner into his position as religious leader, transforming even the most mundane chores into spiritual activities. Had Dowie's career not come to an abrupt end, Faupel writes, his religious organization might have come to resemble the Church of Jesus Christ of Latter-day Saints in even more striking ways.

The third essay in this section draws on a frequent comparison—that between Mormonism and Islam—in order to examine the character of prophetic authority in the LDS Church. Grant Underwood compares Mormons' and Muslims' understandings of their respective founders, Joseph Smith and Muhammad, and the scriptures each man produced. By placing Smith and Muhammad alongside one another, Underwood illuminates aspects of the Mormon understanding of prophethood that would otherwise remain obscured.

A methodology of comparison also informs the final essay in this section, but in Sara Patterson's essay the groups compared are much more closely related than are Mormons and Muslims. Members of the LDS Church have generally characterized the group known as Ex-Mormons for Jesus (EMFJ) or Saints Alive in Jesus (SAIJ), which Patterson examines, as "anti-Mormon,"[28] despite the EMFJ/SAIJ's claim that it acts out of love for Latter-day Saints. In her essay, Patterson demonstrates the extent to which EMFJ/SAIJ faith is shaped by the structures of Mormonism, despite EMFJ/SAIJ members' claims that they have left the LDS Church. Not satisfied with scholars' understanding of "exes" like the EMFJ/SAIJ as "career apostates,"[29] Patterson argues that they have a positive sense of calling and peoplehood based in part on their own claims of difference, much like the Mormons themselves, and she explores how that identity has shifted as the group's mission has changed.

Religious people, of course, are not the only ones who construct boundaries. The academy, shaped as it was by the Enlightenment, has also introduced deep divisions—both by building the walls of the proverbial "ivory tower" and by separating those inside the tower according to their areas of expertise. The final section in this book challenges those divisions. First, Stevan Davies's essay on the identity of Elias, by its very nature, blurs the distinction between insider and outsider among those who think about Mormonism. Davies's essay is an exercise in LDS theology, written from a believer's perspective—but Davies is not, and never has been, LDS. In a thought-provoking prologue to the essay, Davies reflects on doing LDS theology as an outsider.

As always, crossings go in both directions. Eric F. Mason examines the surprising story of Brigham Young University's rise to prominence in the field of Dead Sea Scrolls research. Partnering with the Protestant, Catholic, and Jewish scholars who dominated the field, Mormon scholars worked hard to be taken seriously in this presumptively secular (or at least religiously neutral) field of biblical studies. In order to achieve their goal, Mormon scholars had to convince the scholarly establishment that their treatment of the Dead Sea Scrolls would not be influenced by their church hierarchy nor by their own desires to bolster the evidence for their religion. How they did so is an improbable tale.

Finally, Richard L. Bushman discusses the increasing convergence of Mormon and non-Mormon scholars in Mormon studies. While the divide between Mormons and non-Mormons was once so wide as to seem impassable, Bushman finds encouragement in the growing interest in Mormon studies among non-Mormon scholars.

"Something there is that doesn't love a wall," Robert Frost wrote, imagining the rejoinder of his neighbor, "Good fences make good neighbors." The essays in this collection embody that ambivalence in many ways, talking across religious and scholarly walls even as they examine the fences that separate Mormons from others and the walls that divide Mormonism itself. These boundaries are useful, focusing our attention, but the authors here are careful not to let the boundaries be too limiting. They connect their examinations to larger conversations in theology, comparative religions, American history, and rhetoric, among other fields. This scholarship thus acts like that "something" in Frost's poem "that doesn't love a wall,/ That sends the frozen-ground-swell under it,/And spills the upper boulders in the sun," forcing us to become conscious of the walls that surround and subdivide the religion, prompting a consideration of whether, and in what form, the walls ought to exist.[30]

NOTES

I thank Laurie F. Maffly-Kipp and J. Spencer Fluhman for their comments on an earlier draft of this essay. Still, the views expressed in this introduction are my own and should not be taken to represent the positions of anyone else.

1. Robert Frost, "Mending Wall," in Frost, *North of Boston* (New York: Henry Holt, 1914), 12–13.

2. Jonathan Z. Smith, "Map Is Not Territory," in *Map Is Not Territory* (Chicago: University of Chicago Press, 1993), 294; Jonathan Z. Smith, "Differential Equations: On Constructing the Other," in *Relating Religion: Essays in the Study of Religion* (Chicago: University of Chicago Press, 2004), 230–31.

3. It should be noted that the relationship between religious studies and Mormon studies is reciprocal and might best be envisioned as a Venn diagram: religious studies contributes to Mormon studies, but Mormon studies also contributes to religious studies.

4. This adage is so ubiquitous that its origins are nearly impossible to discover. It appears to have originated in poetry: some attribute it to the German poet Novalis. T. S. Eliot credits the idea to Samuel Taylor Coleridge. T. S. Eliot, *Selected Essays*, new ed. (New York: Harcourt, Brace, 1950), 259. Wherever it originated, the phrase later made its way into anthropology and, indeed, appears to have been adopted as something of a mission statement for the entire field. It is likely that religious studies scholars borrowed the aphorism from anthropology, but it should be noted that the phrase has been greeted enthusiastically in fields from education to marketing to semiotics.

5. Indeed, there is an interesting slippage in the meaning of the term "Mormon history," which is generally considered a part of Mormon studies. Is Mormon history the history of the LDS Church and other groups that followed Joseph Smith, or is it history written by Mormons? Scholars of Mormon history who are also members of the LDS Church often seem to assume that "Mormon history" means history written by, for, and about Mormons. See J. Spencer Fluhman, "Fashioning a Newer Mormon History," *Journal of Mormon History* 35, no. 3 (Summer 2009): 216. There are, of course, noteworthy exceptions to the rule: Jan Shipps, a lifelong Methodist, has been a formative influence on the field of Mormon studies.

6. Although Larry McMurtry might not be considered a scholar in the conventional sense, his review of several books on Joseph Smith in the *New York Review of Books* is a good example of this point. Though the article claims to review five books, McMurtry deals substantively only with Richard Bushman's *Joseph Smith: Rough Stone Rolling* and Fawn M. Brodie's *No Man Knows My History: The Life of Joseph Smith.* Of Bushman's volume, McMurtry writes, "it is when we come to the rather baroque business of the golden plates and their translation that the fact that Professor Bushman is a believing Mormon becomes a shoe that begins to pinch a little. . . . What is difficult to determine is where biography ends and apologetics begins." Larry McMurtry, "Angel in America," *New York Review of Books* 52, no. 18 (November 17, 2005): 35. McMurtry's stance is even clearer in a follow-up letter published some four months later: McMurtry writes that he found *Rough Stone Rolling* "admirable, if bland and rather cautious," but goes on to say that Fawn Brodie "saw the fraud at the heart of Mormonism and she describes it [in *No Man Knows My History*]. Professor Bushman pitty-pats around it." Larry McMurtry, letter to the editor, *New York Review of Books* 53, no. 5 (March 23, 2006): 45.

7. I use the term "ghetto," with its negative connotations, advisedly. I do not mean to imply that those who inhabit this academic enclave are lesser scholars in any way; merely that outsiders may *perceive* them that way.

8. Such warnings are a topic of discussion among young LDS scholars and non-LDS scholars of Mormonism. See, for example, the post and discussion on "The Juvenile Instructor," a shared, self-consciously Mormon blog at www.juvenileinstructor.org/gigantic-and-sometimes-polemical-the-persistent-marginalization-of-mormon-history-as-an-acceptable-field-of-study/, which cites one such warning in the comments of Richard Bushman to students at the Mormon Historical Association meeting in 2005 and characterizes such comments as relatively common. It is worth noting that graduate students are not given similar advice about Catholic or Jewish studies or, for that matter, any of the various lines of research that might be characterized as "Protestant studies."

9. Officially, the policy of the Church History Library (CHL) states, "The Church History Department is committed to making its records available to the public to the extent it can reasonably do so without compromising those that are sacred, confidential, private, or otherwise restricted for legal or ethical reasons." "About the Church History Library," s.v. "*Access*," http://churchhistorycatalog.lds.org/primo_library/libweb/pages/general-about.jsp, accessed June 2, 2011. I thank my colleague Reid L. Neilson, managing director of the Church History Department of The Church of Jesus Christ of Latter-day Saints, for supplying me with this text. Reid L. Neilson, personal communication, June 2, 2011. While most archives follow some version of the CHL's restrictions based on "legal or ethical reasons," the restrictions on "sacred [and] confidential" materials are unique to the CHL, though as I noted above, the LDS Church is not unique among religious bodies in protecting sensitive information.

10. I thank Randy Olsen, director of libraries, Church History Department, Church of Jesus Christ of Latter-day Saints, for providing me with the relevant portions of the Church History Department's current policy statement to clarify the meanings of "sacred," "confidential," and "private." Randy Olsen, personal communication, June 3, 2011.

11. Morris A. Thurston, "A Bundle of Rights," *Journal of Mormon History* 28, no. 1 (Spring 2002): 79. I thank Reid L. Neilson for pointing me to this article. A decade earlier, Edwin S. Gaustad eloquently explained why church records must be more open to scholars, comparing the LDS Church's reluctance to open the archives to that of the Roman Catholic Church in an earlier time. See Gaustad, "History and Theology: The Mormon Connection," in George D. Smith, ed., *Faithful History: Essays on Writing Mormon History* (Salt Lake City: Signature Books, 1992), 65–66. In his essay, Thurston also points out that "a policy [regarding access to archival documents] that seems restrictive on its face, may be much less so in practice. Conversely, an archive whose written policy seems to be open can exercise a great deal of control simply by denying researchers access to certain documents. This can be done overtly, by refusing requests for access to catalogued materials, or covertly, by

failing to catalog documents that the archive does not want examined." Thurston, "A Bundle of Rights," 78n29. Such informal restrictions and relaxations of restrictions are, of course, much more difficult to document, but form part of the lore of archives that circulates among scholars in many subfields, including, but definitely not limited to, both Mormon studies and Catholic studies.

12. The most famous disciplinary proceedings are the so-called September Six, a group of five LDS intellectuals who were excommunicated and one who was disfellowshipped in September 1993. For contemporary coverage of the proceedings, see Special to The New York Times, "Mormons Penalize Dissident Members: 6 Who Criticized Leaders or Debated Doctrine Await Sanctions by Church," *New York Times*, September 19, 1993, A31. For extensive coverage from an LDS intellectual perspective, see "Six Intellectuals Disciplined for Apostasy," *Sunstone*, November 1993, 65–73. Excommunications continued in the 1990s and into the following millennium: Margaret Toscano was excommunicated in 2000 for her outspoken advocacy of feminist perspectives on Mormonism. Peggy Fletcher Stack, "GOD & the Feminist," *Salt Lake Tribune*, August 14, 2004, C1. Simon Southerton was excommunicated in 2005 after publishing *Losing a Lost Tribe: Native Americans, DNA, and the Book of Mormon* (Salt Lake City: Signature Books, 2004), though he had voluntarily left the church several years earlier. Although Southerton believed his excommunication was based on the intellectual claims he made, the articulated basis for the excommunication was having an inappropriate relationship with a woman while separated from his wife. Jennifer Dobner, "Church Excommunicates 'DNA' Author," *Deseret News*, August 5, 2005, B2. Disciplinary proceedings, including excommunications, are carried out at the local level and the LDS Church does not make information regarding these procedures public. Tracking them is therefore much more difficult than it might otherwise be. Mormon graduate students are perhaps particularly vulnerable to intellectual pressures: Janet Bennion recounts being "reprimanded" by a church official for her interest in "contemporary polygamous communities" as a graduate student in the early 1990s. Bennion, "Mormon Women's Issues in the Twenty-first Century," in Cardell K. Jacobson, John P. Hoffman, and Tim B. Heaton, eds., *Revisiting Thomas F. O'Dea's* The Mormons: *Contemporary Perspectives* (Salt Lake City: University of Utah Press, 2008), 152, and personal communication, June 2, 2011. Nearly two decades later, in 2010, colleagues shared with me stories of their LDS graduate students who have been pressured by church officials not to pursue sensitive research topics or risk their church memberships, marriages, and more.

13. Two examples illustrate the unpredictability of these shifts: some of the documents from the LDS Church History Library that Henry J. Wolfinger published as an appendix to his 1975 article, "A Test of Faith: Jane Elizabeth James and the Origins of the Utah Black Community," are no longer accessible to researchers. (Henry J. Wolfinger, "A Test of Faith: Jane Elizabeth James and the Origins of the Utah Black Community," in Clark S. Knowlton, ed., *Social Accommodation in Utah* [Salt Lake City: American West Center Occasional Papers, University of Utah, 1975], 126–72.)

Meanwhile, at least one collection listed as "restricted access" in 2009 is now listed as "open for research" (James Godson Bleak Papers, 1862–1943, ms 21999).

14. See Davis Bitton, "Ten Years in Camelot: A Personal Memoir," *Dialogue: A Journal of Mormon Thought* 16, no. 3 (Autumn 1983): 9–20, for a personal history of Leonard Arrington's time as church historian. See also D. Michael Quinn, "On Being a Mormon Historian (and Its Aftermath)," in George D. Smith, ed., *Faithful History*, 69–70, for a brief description of this period; and Jan Shipps, "Richard Lyman Bushman, the Story of Joseph Smith and Mormonism, and the New Mormon History," *Journal of American History* 94, no. 2 (September 2007): 501–503.

15. See note 12, above.

16. LDS Church Newsroom, "'A Record Kept': Constructing Collective Memory," June 11, 2009, http://newsroom.lds.org/article/a-record-kept-constructing-collective-memory (accessed June 3, 2011). Note that in the same concluding paragraph, this press release also encourages caution, urging "a careful, yet bold presentation of Church history."

17. LDS Church Newsroom, "'Mormon Studies' and the Value of Education," November 2, 2007, http://newsroom.lds.org/article/mormon-studies-and-the-value-of-education (accessed June 3, 2011). Also see Richard Bushman's essay in this volume for further examples of the LDS Church's recent openness to scholarly inquiry. The openness of the church is complemented by the Church History Library making its catalog available on the internet.

18. Moses Rischin, "The New Mormon History," *American West* 6 (March 1969): 49, quoting Leonard Arrington (no citation given).

19. Shipps, "Richard Lyman Bushman," 502. Bushman assumes the Mormon identity of participants in the New Mormon History when he writes that "to avoid the strain between keeping the peace with non-Mormons and showing their colors as believers, the new Mormon historians bypass the early history" of Mormonism. Bushman, "What's New in Mormon History: A Response to Jan Shipps," *Journal of American History* 94, no. 2 (September 2007): 519.

20. See, again, Leonard Arrington as quoted by Rischin, "New Mormon History," 49.

21. Quinn writes in his introduction that his initial selection of essays for the collection "included more than two hundred selections" written by "women and men; Mormon, RLDS, Catholic, Protestant, Jewish, Muslim, and Hindu; American, Belgian, British, Canadian, French, German, Indian, Israeli, Italian, New Zealander, and Palestinian; anthropologists, architects, archivists, artists, biblical scholars, biologists, business administrators, classicists, engineers, English teachers, film critics, folklorists, genealogists, geographers, healthcare specialists, historians, housewives, institute teachers, journalists, lawyers, librarians, linguists, mathematicians, museum curators, philosophers, physicians, physicists, political scientists, psychiatrists, psychologists, sociologists, statisticians, university administrators, as well as leaders of both the Church of Jesus Christ of Latter-day Saints and the Reorganized Church of Jesus Christ of Latter Day Saints." D. Michael Quinn, ed., *The New Mor-*

mon History: Revisionist Essays on the Past (Salt Lake City: Signature Books, 1992), ix–x. Nevertheless, the final selection of essays was authored by a considerably less diverse group. The seventeen authors included fourteen members of the Church of Jesus Christ of Latter-day Saints, one Methodist, one RLDS, and one Roman Catholic. Three authors are women; all are white (though Quinn himself has Latino heritage); and all but two were born and raised in the United States. I thank Jan Shipps for clarifying this information for me. Shipps, personal communication, June 6, 2011.

22. In fact, the Mormon History Association's O.C. Tanner and Grace Tanner Lecture, established in 1980, institutionalizes this welcome of outside scholars. Each year a scholar from outside Mormon studies is invited to speak at the Mormon History Association's annual meeting on a topic at the intersection of Mormon history and his or her own academic specialty. As Martin Ridge's remarks in his Tanner Lecture indicate, this is an unusual practice among academic associations. Martin Ridge, "Mormon 'Deliverance' and the Closing of the Frontier," *Journal of Mormon History* 18, no. 1 (Spring 1992): 137. The first twenty-one Tanner lectures are collected in Dean L. May and Reid L. Neilson, eds., *The Mormon History Association's Tanner Lectures: The First Twenty Years* (Urbana: University of Illinois Press, 2006).

23. Robert B. Flanders, "Some Reflections on the New Mormon History," in George D. Smith, ed., *Faithful History*, 44.

24. Jan Shipps, for example, designates Richard Bushman's *Joseph Smith: Rough Stone Rolling* the "crowning achievement of the 'old' new Mormon history, an intellectual movement that . . . seems to be rapidly passing into history." Shipps, "Richard Lyman Bushman," 516.

25. See the essays included in "What We Will Do Now That New Mormon History Is Old: A Roundtable," *Journal of Mormon History* 35, no. 3 (Summer 2009): 190–233. Many of the contributing scholars also emphasized the need for greater attention to rank-and-file Mormons. This call echoes that made by many other scholars; see, for example, Grant Underwood, "Re-Visioning Mormon History," *Pacific Historical Review* 55, no. 3 (August 1986): 403–26.

26. Recent works in Mormon studies demonstrate a variety of approaches that fit under this rubric. A few of many possible examples include Kathleen Flake, *The Politics of American Identity: The Seating of Senator Reed Smoot, Mormon Apostle* (Chapel Hill: University of North Carolina Press, 2003); Jared Farmer, *On Zion's Mount: Mormons, Indians, and the American Landscape* (Cambridge, Mass.: Harvard University Press, 2008); and W. Paul Reeve, *Making Space on the Western Frontier: Mormons, Miners, and Southern Paiutes* (Urbana: University of Illinois Press, 2007).

27. R. Laurence Moore, *Religious Outsiders and the Making of Americans* (New York: Oxford University Press, 1986), 32, 31. See also Armand L. Mauss, *The Angel and the Beehive: The Mormon Struggle with Assimilation* (Urbana: University of Illinois Press, 1994), on Mormons' movement between what Mauss terms "the predicament of disrepute" and "the predicament of respectability."

28. For the description of EMFJ/SAIJ as "anti-Mormon," see, for example, Armand L. Mauss, "Apostasy and the Management of Spoiled Identity," in David G. Bromley, ed., *The Politics of Religious Apostasy: The Role of Apostates in the Transformation of Religious Movements* (Westport, Conn.: Praeger, 1998), 63.

29. Lawrence Foster uses this phrase to characterize Jerald and Sandra Tanner in "Career Apostates: Reflections on the Works of Jerald and Sandra Tanner," *Dialogue: A Journal of Mormon Thought* 17, no. 2 (Summer 1984): 35–60.

30. Frost, "Mending Wall," 11.

Part 1
Creating and Crossing Internal Boundaries

1
Profits of a Prophet

TOWARD JOSEPH SMITH'S POLITICAL ECONOMY

David Charles Gore

Like Moses, Muhammad, and prophets in all ages of the world, Joseph Smith spoke often about economic justice, including the plight of the oppressed, helpless, and imprisoned.[1] Numerous scholars have commented at length about the failures of Joseph Smith's personal economies, including the failed Kirtland Safety Society and other economic hardships suffered by the early Latter-day Saints.[2] Collectively, these works attend primarily to economic practice rather than economic ideas or rhetoric. But political economy is more than what we do with our money. It includes how we talk about money and how we think about ourselves in relation to matter. Richard Bushman has recently argued that "Joseph had no language of political economy" because he "did not base his reforms on a diagnosis of a diseased economic system."[3] Although perhaps not a systematic theory of political economy, Joseph Smith's prophetic rhetoric regarding matter and social and class distinction illuminates his political economy by way of his political theology.

What does Joseph Smith's prophetic rhetoric, as contained in Latter-day Saint scripture, say about economics and economic justice? What can Smith's prophetic approach teach about the relation between theology and economics? The subject of Smith's political economy is at the nexus of several disciplines and several contested historical facts. It is not the same thing as asking about Smith's economic praxis. The rhetorical level, the level at which we focus on words and their persuasive and argumentative effect, is at once ideal, abstract, and practical.[4] Examining Smith's prophetic style and purpose as rhetoric reveals his reason-making process, which leads this analysis to the subject of political theology—the ways in which beliefs about

God influence political, social, and economic matters.[5] Many hold intense opinions about economics, politics, and religion, and this analysis puts all three in play. Another complication is that political economy is regarded today as a secular social science, a study in political a-theology. With few exceptions, the discipline of economics has largely argued against theological explanations of materiality, choosing instead to see materiality as the driver of human behavior. The intersection of religion and economics is understudied, and there hardly exists an idiom for it, in part because political economy was itself a direct challenge to theological explanations.[6] Related to this lacuna is the contested nature of Smith's theology and its economic consequences. Many in Smith's day considered any fall in profit evidence that he was a fallen prophet.[7] Smith's political economy is not systematic and does not resemble the words of most political economists.[8]

However, Smith's words, like other theologies, provide grounds from which to see the social and material world. Classical political economy depends on an abstraction of preferences derived from human behavior in a context of scarcity. This abstraction sets aside religious and political persuasion.[9] Where Adam Smith and Karl Marx share materialism in common, Joseph Smith deepens the meaning of matter to include all unseen things, injecting matter with spirit. Smith's emphasis on the unseen, his strong preference for social equality, and his focus on the importance of *oikos,* or the household, to political economy underscores how theology can shape economic understanding. To illustrate this point I discuss explanations of political economy about Smith's time, I examine the material aspects of Smith's theology, and I read closely Mormon scripture to show that economic themes are a significant element of his theology.

Political Economy in the Time of Mormon Origins

The work already done showing the distance between Mormon economic ideals and Mormon practice is helpful, but it never highlights how discourse works to bring seemingly disparate ideas together. Smith's sense of equality is always partly economic, partly theological, and partly political. He appears more interested in souls than money, but he clearly sees equality as a way of purifying souls. The economy Smith envisioned is a function of his vision of eternity, not simply an outgrowth of his economic circumstance. This section reviews economic explanations of Smith's political economy and introduces a rhetorical approach to Smith's discourse.

Leonard J. Arrington's powerful *Great Basin Kingdom: An Economic History of the Latter-day Saints, 1830–1900* takes seriously Mormon economic practice and ideals. Arrington's aim is to elaborate on how Mormon economic principles were expressed in practice. This focus naturally renders Smith's economic discourse less prominent. Still, Arrington notes that Smith was "a social theorist of no mean ability" because of his basic economic goals and the organizational structure of the church he founded.[10] Arrington's work ends with a somber note about "the great capitulation," the turn away from a self-sufficient kingdom to full integration with the American economy.[11] It is a story of retreat from ideals to capitalistic practice. Arrington acknowledges, but does not explain, the remaining rhetorical power of Smith's economic ideas. The distance between ideal and practice is a consistent feature of human experience, and the rhetoric of Mormon scripture is one way to grasp Smith's power as a social theorist.

In *The Soul's Economy: Market Society and Selfhood in American Thought, 1820–1920,* Jeffrey Sklansky argues that economic reform during the time of Joseph Smith "was less to transform property relations than to transcend them, to invest the existing economic structure with new social and spiritual value."[12] Ralph Waldo Emerson, Horace Bushnell, and others, each in his own way, wrote to inject new energy and spiritual value into the growing industrial capitalist economy of nineteenth-century America. These thinkers welcomed "the demise of the agrarian republic as a fulfillment rather than a betrayal of freedom and democracy," and their "transcendental psychology could be understood as less a fundamental critique than a newly legitimating conception of market society."[13] Sklansky's proposition would be a broadly true statement of Joseph Smith's economic rhetoric if it were not for the fact that Smith sought transcendence independently, and sometimes in defiance, of the existing theologico-politico-economic structure. Smith's transcendence came not through a new psychology but a new religion.

Of course, Smith was not the only nineteenth-century American to look for religious solutions to the problems presented by capitalism. The religious landscape of the Second Great Awakening was fertile ground for reform-minded movements, most of which had some kind of economic dimension. The Shakers under the leadership of Ann Lee established communities bound together by creative ways of organizing spiritual and economic life. Economically, the Shakers sought a way to avoid the rivalries created by capitalism while emphasizing craftsmanship, diligent work, and avoidance of debt.[14] Owenites, inspired more by socialist ideas than religious impulses, were nevertheless moved to form new communities modeled after new principles of political economy.[15] Whatever their form, it was within a reform-minded society that Joseph Smith preached a new faith that sought emancipation from old ways of organizing social and spiritual life.

Charles Sellers, the foremost historian of Jacksonian political economy, argues that the strange milieu of Jacksonian politics and the secular frustration of many of Smith's contemporaries can explain the appeal of Mormonism and its economic attitudes.[16] The Mormons, according to Sellers, were largely repelled by "elitist," "intellectual" attempts to reinforce the emerging capitalistic order, like those referred to by Sklansky.[17] Early Mormons, according to Sellers, did not turn to psychological explanations, but religious explanations, which they imagined to find a way out of their economic desperation. Sellers's approach reasons that markets and economic fortunes explain everything. He depicts the Smiths and Mormons as economic unfortunates, which they surely were, driven to "fantasy" and "trickery" because of economic difficulties, which is up for interpretation.[18] Moreover, Sellers never quotes Latter-day Saint scriptures in his analysis, and when he does mention them, he reads them too quickly.

It is true that Smith's economic pronouncements came within a complicated economic and religious scene. The emergence of the Book of Mormon took place in a context fraught with economic anxieties. Smith was preoccupied with the idea of preaching for money. In the mid-1820s, the Smiths were on the brink of economic ruin because of debt and the death of their eldest son. Additionally, Smith was implicated in purported money-digging scandals and a series of court trials.[19] Even the "goldness" of the gold plates, from which Smith translated the Book of Mormon, carried economic value. The Book of Mormon, itself, contains stories of buried treasures being cursed and made "slippery" because those who buried them did so out of a sense of selfishness (Helaman 13:31–36). Likewise, the translation and publication of the Book of Mormon required the assistance of Martin Harris, a wealthy benefactor, in order to be completed. The emergence of Mormonism is steeped in a strange milieu of poverty, money-digging, and buried treasure, but Mormonism is more than the sum of these parts.

As Bushman has remarked, Smith's revelations on economic questions "were long on principles and short on detail. They presented a theological message, not a business plan."[20] I presume that Smith was active in shaping these texts and that the words of the text are within his comprehension and style. Some misunderstanding arises from the fact that for many the words reflect the revealed word of God. But Joseph "never considered the wording infallible. God's language stood in an indefinite relationship to the human language coming through the Prophet. The revealed preface to the Book of Commandments specified that the language of the revelations was Joseph Smith's: 'These commandments are of me, and were given unto my servants in their weakness, after the manner of their language, that they might come to understanding.' The revelations were not God's diction, dialect, or native language. They were couched in the language suitable to Joseph's time."[21] Smith's willingness to edit the words of his revelations and the fact that the revelations are in the language of the receiver indicate that treating the words as rhetoric is entirely reasonable. They are words spoken for a persuasive effect, art emphasizing an order of desire. Of course, whether one believes they come from God through Smith or only through Smith will color their persuasive power, but not entirely determine it. Attending to how the words work provides insight into the claims, proofs, and persuasions that result.

Consider the example of an excerpt from Smith's presidential platform from 1844, the year he died.[22] The words resemble what Kenneth Cmiel has called the "democratic idiom," a propensity to value "truth over politeness," a "middling poetics" of "calculated bluntness."[23] The platform decries imprisonment for the abuse of some minor statute "while the duelist, the debauchee, and the defaulter for millions, and other criminals take the uppermost rooms at feasts."[24] Smith's populism sounds indignant, sides with the poor, advocates smaller salaries for public servants and the distribution of surplus revenue to the people, and calls for people to exercise their natural propensity to fraternity. "More economy in the national and state governments," the platform says, "would make less taxes among the people; more equality through the cities, towns and country, would make less distinction among the people; and more honesty and familiarity in societies, would make less hypocrisy and flattery in all branches of community; and open, frank, candid, decorum to all men, in this boasted land of liberty, would beget esteem, confidence, union, and love; and the neighbor from any state, or from any country, of whatever color, clime, or tongue, could rejoice when he put his foot on the sacred soil of freedom, and exclaim the very name of 'American,' is fraught with friendship!"[25] Consistent with the political style of the period, Smith pushes his long sentences to ideal and exalted extremes. The operational political enthymemes, the orator's truncated syllogisms that invite the audience to participate in their own persuasion, are delivered in rapid fashion. He calls for more government restraint, more equality, more honesty, more union, and more love. The invitation is to a politics of friendship. At the same time, Smith's platform asserts that the economy "need[s] the fostering care of government."[26] For Smith, there seems no contradiction in buying the slave's freedom, as he advocates elsewhere in the document, with the plea for more fiscal restraint in the government. The limits of government restraint are measured, apparently, by their effect on constituting friendship, liberty, and equality rather than on the bottom line.

As this brief example shows, attending at the level of the word allows for an appreciation of how words work on more than one level. Smith's rhetoric is religious, but it is also political, social, and economic. Smith was for humbling the rich and exalting the poor, but there is no indication he thought of such humbling and exalting in limited terms (Doctrine and Covenants 84:112; 104:16). Appreciating the wide liberty Smith took with his words allows for an understanding of his political theology because it is enfolded in revelation and prophecy and carries economic effects. Additionally, this approach illustrates the limits of treating political economy as a narrow, atheistic, or a-theological category.

Material Gods, Angels, and Spirits

The LDS doctrine of a material God and physical angels, along with gold plates and seer stones, underscores a new vision of spirit and matter. The vision of fusing spiritual and physical things is integral to the Mormon mind. "For I, the Lord God, created all things of which I have spoken, spiritually, before they were naturally upon the face of the earth," including all the plants, herbs, and humans (Moses 3:5). The Doctrine and Covenants adds that "all things" to the Lord "are spiritual," including his commandments. God's commandments "are not natural nor temporal, neither carnal nor sensual" (Doctrine and Covenants 29:34–35). As Terryl Givens notes, a paradox emerges "from these contrary tendencies . . . a culture that sacralizes and exalts the mundane even as it naturalizes and domesticates the sacred."[27] This allowed Smith to practice "capitalism without the spirit of capitalism. Summing up a day of waiting on customers in the store, he mused 'I love to wait upon the Saints, and be a servant of all, hoping that I may be exalted in the due time of the Lord.'"[28] Shopkeeping becomes a means to exaltation as the distinctions between physical and spiritual reality are dedichotomized.

"There is no such thing as immaterial matter," one revelation said. "All spirit is matter, but it is more fine or pure, and can only be discerned by purer eyes. We cannot see it; but when our bodies are purified we shall see that it is all matter" (Doctrine and Covenants 131:7). If spirit is material, the dualisms of Western thought are rendered, if not immaterial, less important as a lens for looking at economic matters. Yet Smith speaks of a world where material distinctions are minimized in preference to spiritual necessities. Mormon theology offers a way of looking at the economy that respects matter(s) that cannot be seen or can be seen only with purer eyes. The vision of Smith's political economy gives unseen things a credibility as great as that of visible matter.

"Economy" appears once in canonized LDS scripture and once again, interestingly, scrawled across the top of extant manuscripts of one of Joseph Smith's most important revelations. Both the canonized occurrence and the scrawl are on revelations received in early 1832, now canonized as section 76 and section 77 of the Doctrine and Covenants. On two different extant manuscripts of section 76 is written a similar message, providing the reader with a preview of the content of the section. On one manuscript (in the handwriting of Joseph Smith and Frederick G. Williams) is written, "A vision of Joseph & Sidney February 16th 1832 given in Portage County Hiram Township State of Ohio in North America which they saw concerning the Church of the first born and concerning the economy of God and his vast creation throughout all eternity."[29] Known to Smith and his contemporaries as "The Vision," section 76 is about the Latter-day Saint doctrine of various degrees of glory in the afterlife. "The economy of God" concerns the salvation of souls, as Bushman points out, and extends into space to include the vastness of material existence and time.[30] Rather than drawing attention to immanence and the earth as the rhetoric of political economy does,

Smith's revelations—and political theology generally—consider a cosmic and eternal context as grounds for doing social science.

"Economy" appears again in a revelation of March 1832. In connection with Smith's translation of the Bible, he received a revelation explaining the Revelation of St. John:

> Q. What are we to understand by the book which John saw, which was sealed on the back with seven seals?
> A. We are to understand that it contains the revealed will, mysteries, and the works of God; the hidden things of his economy concerning this earth during the seven thousand years of its continuance or its temporal existence. (Doctrine and Covenants 77:6)

This godly economy focuses on the earth, but the emphasis is on realizing that God's aims are hidden as if in a sealed book. Within a theology that sees all spirit as matter and all of nature as spiritually created, the possibility of God's hidden management practices is rhetorical. It becomes the Mormon responsibility to uncover the hidden things by which God governs his economy.

For example, Mormonism invites individuals to consider the spiritual aspects of material possessions and the material consequences of spiritual belief. It means that when one considers the consequences of material decisions, one is caught up in spiritual things. Likewise, the consequences of spiritual decisions may be *material.* According to the revelation mentioned above, only greater purity allows one to see the materiality of spirit. To think and speak in such a way is to invite a new approach to so-called secular behavior, like Smith's manning of the shop counter above. As far as Smith's words go, they constitute scripture in a material sense. The Doctrine and Covenants declares, "It is impossible for a man to be saved in ignorance" (Doctrine and Covenants 131:6). It is likewise impossible for a camel to go through the eye of a needle (see Mark 10:25). For Mormons, the quest for knowledge and the quest for understanding God's purposes are closely related by the notion that mind, spirit, matter, and property share in a oneness.

Because body and spirit are entwined in Smith's theology, he cannot account for the provision of the spirit without accounting for the provision of the body (Doctrine and Covenants 88:15). By conjoining constructs kept separate within contemporary political economy, Smith opens a door for the reevaluation of social constructs such as the city, class, and family. Smith elevates "economics into the sphere of religion and spirituality."[31] Such elevation turns on how much one can think or talk about bodies and spirits as if materiality and spirituality are one. A number of scriptures in the Book of Mormon and Smith's revelations address these issues by way of distinctions between rich and poor. These scriptures underscore that Smith's words invent a faith whereby reconciliation between rich and poor is the essence of heavenly equality. If poverty and wealth, or class distinction, can be reconciled, then the reconciliation of matter and spirit can be demonstrated.

Rich and Poor in LDS Scripture

A significant feature of LDS scripture in both the Book of Mormon and the Doctrine and Covenants is that they focus on the attitudes and tendencies of rich and poor. For example, a poor person who does not give to beggars, but who also *would* not, is considered in need of repentance (Mosiah 4:24–25). A rich person who gives too little or is too proud of his accomplishments will find in the end that his soul is not saved (Doctrine and Covenants 56:16). The priorities are on motive, willingness to sacrifice, and an appreciation of the value of the community. The sermon by King Benjamin, for example, the longest sermon recorded in the Book of Mormon, encompassing Mosiah 2–4, tells those with money that they are not justified in judging those who petition them for charitable assistance. But King Benjamin adds, "I say unto the poor, ye who have not and yet have sufficient, that ye remain from day to day; I mean all you who deny the beggar, because ye have not; I would that ye say in your hearts that: I give not because I have not, but if I had I would give. And now, if ye say this in your hearts ye remain guiltless, otherwise ye are condemned; and your condemnation is just for ye covet that which ye have not received" (Mosiah 4:24–25). King Benjamin's listeners are made spiritually responsible for money that they do not possess. Material relations are here being injected with religious energy by recasting them in terms of what one *would* do.

Smith's revelations warn the poor and criticize the rich. The poor "whose hearts are not broken, whose spirits are not contrite, and whose bellies are not satisfied" are not justified in stealing, greediness, or idleness because of their poverty (Doctrine and Covenants 56:17). The rich who "will not give your substance to the poor" will find "your riches will canker your souls; and this shall be your lamentation in the day of visitation and of judgment, and of indignation: The harvest is past, the summer is ended, and my soul is not saved!" (Doctrine and Covenants 56:16). This declaration suggests that there is no particular virtue in being poor any more than there is virtue in being rich. Instead, each state has its own peculiar pitfalls and challenges for discipleship.

For example, the missionary Alma in the Book of Alma finds that the poor are more inclined to listen to the word of God, in particular because they had been thrown out of the Nephite churches "because of the coarseness of their apparel" (Alma 32:2). They were considered as "filthiness" and "dross" because of their poverty, but "also they were poor in heart." They ask Alma how they are to worship since they have been cast out of the churches because of their poverty, and at this Alma is overcome with "great joy; for he beheld that their afflictions had truly humbled them, and that they were in a preparation to hear the word" (Alma 32:6). He then reminds them that one does not need a church in order to worship God, and that because of their "exceeding poverty" they have been humbled. Yet the humility required by God is qualitatively different from that achieved through circumstance. Alma said, "And now, because ye are compelled to be humble blessed are ye; for a man sometimes, if he is compelled to be humble, seeketh repentance; and now surely, whosoever repenteth shall find mercy; and he that findeth mercy and endureth to the end the same shall be saved. . . . Therefore, blessed are they who humble themselves without being compelled to be humble" (Alma 32:13, 16). The tendency of poverty is humility, but humility is not the exclusive province of the poor. Neither is the humility that comes only from poverty the sort of humility God expects of those who follow him.

Likewise, the rich are not arbitrarily condemned. Jacob, Nephi's younger brother, tells the Nephite rich to "be familiar with all and free with your substance, that they may be rich like unto you" (Jacob 2:17). Then follows a curious passage in the Book of Mormon that reiterates the central idea that being rich or poor does not convey any particular spiritual standing before God: "But before ye seek for riches, seek ye for the kingdom of God. And after ye have obtained a hope in Christ ye shall obtain riches, if ye seek them; and ye will seek them for the intent to do good—to clothe the naked, and to feed the hungry, and to liberate the captive, and administer relief to the sick and the afflicted" (Jacob 2:18–19). There is no injunction against seeking riches for believers in the Book of Mormon, only the directive that one's attitude be right before God. The passage has some similarity to Matthew 6:33, where the faithful are promised that all things shall be added if they seek first the kingdom of God. Both passages border on prosperity gospel talk, and both underscore intention and spiritual standing. Indeed, Jacob's sermon continues by warning strongly against pride, especially pride that comes from "the things which God hath given you" (Jacob 2:20). Religious motivation is given priority, and, in the proper balance, it infuses economic motivation.

The notion of religious motivation superseding self-interest is emphasized in Book of Mormon discussions referring to "exceeding riches," those who are "exceedingly rich," and those in "exceeding poverty." All four instances of "exceeding poverty" in the Book of Mormon occur in the context of Alma and Amulek's mission among the Zoramites.[32] As mentioned above, such poverty made the people more inclined to hear the word of God and more willing to listen to what was taught, but it did not necessarily indicate righteousness. Conversely, every instance of the phrase "exceeding riches" comes with warnings against boasting in human strength and being full of pride.[33] In one instance, the "exceeding riches" of the Nephites are a reason why they did not prosper, were afflicted and smitten, and driven before the Lamanites, until they lost all of their possessions (Helaman 4:12). In another instance, a man named Shez is robbed of his "exceeding riches," which turns out to be a good thing, on balance, because he was threatening to steal the kingdom from his father (Ether 10:3). Of the thirteen passages referring to the "exceedingly rich," only three suggest that it is possible to be "exceedingly rich" and still remain humble.[34] Three more instances occurring in the Book of Ether lean in that direction, but are also part of an intense and rapid pride cycle in which riches lead to loss of heavenly blessings. The most pronounced instance of the "exceedingly rich" maintaining the right balance between riches and righteousness occurs in the first chapter of Alma where, "in their prosperous circumstances, [the church] did not send away any who were naked, or that were hungry, or that were athirst, or that were sick, or that had not been nourished; and they did not set their hearts upon riches; therefore they were liberal to all, both old and young, both bond and free, both male and female, whether out of the church or in the church, having no respect to persons as to those who stood in need" (Alma 1:29). Like Matthew 6:21 and Luke 12:34, the emphasis is on the quality of one's heart. Some of the exceedingly rich "were liberal to all," but most of the exceedingly rich are not able to keep their hearts free from worshipping their wealth.

Even as the poor are inclined to humility, the Book of Mormon reasons that the rich are inclined to pride. God despises the rich and learned who are puffed up.[35] Abinadi, Alma, Helaman, and Nephi the son of Helaman all warn against the tendency for the heart to become set on riches.[36] Indeed, Satan not only tempts persons to set their hearts upon riches, but "to seek for power, and authority, and riches, and the vain things of the world" (3 Nephi 6:15). Repeatedly, the story of the Book of Mormon is one of righteousness leading to prosperity and riches, prosperity and riches leading to pride, and pride leading to wickedness.[37] The cycle of prosperity, pride, and wickedness works as a representative anecdote for human societies and closely resembles the Puritan jeremiad.[38] One difference in the Book of Mormon is the complete awareness that people and peoples cycle through riches and poverty, whereas Puritan sermonizing rested on a philosophy of society that downplayed the possibilities of such cycles, emphasizing instead that God had made some rich and some poor.[39]

The idea that God is the source of riches is a theme in LDS scripture. Although being rich or poor may lead to particular spiritual states, the Lord's voice in the Doctrine and Covenants repeats that "the riches of the earth are mine to give" (38:39). The use of the word "riches" in the Doctrine and Covenants has a deeper meaning than mere materiality. Indeed, the word "riches" is used twelve times in the revelations, only four of which refer to the concept of material wealth: once in the passage just quoted; again in Doctrine and Covenants 56:16, where the Saints are told that riches not shared will canker their souls; a third time in Doctrine and Covenants 42:39, where Saints are told to consecrate riches; and finally in Doctrine and Covenants 45:65, where the Saints are told to "gather up your riches that ye may purchase an inheritance." All the other references to "riches" in the Doctrine and Covenants are to the "riches of eternity" (6:7) and reiterate the charge to "seek not for riches but for wisdom, and behold, the mysteries of God shall be unfolded unto you, and then shall you be made rich. Behold, he that hath eternal life is rich" (11:7). Also, "if ye seek the riches which it is the will of the Father to give unto you, ye shall be the richest of all people, for ye shall have the riches of eternity" (38:39). Elsewhere, LDS scripture underscores that the riches of eternity belong to the Lord, that "the riches of eternity are yours," and that the Saints were offered the riches of eternity, but would not accept them.[40]

The revelations indicate that the Lord disburses worldly wealth, but he prefers to give the riches of wisdom and eternal life. The spiritual riches he offers are worth more than the riches of the earth (Doctrine and Covenants 38:16). One can see that spiritual matters have priority over earthly riches, at least in scripture. When the Saints leave Kirtland, Ohio, after the failure of the Kirtland Safety Society, Joseph Smith receives a revelation directing William Marks and Newel K. Whitney to leave Kirtland immediately and move to Missouri, instead of staying behind to salvage what value remained of their property. The revelation warns,

> Therefore, if they tarry it shall not be well with them.
>
> Let them repent of all their sins, and of all their covetous desires before me, saith the Lord; for what is property unto me? saith the Lord.
>
> Let the properties of Kirtland be turned out for debts, saith the Lord. Let them go, saith the Lord, and whatsoever remaineth, let it remain in your hands, saith the Lord.
>
> For have I not the fowls of heaven, and also the fish of the sea, and the beasts of the mountains? Have I not made the earth? Do I not hold the destinies of all the armies of the nations of the earth?
>
> Therefore, will I not make solitary places to bud and to blossom, and to bring forth in abundance? saith the Lord.
>
> Is there not room enough on the mountains of Adam-ondi-Ahman, and on the plains of Olaha Shinehah, or the land where Adam dwelt, that you should covet that which is but the drop, and neglect the more weighty matters? (Doctrine and Covenants 117:4–8)

Beginning with stern "thus saith the Lord" clauses about leaving property behind, the passage transitions quickly to what Harold Bloom calls "spilled poetry."[41] This poetic bluntness shows the priority of religious obedience over getting a high price for one's property. Following such stern commands is an expansive vision of nature, including the power of God over armies and solitary places, and the glory of "the land where Adam dwelt." The words reach far beyond Kirtland, Ohio, to include the heavens, seas, mountains, and the earth. The turn toward a glorious vision of nature acts as reminder of the bounty and vastness of materiality and its transcendence of human artificiality and real estate. The larger vision offered by this "spilled poetry" compensates for the calamity of lost property, or at least mitigates the loss, by situating it in a far wider context.

Clearly, the passages cited in the Book of Mormon and the Doctrine and Covenants develop ideas about rich and poor that transcend property relations through religion. In particular, they support each other when it comes to making the point that neither rich nor poor are to be entitled to special privileges in the church. The Lord congratulates the poor for their humility, but warns them against selfishness, greediness, and idleness. The Lord tells the rich that he has given them their riches through the abundance of the earth he has made, but warns them against pride, enjoining them to share their riches liberally. These ideas are reiterated in Joseph Smith's retranslation of the Gospel of St. Mark 10:23–27. In this passage Jesus is asked who can be saved if it is easier for a camel to go through the eye of a needle than a rich man to enter the kingdom of heaven. The King James Version of verse 27 reads, "And Jesus looking upon them saith, With men it is impossible, but not with God: for with God all things are possible." The Joseph Smith retranslation says, "With men that trust in riches, it is impossible; but not impossible with men who trust in God and leave all for my sake, for with such all things are possible." By inserting the phrase "trust in riches," Smith's retranslation is consistent with the pronouncements on rich and poor in LDS scripture. By juxtaposing "trust in riches" with "trust in God," the passage suggests that wealth poses a spiritual problem. Indeed, the poor could be guilty of trusting in riches when, for example, they believe that wealth will make them happy. The retranslation underscores how spiritual attitudes toward wealth are more indicative of spiritual standing than mere possession or lack of it, which is an essentially religious idea.

The bulk of canonized revelations regarding rich and poor in the Doctrine and Covenants was received prior to the failure of the Kirtland Safety Society bank. In particular, most such revelations came during 1831 and 1832. Section 78, received in March 1832, stands out among those early revelations for its explicit point about equality. According to the revelations, the United Order (the name given to the organization established in Ohio that held church property in common for the benefit of the poor) was

> For a permanent and everlasting establishment and order unto my church, to advance the cause, which ye have espoused, to the salvation of man, and to the glory of your Father who is in heaven;
>
> That you may be equal in the bonds of heavenly things, yea, and earthly things also, for the obtaining of heavenly things.
>
> For if ye are not equal in earthly things ye cannot be equal in obtaining heavenly things. (Doctrine and Covenants 78:4–6)

The language of this passage is the language of permanence and endurance. It reads as a command to be equal in earthly things as a prerequisite for the reception of heavenly things. Much hinges on the meaning of "equality," which in Smith's usage carries religious, economic, and political connotations, entailing equal consecration, equal opportunities, and equal outcomes.[42] Indeed, since the material and spiritual bleed into one another, the catalog of "earthly things" has no obvious end.

Smith's revelations received when the United Order was "temporarily dissolved," between April and June of 1834, maintain that the purpose of the order was for the benefit of the poor. No person is to say that the treasury holds private accounts, "for it shall belong to you all with one accord" and is to be used "for sacred and holy purposes" (Doctrine and Covenants 104:62, 65). The order failed because the Saints "have not learned to be obedient to the things which I required at their hands, but are full of all manner of evil, and do not impart of their substance, as becometh saints, to the poor and afflicted among them" (Doctrine and Covenants 105:3).

> Therefore, in consequence of the transgressions of my people, it is expedient in me that mine elders should wait for a little season for the redemption of Zion—
>
> That they themselves may be prepared, and that my people may be taught more perfectly, and have experience, and know more perfectly concerning their duty, and the things which I require at their hands. (Doctrine and Covenants 105:9–10)

Preparation, experience, and patience become the watchwords of realizing "equality of earthly things."[43]

Until a divine city can be realized, the Saints must satisfy themselves with tithes and the temple. Bushman argues that the temple is the vital economic center of LDS communities, even as complete consecration must wait for another day.[44] By placing the temple at the center of public life, Mormon political economy becomes centered on the family. We mistake the full power of Smith's rhetoric if we leave the reading of equality at a material level. More than once Smith's revelations refer to brothers and friends, calling on "brother Oliver" and "brother Phillip," and referring to Brigham Young as "dear and well-beloved brother" (Doctrine and Covenants 30:5; 30:10; 126:1).[45] The revelations ask readers to look on Joseph himself as their brother, to seek after "brotherly kindness," and to forgive their brothers. "My dearly beloved brethren and sisters," is an invitation for the Saints to think of themselves as part of a single household, as an *oikos*.[46] Smith's political economy, as Bushman said, establishes no system and is short on a business plan. What it lacks in management specificity it makes up by constituting a society of rich and poor as part of the same family. Smith's emphasis is on *household* rather than *management*, which is why it looks like he is not giving us much by way of political economy. Contemporary students of economics are trained to see only management. Yet the essence of Smith's equality is found among family and friends and it is this language of political economy that has enduring relevance for our times.

Conclusion

"The Prophet Joseph Smith has proved again that economic and social forces do not determine human destiny," wrote Harold Bloom.[47] Smith's theology fuses matter and spirit, filling the whole with religious power. Smith turned toward a religion that invited a politics of friendship and family and sought a unity between social classes. The full extent of these fusions is partially hidden, and Smith taught that they could only be revealed by continued progress in understanding God's will.

The foundation of understanding God's will, for Mormons, is found in the temple and the family. The wisdom contained in connecting households with sound management practices is deep, but not immediately an element of contemporary economics. Most economists and economic historians who study nineteenth-century religious reform movements emphasize economic and political motives. Consistent with their worldview, contemporary economists focus on production and growth rather than the development of sound character and healthy communities. Economic justice, even in so-called secular societies, depends on a vision of human character that accounts for whole persons. The secular science of economics does too little to address the interrelations between the human necessities of belief, creation, and material provision. It acts obliviously to the fact that spirituality has always constituted a significant element of human economies. By ignoring metaphysical aspects of human life, economics may teach societies how to grow richer even as the quality of lives grows poorer.

Smith's words juxtaposed the material with the immaterial, the seen with the unseen, and the *attitude* of rich and poor alike. Two economists recently showed that persuasion—rhetoric—accounts for fully one-fourth, and perhaps as much as one-third, of gross domestic product in the United States.[48] The rhetorician Richard Lanham has observed that a greater proportion of economic value in contemporary societies is made up of what he calls "fluff," as opposed to "stuff." That is, added value in monetary terms derives more from what people think about what they buy, than from the stuff they actually purchase. The scarce resource in such an economy is not information, but attention.[49] By attending to the rhetorical power of Smith's words, I have claimed that there is more to political economy than economic behavior. When considered in the light of a contemporary economy such as ours, where "stuff and fluff" have considerable economic value, Smith's capacity to see matter in spiritual terms and spirit in material terms looks prophetic.

NOTES

1. For this and other reasons, prophets in American history and politics have earned the label "radical." See James Darsey, *The Prophetic Tradition and Radical Rhetoric in America* (New York: New York University Press, 1997). For some background on biblical prophets as the foundation of Western conceptions of economic justice, see E. K. Hunt, *Property and Prophets: The Evolution of Economic Institutions and Ideologies* (London: M.E. Sharpe, 2003), 7–13.

2. For example, see Fawn Brodie, *No Man Knows My History* (New York: Knopf, 1995), 194–207; Leonard J. Arrington, *Great Basin Kingdom: An Economic History of the Latter-day Saints, 1830–1900* (Salt Lake City: University of Utah Press, 1993); Richard T. Ely, "Economic Aspects of Mormonism," *Harper's Monthly Magazine* 106 (April 1903): 667–78; Leonard J. Arrington, "Early Mormon Communitarianism: The Law of Consecration and Stewardship," *Western Humanities Review* 7 (Autumn 1953): 341–69; Marvin S. Hill, C. Keith Rooker, and Larry T. Wimmer, "The Kirtland

Economy Revisited: A Market Critique of Sectarian Economics," *BYU Studies* 17 (Summer 1977): 391–475, later reprinted in book form by Brigham Young University Press, 1978; and O. Kendall White, Jr., "Mormon Resistance and Accommodation: From Communitarian Socialism to Corporate Capitalism," in Scott Cummings, ed., *Self-Help in Urban America: Patterns of Minority Economic Development* (Port Washington, N.Y.: Kennikat Press, 1980), 89–112. For more on the contemporary state of LDS finances, see Richard N. Ostling and Joan K. Ostling, *Mormon America: The Power and the Promise* (New York: HarperSanFrancisco, 2000), 113–29.

3. Richard L. Bushman, *Joseph Smith: Rough Stone Rolling* (New York: Knopf, 2005), 502.

4. For a good overview on using rhetoric to understand economics, see Edward M. Clift, "The Rhetoric of Economics," in Andrea A. Lunsford, Kirt H. Wilson, and Rosa A. Eberly, eds., *The Sage Handbook of Rhetorical Studies* (Thousand Oaks, Calif.: Sage, 2009), 197–213. See also Deirdre N. McCloskey, *The Rhetoric of Economics,* 2d ed. (Madison: University of Wisconsin Press, 1998); Deirdre N. McCloskey, *If You're So Smart: The Narrative of Economic Expertise* (Chicago: University of Chicago Press, 1990); Deirdre N. McCloskey, *Knowledge and Persuasion in Economics* (Cambridge: Cambridge University Press, 1994); James Arnt Aune, *Rhetoric and Marxism* (Boulder, Colo.: Westview Press, 1994); James Arnt Aune, *Selling the Free Market: The Rhetoric of Economic Correctness* (New York: Guilford Press, 2001); and the edited volumes, *Conversations with Economists,* ed. Arjo Klamer (Totowa, N.J.: Rowman & Allanheld, 1984) and *The Rhetoric of the Human Sciences,* ed. John S. Nelson, Allan Megill, and Donald N. McCloskey (Madison: University of Wisconsin Press, 1987).

5. I would love to use the phrase "economic theology," as my central interest is in how theology organizes economic ideas, but that phrase has already been employed to describe the near-fanatic intensity with which economists cling to their mathematical and self-interested theories, as if theology were little more than fundamentalism. See Duncan K. Foley, *Adam's Fallacy: A Guide to Economic Theology* (Cambridge, Mass.: Belknap Press, 2006).

6. For the most crucial work on the subject of economics as countertheology, see John Milbank, *Theology and Social Theory: Beyond Secular Reason,* 2d ed. (Oxford: Blackwell, 2006), especially chapter 2, "Political Economy as Theodicy and Agonistics," 26–47. Other writers have argued for the way particular economic systems, most notably capitalism, support Christian ideals. For more on this, see Michael Novak, *The Spirit of Democratic Capitalism* (New York: Madison Books, 1991); Deirdre N. McCloskey, "Capital Gains: How Economic Growth Benefits the World," *Christian Century* 121 (May 4, 2004): 24–30; and a variety of viewpoints in William Schweiker and Charles Mathewes, eds., *Having: Property and Possession in Religious and Social Life* (Grand Rapids, Mich.: Eerdmans, 2004).

7. Complicating the picture is the twentieth century's Cold War residue that leads many to see political economy as either capitalist or Marxist. Indeed, after I

presented an early draft of this essay at the 2006 Mormon History Association conference in Casper, Wyoming, a listener congratulated me for showing that Smith's economic orientation was Marxist. This was not my intention. There are, of course, similarities with Marx as there are, probably, with the capitalistic rhetoric of LDS business leaders like Mitt Romney and Steven Covey, but that is beside my point.

8. As far as I am concerned, Joseph Smith is a prophet because he talks like a prophet. He does not talk like a political economist. A communicative or literary approach to discourse may assert confidently that we are dealing with prophetic texts. See Harold Bloom's justification for a similar approach to reading the Book of Mormon in Harold Bloom, *The American Religion* (New York: Chu Hartley, 1992), 78–79.

9. See Peter Minowitz, *Profits, Priests, and Princes: Adam Smith's Emancipation of Economics from Politics and Religion* (Stanford, Calif.: Stanford University Press, 1993).

10. Arrington, *Great Basin Kingdom,* 35.

11. Ibid., 409.

12. Jeffrey Sklansky, *The Soul's Economy: Market Society and Selfhood, 1820–1920* (Chapel Hill: University of North Carolina Press, 2002), 7.

13. Ibid., 38.

14. Bernard Bailyn, David Brion Davis, David Herbert Donald, John L. Thomas, Robert H. Wiebe, and Gordon S. Wood, *The Great Republic: A History of the American People* (Boston: Little, Brown, 1977), 538.

15. On the Owenites, see John Harrison, *Robert Owen and the Owenites in Britain and America: The Quest for the New Moral World* (New York: Routledge, 2009).

16. Charles Sellers, *The Market Revolution: Jacksonian America, 1815–1846* (New York: Oxford University Press, 1991), 217–25.

17. Ibid., 219.

18. Ibid., 220, 222.

19. For more on this milieu, see Alan Taylor, "The Early Republic's Supernatural Economy: Treasure Seeking in the American Northwest, 1780–1830," *American Quarterly* 38 (Spring 1986): 6–34. Taylor posits Joseph Smith's treasure seeking as a means to discovering a supernatural economy "as an alternative to the disappointing natural economy" and argues that early Mormonism avoided the fate of other treasure-seeking groups through institutionalizing their leadership and pointing followers to riches in the hereafter. While I do not disagree with the probable motives identified by Taylor or Sellers, I am more interested in the possibilities presented by supernatural economic rhetoric.

20. Bushman, *Joseph Smith,* 182.

21. Ibid., 174.

22. Samuel Brown has shown convincingly that the words of the presidential platform are those of Joseph Smith's ghostwriter, W. W. Phelps, who was instructed

to write the piece by Smith. See Samuel Brown, "The Translator and Ghostwriter: Joseph Smith and W. W. Phelps," *Journal of Mormon History* 34 (Winter 2008): 26–62.

23. Kenneth Cmiel, *Democratic Eloquence: The Fight over Popular Speech in Nineteenth-Century America* (New York: William Morrow, 1990), 63.

24. Joseph Smith, *General Smith's Views of the Powers and Policy of the Government of the United States* (Nauvoo, Ill.: John Taylor, 1844), 3.

25. Ibid., 7.

26. Ibid., 4.

27. Terryl Givens, *People of Paradox: A History of Mormon Culture* (Oxford: Oxford University Press, 2007), 42.

28. Bushman, *Joseph Smith,* 503.

29. Robert J. Woodford, "The Historical Development of the Doctrine and Covenants," 3 vols. (Ph.D. dissertation, Brigham Young University, 1974), 2:935–36.

30. Bushman, *Joseph Smith,* 197, 199.

31. Leonard J. Arrington, "Religion and Economics in Mormon History," *BYU Studies* 3 (Spring/Summer 1961): 15.

32. Alma 32:5, 12, 15; 34:40.

33. Alma 4:6; Helaman 4:12; 4 Nephi 1:43; Ether 10:3.

34. For passages mentioning the "exceedingly rich," see Jarom 1:8; Alma 1:29, 45:24, 50:18, 62:48–49; Helaman 3:36, 6:9, 7:26; 3 Nephi 6:10; 4 Nephi 1:23; Ether 6:28, 9:16, 10:12. I consider only Alma 1:29; Alma 62:48–49; and, on a stretch, 4 Nephi 1:23 to be instances where "exceedingly rich" is not condemned within the same verse. The reference to 4 Nephi is questionable because 1:24 shows that the exceeding riches led quickly to pride and wickedness. Still, the references in Ether are instances where "exceeding riches" are not immediately condemned, but they come in the context of being so short-lived and ineffective that they ought to be read differently.

35. 2 Nephi 9:42; 28:15.

36. Mosiah 12:29; Alma 5:53; 7:6; Helaman 4:12; 7:21.

37. This was an important theme in the ministry of the late president of the LDS Church, Ezra Taft Benson. See Ezra Taft Benson, "Beware of Pride," *Ensign* (May 1989): 4–7.

38. See Perry Miller, *The New England Mind: From Colony to Province* (Cambridge, Mass.: Harvard University Press, 1953); and Sacvan Bercovich, *The American Jeremiad* (Madison: University of Wisconsin Press, 1979). The jeremiad, named for the prophet Jeremiah, is a thematic structure for sermons noted originally in the books of Jeremiah and Isaiah that follows a description of God's relations with his people as covenant, declension, and prophecy. God chooses and makes special his people, they often neglect his commands and fall into error, but there is prophetic hope that if they change their ways they can be redeemed. The themes appear in many early Puritan discourses as well as more generally and repeatedly in American political discourse.

39. Miller, *New England Mind,* 400–401.

40. Doctrine and Covenants 67:2; 78:18; 43:25.

41. Bloom, *American Religion,* 70.

42. For more on Smith's sense of equality, see Bushman, *Joseph Smith,* 155.

43. See also Bloom, *American Religion,* 81–90.

44. See Bushman, *Joseph Smith,* 504, where Bushman juxtaposes the temple "soul" of Nauvoo with Chicago's "soul" at the Board of Trade, reasoning, I think justly, that the respective economies of the towns were, likewise, different. Traditionally, temples in agricultural societies were a repudiation of the economic order because they were constituted of large chunks of land that were left uncultivated. See Josef Pieper, *Leisure: The Basis of Culture* (Indianapolis: Liberty Fund, 1952), 44–48, for a discussion of the Sabbath and temples as economic transcendence. Using contemporary economic methods one might consider an LDS temple as revenue producing, in the sense that it promotes continued faithfulness and the desire to pay tithes, and is thus not a revenue-consuming asset. This is the idea adopted by Ostling and Ostling, *Mormon America,* but it conflicts with the rhetoric of the late church president Gordon B. Hinckley, who publicly expressed anxiety that the building of new temples is an economic burden to the church.

45. There are numerous references to "friends" in the revelations, but see Doctrine and Covenants 82:22 and 93:45 where "friends" intersects with economic commands.

46. The etymology of "economy" is hybrid of the Greek words *oikos* and *nomos,* "household" and "management" or "law," respectively.

47. Bloom, *American Religion,* 89.

48. Arjo Klamer and Deirdre McCloskey, "One Quarter of GDP Is Persuasion," *American Economic Review* 85 (May 1995): 191–96.

49. See Richard Lanham, *The Economics of Attention: Style and Substance in the Age of Information* (Chicago: University of Chicago Press, 2006).

2

"Is There No Blessing for Me?"

JANE JAMES'S CONSTRUCTION OF SPACE IN LATTER-DAY SAINT HISTORY AND PRACTICE

Quincy D. Newell

Behold, there shall be a record kept among you.

—*Doctrine and Covenants 21:1 April 6, 1830*

Though she did not write it herself, Jane Elizabeth Manning James still managed to leave a record of her life as an African American Latter-day Saint.[1] Like many nineteenth- (and twentieth-) century Mormons, she left an autobiography to testify to her "faith in the Gospel of Jesus Christ of the Latter-day Saints," which, she affirmed, "is as strong today, nay, it is if possible stronger than it was the day I was first baptized."[2] James listed her religious practices as support for the strength of her faith: "I pay my tithes and offerings, keep the word of wisdom, I go to bed early and rise early, I try in my feeble way to set a good example to all; I have had eighteen grand children eight of them are living, also seven great grand children."[3] Of course, she kept a record as well, by dictating her autobiography to Elizabeth J. D. Roundy sometime between 1901 and her death in 1908.[4] She also contributed her reminiscences of the prophet Joseph Smith to the LDS Church–published *Young Woman's Journal* for the centenary of his birth in 1905.[5]

In telling her life story, Jane James positioned herself near the center of the Latter-day Saint story, inserting herself into LDS myth-history. In this way, she carved out a space for herself in LDS history and practice despite the efforts of the church hierarchy to marginalize her because of her race. This essay focuses primarily on the autobiography in order to understand how and why James inserted herself into the center of the LDS story. James's membership in the LDS community began with her conversion, so the first part of this essay focuses on James's conversion story. I show how it fits the conventions of nineteenth-century Latter-day Saint conversion narratives and uses rhetorical devices that were particularly powerful for LDS audiences. In the second section, I examine James's account of gathering at Nauvoo, Illinois. Gathering was a major religious impulse, particularly in early Mormonism, but James responded to the call too late to experience much of the persecution that eventually drove the Saints to Nauvoo.[6] Nevertheless, James absorbed this history of persecution into her own story by emphasizing the similarity of her experiences to those of other Saints, and by using her gathering story to stand in for the story of the hardships and trials that all the Saints experienced on the way from Nauvoo to the Great Salt Lake Valley. The third section of this essay examines the portion of James's narrative that she set in Nauvoo, the longest section of the autobiography. In this portion of the autobiography, James emphasizes her intimacy with Joseph Smith and his family; her access to sacred objects; and her acquisition of sacred knowledge, emphatically positioning herself as an insider in the LDS community. Finally, in the last section of this essay I place James's autobiography within the context of her concern over her spiritual welfare. I argue that the autobiography was the fullest of James's many attempts to carve out space for herself in Mormon practice, despite her race, by appealing to the position she had occupied in Mormon history.

Scholarship on Jane James has been surprisingly limited, given the available sources. Although James is relatively well known among twenty-first-century Mormons—and among scholars of African American Mormon history—most discussions of her life have been produced for popular consumption and therefore include little, if any, analysis of James's religious experience.[7] Scholarship on African Americans in the LDS Church more generally has tended to be policy-oriented: after Joseph Smith's death in 1844, the church leadership instituted a policy that came to be known as the "priesthood ban," barring people of African descent from sharing in the "blessings of the priesthood." This policy, which came to be understood as doctrine, prevented black men from being ordained to the priesthood, which was held by all other worthy male members of the church. A less frequently discussed implication of this policy was that black women were prohibited from participating in most ceremonies in LDS temples because of these ceremonies' dependence on the exercise of priesthood authority within a marital relationship. While these policies clearly shaped James's religious experience, description and analysis of the church's "Negro Doctrine" cast only a faint light on James's religious life. James is often noted as an early African American convert, but scholarship on African Americans' experiences in the LDS Church has focused on the period since 1978, when the priesthood ban was lifted.[8] Studies of nineteenth-century African American religion more broadly have completely ignored African American Mormons, probably because their numbers seemed too small to merit sustained consideration.[9] While the number of African Americans who converted to Mormonism was relatively small, this fact does not make these converts insignificant. Rather, despite their small number, the experiences of African American Mormons like Jane James illuminate a number of important and understudied facets of nineteenth-century Mormonism, including the intersection of religious and racial identity in the LDS Church; the religion's shifting structures of authority; and the tension between institutional doctrine and personal experience.

"Fully Convinced That It Was the True Gospel"

Jane Elizabeth Manning James was, during her lifetime, something of an anomaly as an African American Mormon. Few other African Americans converted to the LDS faith during the lifetime of its founding prophet, Joseph Smith, and after his death in 1844 the church slowly moved to systematically discourage proselytization among African Americans.[10] Nevertheless, some African Americans, including a young Jane James, joined the church.

Jane James's conversion story is brief—just a few lines. As she recalled it, James went to hear Charles Wesley Wandell, a Mormon missionary, preach "and was fully convinced that it was the true Gospel he presented and I must embrace it[.] The following Sunday I was baptized and confirmed a member of the Church of Jesus Christ of Latter-day Saints. About three weeks after while kneeling at prayer the Gift of Tongues came upon me, and frightened the whole family who were in the next room."[11] Although short, James's story bears the hallmarks of typical nineteenth-century Mormon conversion narratives. In an analysis of the conversion narratives of early Mormon converts, Steven C. Harper writes that for many people, Mormonism combined empirical evidence and supernatural experience in a way that "simultaneously catered to the metaphysical, rationalistic, and democratic—coexisting features of the intellectual framework that most frequently informed conversion."[12] These three features figured in James's conversion as well. She accepted the missionary's message on a rational level; experienced confirmation of the message metaphysically in her experience of glossolalia; and found in the LDS Church a more egalitarian community than was available to her elsewhere.

James's matter-of-fact tone in her statement that she "was fully convinced that it was the true Gospel [Wandell] presented," emphasizing the superiority of Wandell's message to those previously available to her, matches that of other nineteenth-century LDS converts.[13] Eliza Gibbs, a white convert from the late 1830s, used very similar language: a young Mormon man named Elijah Austin, Gibbs later remembered, "enlightened my mind" with regard to the principles of the LDS Church. These principles made sense to Gibbs because they corresponded with how she understood the Bible. "As soon as he began to preach his doctrine I perceived it was Bible Doctrine, and as he progressed in explaining his faith I also discovered that the principles he taught were the same I had adopted," she recalled. The logical response, for Gibbs, was to "embrace the gospel," just as Jane James would do a few years later.[14] Rational persuasion also seems to have formed the core of the conversions of Benjamin Ashby and his parents, white Americans who converted to Mormonism around the same time as Jane James. After hearing Erastus Snow preach in Salem, Massachusetts, Ashby recalled, "my mind soon became enlightened upon the plan of salvation. I firmly believed in the divinity and sacred character of the Book of Mormon which I read." His mother, likewise, "attended the [Mormon] meetings in the Masonic Hall and became convinced of the truth of the gospel."[15] For James, as for Gibbs and the Ashbys, conversion to Mormonism was a rationalistic response to what they perceived to be a logically superior message.

This rationalistic response was confirmed by what converts understood as metaphysical experiences. Although Ashby's initial conversion focused on the process of rational persuasion, he also experienced a physical healing that he attributed to his baptism. For Ashby, this healing validated his decision to accept baptism, thereby cementing his conversion to Mormonism. Jane James had a similar experience of supernatural power that confirmed her selection of Mormonism as the "right" religion when she experienced "the Gift of Tongues" some three weeks after her baptism.[16] Harper points to this combination of rational persuasion and supernatural experience—the apparent truthfulness and reasonableness of the Mormon message paired with "proof of spiritual efficacy"—as the key characteristic of nineteenth-century Mormon conversion narratives.

While James's conversion story shows how, in Harper's terms, Mormonism "catered to the metaphysical [and] rationalistic" aspects of her intellectual framework, its appeal to the third aspect that Harper identifies, the "democratic" side of her thinking, is less apparent. Still, it is possible that Mormonism did, in fact, strike Jane James as more democratic than the other religious options available in Wilton, Connecticut. The Mormons' willingness to baptize James and claim her as a full-fledged member of their church may have contributed to this impression. In an era when most Protestant denominations segregated their members, relegating black members to seats in galleries or to entirely separate congregations, the LDS Church does not appear to have enacted any policy that distinguished between believers on the basis of race at that early point in its history.[17] James may thus have seen the LDS Church as more egalitarian than other religious organizations at the time.

In her autobiography, James implicitly compared the LDS Church to the Presbyterian Church, which she said she joined about a year and a half before hearing Wandell, the Mormon missionary, preach. She narrated her conversion to Mormonism immediately after noting that her pastor "forbid me going to hear [Wandell] as he had heard I had expressed a desire to hear them." While the pastor's opposition may have been rooted in theological disagreement or simple prejudice against Mormonism, in this context it reads as obstructionist opposition to James's sincere search for truth. Nathan Hatch cautions scholars against seeing such conflicts in straightforward theological or intellectual terms, writing that "the most profound religious debates in the early republic followed social and class lines rather than merely intellectual ones."[18] Though James's story takes place slightly later than the period Hatch discusses, the same social and cultural cleavages pertained: the Presbyterian clergy represented an educated intellectual and cultural elite, whereas the Mormons saw themselves and were seen by others as socially and culturally marginalized. James may thus have believed her pastor's hostility to the Mormons was based less in theological differences than in the pastor's attachment to the established social hierarchy and his elevated place in it. Although both Wandell and her pastor were white men, James may have felt she was closer in status, as a free black woman, to the Mormon than to the educated minister. In her telling, she voted with her feet, choosing the egalitarian church of the outsiders over the hierarchical religious establishment.

Although James said she joined the Presbyterian Church—and, indeed, that her pastor had opposed her plan to listen to the visiting Mormon missionary—a search of local church records has yet to turn up evidence of James's membership in any other congregation prior to her Mormon conversion. In fact, there was no Presbyterian church in Wilton, Connecticut. In 1801, acknowledging their theological commonalities, the Presbyterian and Congregational Churches joined together in what was known as the "Plan of Union," a scheme to evangelize the entire fledgling United States. The two churches divided up the territory to be covered and agreed not to interfere with each other's missionary work. Southwestern Connecticut, where James lived, was assigned to the Congregationalists. According to historian George M. Marsden, "in Connecticut the term Presbyterian had become acceptable and common usage for designating Congregational affiliation."[19] Thus, it is possible that James may have meant that she joined the Congregational Church in Wilton. However, no record of her membership in the Congregational Church exists. A major religious revival took place in Wilton in 1842, and it is around this time that James claimed to have joined the Presbyterian Church. The revival was jointly sponsored by the local Methodist and Congregational Churches, raising the possibility that Jane James joined the Methodists, but no record of her membership has been found there.[20] Joseph Fitch, the patriarch of the family for whom James worked as a girl, was a chorister in the local Episcopal Church, but she does not appear in that congregation's membership records either.[21] James's absence from the records is not a result of her race: all of these denominations kept records of both white and black members in the nineteenth century. It is possible, of course, that records of her membership have simply been lost. It is also possible, however, that James did not officially join any of the churches in Wilton, though she may have become a regular attendee at one of them.

Regardless of its veracity, James's claim to have joined the Presbyterian Church served important rhetorical purposes in her narrative. "When about fourteen years old I joined the Presbyterian Church," James recalled, "yet I did not feel satisfied[.] It seemed to me there was something more that I was looking for."[22] Appearing in the first lines of James's narrative, this statement immediately signaled her seriousness with regard to religious matters and categorized her as a religious seeker. James's search was relatively short compared with that detailed in some nineteenth-century Mormon conversion narratives, since she only tried one other church before finding the "true Gospel" in the LDS Church. Nevertheless, James's sojourn in the Presbyterian Church was the element necessary to structure this portion of the narrative as a quest for complete truth, a common motif in the conversion stories of James's contemporaries. Joseph Smith's own story, perhaps the paradigmatic conversion narrative for members of the LDS Church, began with confusion about which denomination was correct. It was Smith's earnest search for religious truth, Mormons believed, that led him to pray for answers, thus setting in motion the events that led to the founding of the LDS Church.[23]

In Jane James's narrative, as in many nineteenth-century LDS conversion narratives, the Presbyterians functioned as a foil for the Mormons, providing a background of inadequacy against which the completeness of Mormonism's message—its possession of that "something more" that Jane James sought—stood out in bold relief. Mormons had long used the Presbyterians for contrast in this way; animosity between the two groups had existed since the very beginning of the LDS Church. Both Joseph Smith and his mother, Lucy Mack Smith, singled out the Presbyterians as a source of particular antagonism in the LDS Church's early days.[24] Mormons' use of the Presbyterians as a contrast to their religion continued well after Joseph Smith's death. Leaders like George Albert Smith, a nephew of Joseph Smith, Jr., and Wilford Woodruff, the president of the LDS Church near the end of the nineteenth century, both discussed their personal encounters with Presbyterianism as a way of showing the inadequacy of ordinary Protestantism and the completeness of the LDS message. Smith told a Salt Lake City audience in 1857 that the Presbyterian Church and its ministers lacked "force" with regard to spiritual matters.[25] In a similar vein, Woodruff remarked in 1898 that the Presbyterians had no "power to unlock the heavens and give you converse with God and angels, and give you gifts and graces and power." In Mormonism, on the other hand, he found all this as well as "a Prophet"—an office he eventually occupied himself.[26] Whether or not Jane James heard these particular speeches, she recalled her experience with Presbyterians in similar terms. Like Smith and Woodruff, James also found something missing in the conventional Protestant denominations. And like Smith and Woodruff, she also found that "something more" in the LDS Church.[27]

"We Went on Our Way Rejoicing"

By the time Jane James dictated her autobiography in the early 1900s, the Saints were following their fifth prophet. They had been driven from New York to Ohio; Ohio to Missouri; Missouri to Illinois (where James joined the group); and finally from Illinois to Utah. The Saints had adopted, and then given up, their distinctive practice of polygamy and were elaborating new markers of peoplehood, negotiating what it meant to be a Latter-day Saint if it did not mean practicing plural marriage.[28] To James, Latter-day Sainthood meant participating in the group's tumultuous history, experiencing its earthly persecutions and its spiritual manifestations. The Utah Saints were in the process of ritualizing this history, focusing especially on the heroic pioneer generation that originally settled the Great Salt Lake Valley and on the restoration of the gospel through Joseph Smith.[29] In her autobiography, Jane James placed herself near the center of this history.

As she told her story, James absorbed the Latter-day Saints' history into her own personal narrative. James said little about the exodus from Nauvoo to Utah in 1846 and 1847. Instead, she focused on her journey from Connecticut, where she was baptized, to Nauvoo. In James's narrative, this trip stood for both the persecutions of the Mormons before they went to Illinois and for the hardships of the final exodus to the Great Salt Lake Valley. James and several other African Americans began the journey as part of an interracial group led by Charles Wesley Wandell, the missionary who had baptized James. Among the African Americans were James herself (who was at that point unmarried, and therefore still known by her maiden name,

Manning), James's mother and stepfather, her five siblings and two siblings-in-law, James's first child, and two former slaves.[30] Though the entire group began the journey by boat, the African American migrants were forced to abandon this mode of transportation when they reached Buffalo, New York, and to walk the remainder of the distance (which James estimated on three separate occasions at eight hundred, nine hundred, and one thousand miles), much like the handcart pioneers when they traveled to Utah.[31] In James's account of this journey, two motifs emerged: the suffering of the people and the providence of God.[32]

James left no doubt that she and her family suffered in their quest to join the Saints in Nauvoo. They faced the threat of jail in Peoria, because they carried no documentation to prove their status as free blacks. In addition to fright, the threats apparently caused considerable confusion: "we didnt know at first what he meant for we had never been slaves," James recalled. More serious than the mental anguish that the authorities' harassment brought on, though, were the physical sufferings the party endured. "We walked until our shoes were worn out," James remembered, "and our feet became sore and cracked open and bled until you could see the whole print of our feet with blood on the ground." Nevertheless, they continued, wading through a stream that reached "up to our necks," sleeping on the ground with "frost . . . so heavy that it was like a light fall of snow" and, the following morning, "walking through that frost with our bare feet."[33] To confirm that the physical and emotional trials she and her family endured were enough to test the faith of the most devout Latter-day Saint, James recalled an exchange between Joseph Smith and John M. Bernhisel on the evening that she arrived in Nauvoo. Bernhisel was an important man in the LDS community at the time and was later elected to be Utah's first delegate to Congress in 1853.[34] After the two men had heard the story of James's journey to Nauvoo, she said, "Brother Joseph slapped Dr Bernhisel on the knee and said, what do you think of that Dr, isn't that faith, the Dr, said, Well I rather think it is, if it had have [*sic*] been me I fear I should have backed out and returned to my home!"[35] For a prominent Mormon like Bernhisel to admit that James had been through more than he could have endured demonstrated the depth of her suffering.

In James's account, the journey was only endurable because of God's providence and miraculous intervention. When their feet were cracked and bleeding, she recalled, "We stopped and united in prayer to the Lord, we asked God the Eternal Father to heal our feet and our prayers were answered and our feet were healed forthwith." God's assistance became a motive for celebration, and as she and her family walked barefooted through the frost, James said, "we went on our way rejoicing singing hymns and thanking God for his infinite goodness and mercy to us, in blessing us as he had, protecting us from all harm, answering our prayers and healing our feet."[36] God's providence apparently extended through James and her family to other people. "At La harpe [Illinois]," James recalled, "we came to a place where there was a very sick child, we administered to it, and the child was healed[.] I found after the elders had before this given it up as they did not think it could live."[37] The implication was clear: James and her party had greater faith than the Mormon elders and were therefore able to heal the child when the elders could not.

Because James was baptized in 1842 and went directly to Nauvoo in 1843, she did not experience the persecution directed against the Saints in Missouri and elsewhere. James's account, however, assured her audience that, though she was not driven out from anywhere at gunpoint, she experienced equivalent hardship. Though she did not suffer alongside the Saints, she nevertheless believed that God still accompanied and provided for her and her family. Thus, though she did not experience the same persecution that many other early Latter-day Saints did, James constructed herself as an insider by substituting her suffering on the journey from Connecticut to Nauvoo.

James's story of the hardships she endured between Connecticut and Nauvoo also anticipated the suffering of the Saints during their last collective migration from Nauvoo to the Great Salt Lake. James's account of the trek from Nauvoo to Utah is surprisingly brief in comparison with her recollection of the earlier trip from Connecticut to Nauvoo. "In the spring of 1846 I left Nauvoo to come to this great and glorious Valley," she remembered.[38] She spent the winter at Winter Quarters, an LDS settlement built on the west bank of the Missouri River outside what is now Omaha, Nebraska, where she and her new husband welcomed her second son.[39] The journey recommenced in the spring and, as James recalled, "We arrived here on the 22nd day of September 1847 without any serious mishaps, the Lords blessing was with us and protected us all the way, the only thing that did occur worth relating was when our cattle stampeded, some of them we never did find."[40]

James's omission of the hardships of this trek is a curious choice. By the first decade of the twentieth century, the journey from Nauvoo to the Great Salt Lake had acquired legendary status among Latter-day Saints. Pioneer Day, which marked the arrival of the first LDS company into the Great Basin, was (and still is) celebrated annually with more fanfare than the Fourth of July. In 1897, James had been photographed along with other 1847 pioneers as part of the fiftieth anniversary celebrations.[41] James's participation in the group photo and other activities suggests that the journey to Utah was an important memory for her. She may have placed less emphasis on the migration from Illinois to Utah than on other parts of her narrative because she assumed that her audience would be familiar with this well-known event in LDS history. Discussing this journey only briefly may thus have been, for James, another way of marking herself as an insider—as someone who knew what did *not* need to be said. Alternatively, James may have seen the migration from Nauvoo to the Great Salt Lake as fundamentally less important than earlier portions of her narrative because some of the most important characters—Joseph Smith and his family—no longer figured in the story.

"Our Destined Haven of Rest"

Though James had lived more than half a century in Salt Lake City by the time she dictated her autobiography, the central portion of the manuscript concerns the few years she spent in Nauvoo.[42] Her focus on this location, rather than on Salt Lake, suggests that Nauvoo held a mythic status in James's mind akin to the Garden of Eden. "We have now arrived to our destined haven of rest, the beautiful Nauvoo!" she exclaimed when she reached that point in her narrative.[43] Just as Adam and Eve walked and talked with God in Eden, James had daily contact with the prophet of God, Joseph Smith, in Nauvoo. Indeed, James's description of Nauvoo centers around the person of Joseph Smith, at whose home she arrived, and where she stayed as a guest and, once the rest of her traveling companions had found jobs elsewhere, as a servant. He and his family attended personally to her needs—from temporal considerations such as shelter, clothing, and employment, to spiritual necessities such as divine guidance and heavenly exaltation. In James's narrative, it was in Nauvoo that God's presence and providence were most tangible.

In this central portion of her autobiography, James forcefully constructed her position near the center of LDS history. In a series of six anecdotes, James established her intimacy with Joseph Smith and his family, her access to sacred objects, and her knowledge of sacred information and obedience to divine commands received through both natural and supernatural means. She suggested that this intimacy, access, and knowledge ought to be more important than her black skin in determining her position in the LDS church.

As a guest and then as a servant, James had daily contact with Joseph Smith and his family. When she arrived with her own family in Nauvoo, James found a warm welcome at Smith's home, in contrast to the "hardship, trial and rebuff" that her party experienced elsewhere in Nauvoo before reaching the Smith home. James made it clear that Joseph Smith found her dark skin no obstacle to fellowship: not only did Joseph and his wife Emma Smith welcome James and her family, but "Brother Joseph said to some white Sisters that was present, Sisters I want you to occupy this room this evening with some brothers and sisters that have just arrived." According to James's account, everyone enjoyed the evening of storytelling and sharing that followed.[44]

James's marking of race in this episode is subtle, yet telling: in her recollection, Smith made no reference to her race; he simply invited James and her family to join that evening's gathering. By noting the race of the "Sisters," James shows that Smith's invitation created an interracial group, integrating white and black Mormons. She also signals her own consciousness of race—her own and that of those around her—by noting that the "Sisters" were white, and she subtly engages her audience's racial consciousness as well. She seems to be telling her audience, composed primarily of her mostly white coreligionists, that she has not forgotten that her race separates her from most of them—but that that separation was insignificant to Joseph Smith and the Saints closest to him in Nauvoo.

James emphasized Joseph Smith's friendly treatment of her and her family, driving home the point that he found her race irrelevant. As James remembered it, Smith was the consummate host, extending a hearty welcome to the group on the evening of their arrival, and "[coming] in every morning to say good morning and ask how we were."[45] Once the rest of her family had found jobs and homes, Smith's solicitude for James led him to offer her a post in his own home. When she was a servant, James recalled, Joseph continued to treat her cordially, greeting her in the morning and shaking hands with her.[46]

James's experience of Smith was the practical translation of his racial attitudes into everyday life. Scholars have shown that Smith's views on race were quite complex: he opposed racially mixed marriages, but believed that black people had just as much innate potential as white people. He opposed slavery, but disagreed with the methods of the abolitionist movement. He proclaimed a message of salvation available to all people, but wrote that "it would be much better and more prudent, not to preach at all to the slaves, until after their masters are converted."[47] Like most white Americans of his time, he believed that black skin was a mark of divine curse, but he allowed the ordination of black men in the LDS Church and looked forward to the day when people of all races would worship together.[48] In James's case, Smith welcomed her into his home, but treated her as a child.

Working in the Smith home allowed James access to other members of the Smith family as well. She recalled in her narrative that "I had to pass through Mother [Lucy Mack] Smiths room to get to mine," and the elder Mrs. Smith confided in James, bringing her into the family's circle of intimates. As James passed through Lucy Smith's room, she remembered, the mother of the Prophet "would often stop me and talk to me, she told me all Brother Josephs troubles, and what he had suffered in publishing the Book of Mormon."[49] Through Lucy Mack Smith, then, James participated more directly in the life of the first Mormon prophet than did many of his followers.

James emphasized her closeness to the Smiths by narrating her brush with membership in the family. "Sister Emma [Smith] asked me one day if I would like to be adopted to them as their child," James remembered. "I did not answer her, she said I will wait a while and let you consider it; she waited two weeks before she asked me again." When the wife of the Prophet returned to reiterate the offer, James declined. Although in 1843 Joseph Smith had dictated the revelation that underlay the concept of sealing children to parents, so that families would remain intact for eternity, a ritual for sealing members of different generations in the temple was not developed until after Smith's death in 1844. During Smith's lifetime, the focus was on rituals that would seal men and women as husbands and wives for eternity and ensure eternal life for believers. Development of the parent-child sealing ritual occurred only later, during Brigham Young's tenure as the leader of the Saints.[50] In this later period, the law of adoption became a way of knitting members of the LDS Church together in an extended family that would endure for eternity. With the clarification of this conception of adoption in the LDS Church, James tried to reverse her decision, claiming several times that she did not understand what Emma Smith's offer meant.[51] James almost certainly did not take the initial offer to mean that she would be permanently linked with Joseph Smith, allowing her to share in his exaltation; she may have believed that the adoption would lock her into a position of subservience that she did not wish to hold forever. She also may have anticipated a temple marriage sometime in the future that would have rendered unnecessary her adoption into Smith's family by giving her an eternal family of her own: since the Nauvoo Temple was not completed until after Joseph Smith's death, James might reasonably have expected to be allowed to participate in temple ceremonies along with white Mormons.[52]

Although James declined to be formally adopted into the Smith family, she was still treated like part of the family by the Smiths—most importantly, by the Prophet. "He'd always smile," James recalled in her 1905 reminiscence for the *Young Woman's Journal*. In fact, she continued, he smiled at her "always just like he did to his children. He used to be just like I was his child."[53] James later emphasized her status as a quasi-child (instead of a servant) in her autobiography and other recollections of her time in the Smith home in order to bolster her claims to intimacy with the Prophet and his family despite her dark skin.

James's narrative emphasized her intimacy with the Smith family by recounting the way the Smiths treated her as a member of the family, but her status as a servant also gave James access to the Smiths' dirty laundry—quite literally. As an employee of the Smith family, James was in charge of washing the Smiths' clothes, including Joseph's temple robes. By the twentieth century, few Saints could claim to have seen the Prophet's ceremonial robes, and James used her routine access to these articles of clothing to further reinforce her claim to have had privileged access to the Prophet.

The ceremonial clothing Smith wore during temple rituals, in particular, held the status of sacred objects in James's understanding. In her account of the first time she washed them, the robes were immediately striking. "Among the clothes I found brother Josephs Robes. I looked at them and wondered, I had never seen any before," she recalled. James's wonder was so profound that it led to a mystical experience: "I pondered over them and thought about them so earnestly that the spirit made manifest to me that they pertained to the new name that is given the saints that the world knows not off [*sic*]," she remembered. "I didnt know when I washed them or when I put them out to dry."[54] Although they might have appeared to be ordinary articles of clothing, the robes thus revealed themselves as sacred objects, capable of inducing a trance state and catalyzing communication with the divine. Though James was not permitted to participate in the temple ceremonies for which the robes were designed, she nevertheless had access to the robes of the most important person in the church—the Prophet himself.

The temple robes were not the only sacred objects to which James had access in Nauvoo. One day, as she was passing through Lucy Mack Smith's room, James recalled, the prophet's mother asked her to retrieve a bundle from the bureau in the room. When James had done so, Mrs. Smith somewhat mysteriously "placed the bundle in my hands and said, handle this and then put [it] in the top drawer of my bureau and lock it up.[55] Once James had followed these instructions, she recalled, the older woman asked her, "Do you remember that I told you about the Urim and Thumim [*sic*] when I told you about the book of Mormon? . . . She then told me I had just handled it, You are not permitted to see it, but you have been permitted to handle it. You will live long after I am dead and gone And you can tell the Latter-day Saints, that you was permitted to handle the Urim and Thumim [*sic*]."[56] James's narration of this episode—particularly the remarks she attributed to Lucy Mack Smith—made clear that handling the Urim and Thummim, the seer stones that Joseph Smith had retrieved with the gold plates and used to translate the plates into the Book of Mormon, was a privilege few Saints could expect to have. Like seeing the golden plates from which the Book of Mormon was translated, or serving as a secretary during the translation, handling the Urim and Thummim materially linked James to the translation of the Book of Mormon and what the Latter-day Saints believed was the restoration of the Gospel. In this way, she joined an elite group of Saints who had connections to that early (and in the LDS imagination, glorious) period of Mormon history.

James further bolstered her claim to a place near the center of LDS history through the sacred knowledge she acquired from both divine and human sources. This knowledge began with the "Gift of Tongues" shortly after her baptism, which confirmed her conviction of the truth of Mormonism, and it continued with a dream or vision of Joseph Smith that she experienced in Connecticut, allowing her to recognize him as a true prophet upon her arrival in Nauvoo.[57] This contact with the divine continued during her time as a servant in Joseph Smith's house. As mentioned earlier, James recalled that, while she was washing Joseph Smith's temple robes, "the spirit made manifest to me that they pertained to the new name that is given the saints that the world knows not off [*sic*]."[58] As James indicated, "the world [knew] not" about this "new name" because the Mormons closely guarded information about their temple rituals. This knowledge, then, was privileged information about sacred rites that the Holy Spirit had apparently seen fit to share directly with James. Though church leaders had repeatedly denied her permission to participate in those temple rituals by the time she dictated her autobiography, James made it clear that they could not fully exclude her from the knowledge imparted in those ceremonies.

James acquired similarly privileged sacred knowledge through human channels. In her autobiography, James told of a conversation with four women in which she learned of the doctrine of plural marriage. "Sarah [Lawrence] said what would you think if a man had more wives than one?" James remembered. "I said that is all right!" Seeing James's enthusiasm, Sarah's sister Maria Lawrence replied, "Well we are all four Brother Josephs wives! I jumped up and clapped my hands and said that's good, Sarah said she is all right, just listen she believes it all now."[59] The disclosure of the plural marriage doctrine to James in a private setting suggests that polygamy had not yet been announced to the majority of the Saints.[60] This conversation thus highlighted her status as an insider in the LDS community, with access to sacred knowledge of limited circulation. James's immediate and enthusiastic acceptance of this doctrine, a teaching that proved very difficult for other Saints to embrace, justified this privileged status.

James may also have believed that she acquired sacred knowledge through Joseph Smith's mediation. "I saw Brother Joseph and asked him if I should go to Burlington and take my sister Angeline with me," recalled James. "He said yes go and be good girls, and remember your profession of faith in the Everlasting Gospel, and the Lord will bless you."[61] During Smith's lifetime, it was not uncommon for his followers to ask the Prophet for revelations or "commandments" to guide their personal lives. While a few of these revelations were canonized in the Doctrine and Covenants, most were not.[62] James may have seen this command to go to Burlington with Angeline as just such a noncanonical revelation. Smith's promise that the Lord would bless the sisters if they remembered their profession of faith added a sacred dimension to the otherwise secular journey.[63] The trip acquired added importance in James's memory for another reason: "During this time," she recalled, "Joseph and Hyrum were killed."[64] Thus, the command to go to Burlington was not only a revelation to James through Joseph Smith, but also the Prophet's last words to her and perhaps, for that reason, particularly poignant.

"Is There No Blessing for Me?"

According to Elizabeth J. D. Roundy, who transcribed Jane James's autobiography, James "wishe[d] it read at her funeral."[65] However, James may have hoped that her autobiography would serve not only as a eulogy, but also as an instrument of persuasion. Since at least 1884, James had been petitioning various church officials for the right to perform various rituals that would ensure her salvation and exaltation after death.[66] James was clearly concerned about her eternal welfare and that of her loved ones. Access to temple rituals was the only way to ensure that she would be with her family and that she would achieve the degree of glory to which she aspired.

Since Brigham Young assumed leadership of the church, African Americans had been denied ordination to the priesthood and access to temple rituals such as endowments. James's marriage to Isaac James, which almost certainly occurred after Smith's death, thus could not be consecrated in temple ritual. James clearly disagreed with this policy. Her color, she tried to persuade the men to whom she wrote, should not matter. "My race was handed down through the flood & God promised Abraham that in his seed all the nations of the earth should be blest," she wrote to President John Taylor in 1884, "& as this is the fullness of all dispensations is there no blessing for me[?]"[67] This letter is the only extant evidence that James tried to argue from the Bible for a color-blind policy regarding temple endowments.

Possibly because her biblical exegesis did not persuade the men to whom she wrote, James also consistently referred to Emma Smith's offer to adopt James as a child. To President Taylor, she wrote, "Sister Emma came to me & asked how I would like to be adopted to them as a Child[.] I did not comprehend her & she came again[.] I was so green I did not give her a decided answer & Joseph died & [I] remain as I am[.] [I]f I could be adopted to him as a child my Soul would be satisfied[.]"[68] James's explanation that she refused adoption at the time Smith offered it because she "did not understand the Law of adoption" is in all but one of her extant petitions.[69]

James occasionally bolstered her petition by pointing to her exemplary life as a Saint and her close association with Joseph Smith and his family. "You know my history & according to the best of my ability I have lived to all the requairments [*sic*] of the Gospel," she wrote in her petition to President Taylor. "When we reached Nauvoo . . . Bro Joseph Smith took us in & we staid [*sic*] with him until a few day[s] of his death."[70] To Apostle Joseph F. Smith, the nephew of the first Mormon prophet, she wrote, "I think you are somewhat Acquainted with me—I Lived in the prophets family with Emma and others, about a year."[71] Implicit in the inclusion of this information is the idea that James's conformity to LDS behavioral standards and proximity to Joseph Smith should override, or at least mitigate, the color of James's skin in church officials' consideration of her petition.

Coming as it did toward the end of James's campaign to receive her endowments and be sealed in the temple, James's autobiography was perhaps the fullest expression of her idea that proximity to the first Mormon prophet and conformity to the Mormon gospel should be the measure of one's worthiness. Particularly in her account of the Nauvoo period, James suggested implicitly that if Joseph Smith were still alive, he would have welcomed James into the temple just as he welcomed her into his home. By positioning herself near the center of LDS history—from the gathering, through Nauvoo, and into Salt Lake—James also reminded the church officials that she had shared these experiences with them. Instead of an outsider and an underling, she made herself an insider in the LDS community with access to important people, sacred objects, and privileged information. As a full-fledged member of the LDS community, she implied, there should have been a blessing for her too.

Conclusion

Jane James is relatively well known among twenty-first-century Latter-day Saints in part because she was an anomaly. After the 1978 revelation extending the priesthood to "all worthy male members" of the LDS Church—and therefore removing the obstacles that had prevented black women like James from participating in temple ceremonies—she was one of few early black converts to whom the church could point as evidence of a racially diverse past. But rather than demonstrating harmony in the early LDS Church, James's life illustrates the tensions that ran through it. James constructed her life story so that it fit with the stories her white coreligionists told: her conversion narrative valued the rationalistic, metaphysical, and democratic aspects of the LDS message; her story of gathering emphasized both suffering and divine providence; and her accounts of life in Nauvoo told of intimacy with the Smith family, access to sacred objects, and acquisition of sacred knowledge. James used these stories to accentuate the things she held in common with other members of the church, constructing herself as an insider.

However, James's story was necessarily different from the stories white Mormons told, because as a black person she was excluded from the temple ceremonies that came to form the core of LDS ritual life. Her experience of the divine, then, had to come through back channels—noncanonical revelations, dirty laundry, and family secrets. James's racial identity meant that her contact with God would be informal and spontaneous, not susceptible to the regularizing authority of church leaders. James's encounters with the divine, and her sustained contact with Joseph Smith, persuaded her that she was just as worthy as any white member of the church to participate in the temple ceremonies necessary for her to reach the highest degree of exaltation after her death. Perhaps it was the weight of these experiences that gave her the courage to continue pestering church leaders for permissions. With each new president of the church, she renewed her petitions, asking again: "[I]s there no blessing for me[?]"

NOTES

1. The subject of this essay, Jane Elizabeth James, was born Jane Elizabeth Manning. However, to avoid confusion for the reader, I shall refer to her as Jane James throughout this essay. James claimed she could both read and write: she told the *Young Woman's Journal* in 1905 that "I used to read in the Bible so much and in the Book of Mormon and Revelations [*sic*]" and mentioned that the Smith family "was looking for us [when she and her party arrived in Nauvoo] because I wrote them a letter." ("Joseph Smith, the Prophet," *Young Woman's Journal* 16, no. 12 [December

1905]: 551, 552.) However, surviving letters and other documents from Jane James appear to have been written by other people following her dictation. See Henry J. Wolfinger, "A Test of Faith: Jane Elizabeth James and the Origins of the Utah Black Community," in Clark S. Knowlton, ed., *Social Accommodation in Utah* (Salt Lake City: American West Center Occasional Papers, University of Utah, 1975), 169n76.

2. Jane E. James, "Autobiography [ca. 1902]," [microfilm] LDS Church Archives, Salt Lake City, Utah, fol. 4v.

3. Ibid.

4. Although the text was belatedly dated 1893, James's comment near the end of the narrative about Joseph F. Smith leading the LDS Church clearly indicates that she could not have dictated the autobiography before 1901, when Smith became the church's sixth prophet.

5. Both of these texts, as oral narratives transcribed by someone other than Jane James, are problematic sources. It is difficult, if not impossible, to know how heavily these accounts were edited by those who wrote down James's words. It is just as difficult to know how James shaped her account to fit her audience—both the interviewer/scribe and the imagined reading or listening public.

6. For an interpretation of gathering as an eschatological event, see Grant Underwood, *The Millenarian World of Early Mormonism* (Urbana: University of Illinois Press, 1993), 29.

7. Retellings of James's life in the modern era begin with Kate B. Carter, comp., *The Story of the Negro Pioneer* (Salt Lake City: Daughters of the Utah Pioneers, 1965). More recent popular versions include Linda King Newell and Valeen Tippetts Avery, "Jane Manning James: Black Saint, 1847 Pioneer," *Ensign* 9 (August 1979): 26–29; Margaret Blair Young and Darius Aidan Gray, *Standing on the Promises*, 3 vols. (Salt Lake City: Bookcraft, 2000–2003); and *Jane Manning James: Your Sister in the Gospel*, DVD (Layton, Utah: Freebairn Entertainment and Hey You Pictures, 2005). The most extensive scholarly treatment of James's life is Wolfinger, "Test of Faith," 126–72. Ronald G. Coleman has also examined Jane James's life in "'Is There No Blessing for Me?' Jane Elizabeth Manning James, a Mormon African American Woman," in Quintard Taylor and Shirley Ann Wilson Moore, eds., *African American Women Confront the West, 1600–2000* (Norman: University of Oklahoma Press, 2003), 144–62.

8. The definitive statement on the origins of the priesthood ban is Lester E. Bush, Jr., "Mormonism's Negro Doctrine: An Historical Overview," *Dialogue* 8, no. 1 (Spring 1973): 11–68. Other important works include Newell G. Bringhurst, *Saints, Slaves, and Blacks: The Changing Place of Black People Within Mormonism* (Westport, Conn.: Greenwood Press, 1981), which deals with LDS racial doctrines and attitudes from 1820 to approximately 1980; Lester E. Bush, Jr., and Armand L. Mauss, eds., *Neither White Nor Black: Mormon Scholars Confront the Race Issue in a Universal Church* (Midvale, Utah: Signature Books, 1984), which is a collection of essays previously published in *Dialogue* (including Bush's "LDS Church's Negro Doctrine," cited above) that are concerned primarily with the LDS Church's racial

attitudes and policies, though it also includes an essay by Newell Bringhurst that explores the implications of those policies for nineteenth-century black Mormons; Jessie L. Embry, *Black Saints in a White Church: Contemporary African American Mormons* (Salt Lake City: Signature Books, 1994), which focuses on the experiences of black Mormons in the post-1978 LDS Church; and Armand L. Mauss, *All Abraham's Children: Changing Mormon Conceptions of Race and Lineage* (Urbana: University of Illinois Press, 2003), which analyzes the ways in which LDS thought about race and descent have changed throughout the religion's history.

9. The LDS church does not merit a single mention, for example, in Lawrence Neale Jones, *African Americans and the Christian Churches, 1619–1860* (Cleveland: Pilgrim Press, 2007); Milton C. Sernett, ed., *African American Religious History: A Documentary Witness*, 2d ed. (Durham, N.C.: Duke University Press, 1999); Larry G. Murphy, ed., *Down By the Riverside: Readings in African American Religion* (New York: New York University Press, 2000); Marvin A. McMickle, *An Encyclopedia of African American Christian Heritage* (Valley Forge, Pa.: Judson Press, 2002); or Albert J. Raboteau, *African-American Religion* (New York: Oxford University Press, 1999).

10. Bush, "Mormonism's Negro Doctrine," 38–39. In 1835, the LDS Church instructed missionaries not to teach enslaved people except with the consent of masters. See Bush, "Mormonism's Negro Doctrine," 13.

11. James, "Autobiography," fol. 1r.

12. Steven C. Harper, "Infallible Proofs, Both Human and Divine: The Persuasiveness of Mormonism for Early Converts," *Religion and American Culture* 10, no. 1 (Winter 2000): 112.

13. James, "Autobiography," fol. 1r.

14. "Eliza Gibbs, Autobiography," transcribed in "Writings of Early Latter-day Saints and Their Contemporaries," compiled by Milton V. Backman, Jr., in cooperation with Keith W. Perkins, *LDS Collectors Library* [CD-Rom] (Provo, Utah: Infobases Incorporated, 1995), n.p. On early LDS conversions more generally, see Richard L. Bushman, "Theories of Conversion," paper delivered at the Mormon History Association Annual Meeting, Aalborg, Denmark, July 1, 2000.

15. Benjamin Ashby, "Autobiography of Benjamin Ashby," transcribed in "Writings of Early Latter-day Saints and Their Contemporaries," *LDS Collectors Library* [CD-Rom], n.p.

16. James, "Autobiography," fol. 1r. James did not say whether the frightened family was the Mannings or the Fitches, the white family that employed and housed her for many years.

17. Jones, *African Americans and the Christian Churches*, 151–60; Jeremiah Asher, "Protesting the 'Negro Pew,'" from *Incidents in the Life of the Rev. J. Asher, Pastor of Shiloh (Coloured) Baptist Church, Philadelphia, and a Concluding Chapter of Facts Illustrating the Unrighteous Prejudice Existing in the Minds of American Citizens toward Their Coloured Brethren* (London: Charles Gilpin, 1850), 43–48, reprinted in Sernett, ed., *African American Religious History*, 224–27.

18. Nathan Hatch, *The Democratization of American Christianity* (New Haven, Conn.: Yale University Press, 1989), 35.

19. George M. Marsden, *The Evangelical Mind and the New School Presbyterian Experience* (New Haven, Conn.: Yale University Press, 1970), 10. I thank my colleague John Matzko for bringing this information to my attention.

20. Robert Russell, *Wilton, Connecticut: Three Centuries of People, Places, and Progress* (Wilton, Conn.: Wilton Historical Society, 2004), 184, 191.

21. Russell, *Wilton, Connecticut,* 77. I am grateful to Robert Russell, historian of the Wilton Congregational Church; Mark Shenise, associate archivist, United Methodist General Commission on Archives and History; and Bette Johnson Sohm, archivist, New York Annual Conference of the United Methodist Church, for their help in searching for Jane James's church membership records.

22. James, "Autobiography," fol. 1r.

23. Terryl L. Givens, *People of Paradox: A History of Mormon Culture* (New York: Oxford University Press, 2007), 27–28.

24. For more on the relationship between Presbyterians and early Mormons, see John Matzko's essay in this volume.

25. George A. Smith, "Discourse by Elder George A. Smith: Joseph Smith's Family—Details of George A. Smith's Own Experience, Etc.," August 2, 1857, Salt Lake City, *Journal of Discourses,* vol. 5, 104–106.

26. Wilford Woodruff, Discourse, February 13, 1898, Salt Lake City, in Brian H. Stuy, ed., *Collected Discourses,* vol. 5 (Woodland Hills, Utah: B. H. S. Publishing, n.d.), n.p., on *LDS Library 2006* [CD-Rom] (Salt Lake City: Deseret Book, 2006).

27. That James's rejection of the Presbyterians would have played well with LDS audiences makes it unsurprising that she would have emphasized this detail. It does not mean, however, that she would have invented this detail. It is more likely, in my view, that she sincerely believed she was telling the truth, but that some details became fuzzy over time and that James's recollection was shaped by her immersion in the LDS community and its narrative conventions.

28. On the Mormons' negotiation of this question, see especially Kathleen Flake, "Re-placing Memory: Latter-day Saint Use of Historical Monuments and Narrative in the Early Twentieth Century," *Religion and American Culture* 13, no. 1 (Winter 2003): 69–109.

29. Davis Bitton, "The Ritualization of Mormon History," *Utah Historical Quarterly* 43 (Winter 1975): 67–85.

30. Russell, *Wilton, Connecticut,* 191; James, "Autobiography," fol. 1r; Elizabeth J. D. Roundy, in James, "Autobiography," fol. 5r.

31. James, "Autobiography," fol. 1r; Jane E. James to President John Taylor, Salt Lake City, December 27, 1884, transcribed in Wolfinger, "Test of Faith," 148; "Joseph Smith, the Prophet," 552.

32. There are suggestive parallels and interesting divergences between the Mormons' self-understanding as a chosen people who were "recapitulating" the events

of the Hebrew Bible and African Americans' self-identification with the oppressed Israelites of the same text, but they are beyond the scope of this essay.

33. James, "Autobiography," fol. 1v.

34. For the identification of "Dr. Bernhisel" as John M. Bernhisel, see Wolfinger, "Test of Faith," 170n92. According to Wolfinger, Bernhisel was a "prominent churchman who later served as Utah's delegate to Congress." Wolfinger, "Test of Faith," 170–71n92. Andrew Jenson corroborates this assessment: he writes that Bernhisel, upon joining the Latter-day Saints in Nauvoo, "became at once a prominent factor in the community at that place." Andrew Jenson, *Latter-day Saint Biographical Encyclopedia,* vol. 1 (1901; reprint, Salt Lake City: Western Epics, 1971), 723.

35. James, "Autobiography," fol. 2r. James narrated this same exchange in very similar terms in "Joseph Smith, the Prophet," 552.

36. James, "Autobiography," fol. 1v.

37. Ibid., fol. 2r.

38. Ibid., fol. 3v.

39. Jane Manning married Isaac James while working in Brigham Young's house in Nauvoo, sometime after Joseph Smith's death and before Brigham Young left Nauvoo. See James, "Autobiography," fol. 3v.

40. Ibid., fol. 3v–4r.

41. The photo, taken by George Anderson, can be viewed on the Daughters of Utah Pioneers website at www.dupinternational.org/jubilee/pioneers.htm.

42. The Nauvoo portion of the "Autobiography" runs from fol. 2r through 3v.

43. James, "Autobiography," fol. 2r.

44. Ibid.

45. Ibid., fol. 2v.

46. Ibid., fol. 3r; see also "Joseph Smith, the Prophet," 551.

47. Bush, "Mormonism's Negro Doctrine," 14, quoting an article by Joseph Smith, Jr., in the *Messenger and Advocate* 2 (April 1836): 289–301.

48. Richard L. Bushman, *Joseph Smith: Rough Stone Rolling* (New York: Alfred Knopf, 2005), 289, 516–17; Bush, "Mormonism's Negro Doctrine," 11–22.

49. James, "Autobiography," fol. 3r.

50. Rex Eugene Cooper, *Promises Made to the Fathers: Mormon Covenant Organization* (Salt Lake City: University of Utah, 1990), 112–13.

51. See James, "Autobiography," fol. 3v; Jane E. James to President John Taylor, December 27, 1884, transcribed in Wolfinger, "Test of Faith," 148; Jane E. James to Apostle Joseph F. Smith, February 7, 1890, transcribed in Wolfinger, "Test of Faith," 149; Zina D. H. Young to Apostle Joseph F. Smith, January 15, 1894, transcribed in Wolfinger, "Test of Faith," 150.

52. Cooper, *Promises Made to the Fathers,* 153; Bush, "Mormonism's Negro Doctrine," 17–18; Newell Bringhurst, "Elijah Abel and the Changing Status of Blacks within Mormonism," in Bush and Mauss, eds., *Neither White Nor Black,* 137–38.

53. "Joseph Smith, the Prophet," 551.

54. James, "Autobiography," fol. 2v–3r.

55. Ibid., fol. 3r.

56. Ibid., fol. 3r–3v.

57. "Joseph Smith, the Prophet," 552, 553. James draws no clear distinction between a dream and a vision. She says, first, that she recognized Smith upon her arrival in Nauvoo "because I had seen him in a dream" (552) but later says that "I saw him back in old Connecticut in a vision, saw him plain and knew he was a prophet" (553). I find it unlikely that these two remarks refer to different episodes.

58. James, "Autobiography," fol. 3r.

59. Ibid.

60. The four women to whom James referred in her autobiography were Emily Dow Partridge, Eliza Maria Partridge, Maria Lawrence, and Sarah Lawrence. Sisters Emily and Eliza Partridge married Joseph Smith in March 1843, and sisters Maria and Sarah Lawrence married him in May of the same year. Todd Compton, *In Sacred Loneliness: The Plural Wives of Joseph Smith* (Salt Lake City: Signature Books, 1997), 6. The revelation on the "Eternity of the Marriage Covenant and Plural Marriage," now Doctrine and Covenants, section 132, was recorded on July 12, 1843. (It was not publicly acknowledged until 1852, when the Saints had safely removed themselves to Utah.) That provides a short, one- to two-month window for this conversation to have taken place.

61. James, "Autobiography," fol. 3r. James was probably referring to the town of Burlington, Iowa, a short distance up the Mississippi River from Nauvoo.

62. Richard L. Bushman, personal communication, July 20, 2005; Grant Underwood, personal communication, July 20, 2005. For examples of personal revelations that were canonized, see Doctrine and Covenants, section 4 (directed to Joseph Smith, Sr.); sections 8 and 9 (directed to Oliver Cowdery); section 30 (directed to David, Peter, and John Whitmer); and section 31 (directed to Thomas B. Marsh).

63. It is likely that James undertook this trip to look for work, since Smith's Mansion House had by that time ceased to function as a business. On the LDS presence in Burlington, see Robert Goodwin, "Among the Poorest of Saints: Mormon Migration to and through Burlington, Iowa, 1846–1887," *Mormon Historical Studies* 4, no. 2 (Fall 2003): 97–112. I am grateful to Troy Ramsey for bringing this article to my attention.

64. James, "Autobiography," fol. 3r.

65. Ibid., fol. 1r.

66. The earliest documentary evidence of James's quest that Wolfinger found is a letter dated December 27, 1884, to President John Taylor, requesting that James be allowed to be adopted as a child into the Smith family. See Wolfinger, "A Test of Faith," 148.

67. Jane E. James to President John Taylor, Salt Lake City, December 27, 1884, transcribed in Wolfinger, "Test of Faith," 148.

68. Ibid.

69. James to Taylor, December 27, 1884; Jane E. James to Apostle Joseph F. Smith, Salt Lake City, February 7, 1890; Zina D. H. Young to Apostle Joseph F. Smith, Salt Lake City, January 15, 1894, all transcribed in Wolfinger, "Test of Faith," 148–51. The quotation is from James to Smith, February 7, 1890, in Wolfinger, "Test of Faith," 149. James's only extant petition that fails to mention Emma Smith's offer to adopt her is Jane E. James to President Joseph F. Smith, Salt Lake City, August 31, 1903, transcribed in Wolfinger, "Test of Faith," 151. This letter, the last of James's extant petitions, simply asks, "if I can get my endowments and also finish the work I have begun for My dead."

70. James to Taylor, December 27, 1884, in Wolfinger, "Test of Faith," 148.

71. James to Smith, February 7, 1890, in Wolfinger, "Test of Faith," 149.

Part 2
Border Crossings
TALKING AND MOVING ACROSS RELIGIOUS LINES

3
The Young Joseph Smith and Presbyterianism

John Matzko

Of the Protestant denominations vying for converts in western New York during the early nineteenth century, it was Methodism that made the greatest impression on the young Joseph Smith. Oliver Cowdery said that Smith had been "awakened" during a sermon by the Methodist minister George Lane. Smith himself said he became "somewhat partial to the Methodist sect" and "felt some desire to be united with them."[1] At some point between 1821 and 1829, Smith served as "a very passable exhorter" at Methodist camp meetings near Palmyra.[2] His wife, Emma Hale, was a Methodist, and, shortly after her first pregnancy ended in a stillbirth, Smith briefly joined a Methodist class meeting that convened at the home of Emma's uncle, the Reverend Nathaniel Lewis.[3] Two years later, when Smith organized the Church of Christ, both its conferences of elders and its commissioning of minimally trained missionaries had a Methodist flavor.[4]

Nevertheless, if Methodism most impressed the young Joseph Smith, Presbyterianism and its characteristic Calvinist theology also played an influential, if more negative, role in his religious development. When Joseph reported his earliest vision to his mother, he did not tell her that all Christian sects were equally false. He said that "Presbyterianism [was] not true."[5]

In early-nineteenth-century America, Presbyterians differed from most other Protestant denominations in holding to an elaborately refined theological system dating to the Reformation. Like other branches of the Calvinist or "Reformed" tradition, Presbyterianism emphasized the sovereignty of God in the saving of souls. Presbyterians insisted that men and women were unable to contribute to their own salvation, that God predestined the elect to everlasting life, that Christ's atonement was limited to those who would be saved, that God's call to the elect was irresistible, and that it was impossible for any soul sanctified by God's spirit to fall from the state of grace. In other words, Calvinists maintained that saving grace sprang from an immutable decree of God rather than through the ability of individuals to acquire it by their own effort. By the beginning of the nineteenth century, Calvinism was in decline, especially beyond the older coastal settlements. Pioneers traveled faster than preachers, and easterners feared the frontier would ultimately degenerate into a haunt of lawlessness as well as religious indifference. Then, beginning in 1801, a wave of revivals convulsed the trans–Appalachian West, beginning with a spectacular outpouring of religious emotion at Cane Ridge, Kentucky.[6]

During this period of religious fervor, Presbyterian insistence on an educated ministry put the denomination at a disadvantage to Methodists and Baptists who had more numerous but less educated clergy and who therefore outstripped Presbyterians in competition for western converts. Eventually, even committed Calvinists accommodated to an informal Arminianism—roughly, the belief that human free will *does* play a role in salvation. Some "New School" Presbyterians (most notably, Charles Finney) eventually abandoned Calvinism altogether, and in 1838, American Presbyterians rancorously divided into "Old School" and "New School" factions.[7]

Nevertheless, the influence of Presbyterianism during the first half of the nineteenth century should not be underestimated. In 1854, the eminent church historian Philip Schaff asserted that Presbyterians were "without question one of the most numerous, respectable, worthy, intelligent, and influential denominations" and one with a "particularly strong hold on the solid middle class."[8] By the Plan of Union of 1801, Presbyterians and Congregationalists joined to evangelize the West, and the combined effort largely benefited the Presbyterians. Even in Connecticut, Congregationalists began calling themselves Presbyterians, and the upshot was that membership in the Presbyterian Church grew through both conversions and the addition of Congregationalists.[9]

Like many other New Englanders, the Joseph Smith family emigrated to western New York during the early nineteenth century. Lucy Mack Smith had been reared by a devout Congregationalist mother and thus, not surprisingly, developed a connection with the Presbyterian Church in Palmyra, New York, even though at first she did not join.[10]

Presbyterians established a Palmyra church in 1797, but not until after a religious revival in 1816 was a new congregation, the Western Presbyterian Church, organized. Although land for the first meetinghouse—the only meetinghouse that existed in Palmyra during Joseph Smith's childhood—was donated for a union church, the building was constructed almost entirely by Presbyterians.

The white, rectangular structure, built in the New England tradition, featured green blinds and a steeple with a gilded weather vane. Inside, a gallery reached by stairways on either side faced "a high pulpit . . . of primitive fashion."[11] Sunday sermons, delivered both morning and afternoon, were long and doctrinal. Pews were rented, and church discipline was rigorously enforced. Members were excommunicated not only for "intemperate use of spirituous liquors," "having intercourse with females of bad character," and reneging on bad debts, but also for having "denied the Bible" by declaring that "all men would be saved." Furthermore, the elders and deacons who enforced this church discipline were sturdy representatives of the local elite.[12]

Late in life, Lorenzo Saunders, a childhood acquaintance of Smith's, recalled that the first time he ever attended Sabbath School, he went with "young Joe Smith at the old Presbyterian Church."[13] Nevertheless, the relationship between Joseph Smith and the Presbyterian Church seems to have soured after the sudden and still-mysterious death of his eldest brother, Alvin, on November 19, 1823. In old age, Joseph's younger brother, William, claimed that at Alvin's funeral the Reverend Benjamin B. Stockton, a Presbyterian minister, had "intimated very strongly" that Alvin had gone to hell.[14] Nothing of the sermon remains. Perhaps Stockton simply made an evangelistic appeal that William Smith misremembered.

The latter seems likely because the Palmyra revival of 1824–25 followed hard on Alvin's death, and Stockton served as a leader of that religious resurgence. Lucy Smith later recalled that "the whole neighborhood was very much aroused" by the revival and that the Smith family "flocked to the meeting house to see if there was a word of comfort for us." Lucy Smith never expressed displeasure with either Stockton's theology or his remarks at Alvin's funeral. In fact, sometime before 1828, she and three of her children—Hyrum, Samuel, and Sophronia—joined the Western Presbyterian Church where Stockton had been called as pastor.[15]

Although Presbyterians were the most prestigious denomination in the neighborhood and the only ones with a meetinghouse, it is unlikely that the religiously minded Lucy Mack Smith would have joined primarily for social reasons. More than twenty years earlier, when the Smiths had lived in Randolph, Vermont, Lucy had sought spiritual comfort from a Presbyterian minister, and she described the encounter as "emptiness, vanity, [and] vexation of spirit" that failed to satisfy "the craving hunger of the soul."[16]

Joseph Smith later wrote that his "Father's family [had been] proselyted to the Presbyterian faith." But the death of Alvin and the arrival of Stockton seem to have driven both Smith and his father (who glided easily between skepticism and folk religion) further from the Presbyterian Church and its Calvinistic doctrine.[17] It was probably during this period that Joseph "became partial to the Methodist sect," whose opposition to Reformed doctrine was notorious. Smith recalled that the "Presbyterians were most decided against the Baptists and Methodists, and used all their powers of either reason or sophistry to prove their errors, or at least to make the people think they were in error. On the other hand the Baptists and Methodists in their turn were equally Zealous in endeavoring to establish their own tenets and disprove all others."[18] A possible implication of this phrasing is that, to Joseph, Presbyterians stood on one side of a Calvinist-Arminian divide, Baptists and Methodists on the other.[19] Furthermore, Presbyterians gloried in the Protestant Reformation, whereas Francis Asbury, the effective founder of American Methodism, argued that the apostolic order had been lost during the first century and was only then about to be restored.[20]

After Joseph's death, Lucy Smith recalled her son warning that although it would do the family "no injury" to join the Presbyterians, he believed her ignorant of "the wickedness of their hearts." According to Lucy, Joseph predicted that "Deacon Jessup" of the Presbyterian Church would "not scruple to take the last cow" from a widow with eight little children in order to satisfy a debt; and so, she said, it turned out.[21]

Joseph Smith began dictating the Book of Mormon at about the same time that Stockton left the pastorate of the Western Presbyterian Church. Concurrently, Lucy and her children stopped attending the church. On March 10, 1830, after eighteen months of procedural delay, the communicants of the Smith family were formally disfellowshipped after a visit from three church officials. Lucy later claimed that the three Presbyterians had conspired to destroy the Book of Mormon, although church records note only that the Smiths "did not wish to unite with us any more."[22]

The Presbyterians more than had their revenge. In 1833, when D. P. Hurlbut busied himself collecting anti-Smith affidavits from Palmyra residents, at least ten Presbyterians, all members of the local elite—including Henry Jessup—swore that "Joseph Smith, Senior, and his son Joseph in particular," were "entirely destitute of moral character, and addicted to vicious habits."[23]

Once the nature of Smith's "golden Bible" became known, Joseph's uncle, Jesse Smith, a staunch Calvinist with whom Joseph had lived for some months as a child, assailed the book as "a work of deception."[24] The *Rochester Observer,* a Presbyterian newspaper, introduced the Book of Mormon below the title "Blasphemy!" And the *New York Evangelist* of New York City, another Presbyterian periodical, scorned the new scripture as a plagiarism of the Bible and its followers as persons carried away by a "strange delusion."[25]

In 1830, when Smith tried to organize his new converts in Colesville Township, southern New York, he came to believe—with some reason—that Presbyterians had engaged in a conspiracy against him. On the day before a June baptismal service, Rev. John Sherer, a local Presbyterian pastor, attempted what some modern people might call a "cult rescue." One of his parishioners, Emily Colburn, the sister-in-law of Mormon stalwart Newel Knight, had expressed interest in becoming a Mormon. Through a ruse, Sherer met Colburn in a nearby grove and, taking her firmly by the hand, tried to lead her away. A knot of Mormons materialized, and Sherer was forced to retreat. Nevertheless, the next day Colburn was returned to her family through a power of attorney signed by her father. Emily Colburn at first made her peace with the Presbyterian Church that had disciplined her, but later that year she rejoined the Knights and was baptized a Mormon.[26]

Joseph Smith's troubles in Colesville had only begun. Presbyterians Abram W. Benton, Nathan Boynton, and Cyrus McMaster had Joseph arrested as a "disorderly person," and when he was acquitted the following day, they had him arrested again. After being acquitted a second time, he was forced to flee when local residents threatened mob violence.[27] No wonder Smith avowed in Nauvoo that he had been "ground" in "a Presbyterian smut machine."[28]

Given Smith's early chafing against Presbyterianism, one might have expected more explicit antagonism toward Presbyterian doctrine in the Book of Mormon. Certainly the Book of Mormon seems to contradict all five points of Calvinism: total depravity (an inherited sinful nature),[29] unconditional election (salvation is by God's choice),[30] limited atonement (only some are saved),[31] irresistible grace (humans cannot resist the call of God),[32] and perseverance of the saints (salvation cannot be lost).[33] In contrast, the Book of Mormon emphasizes a cheerier view of the Fall[34] and declares that salvation is "free for all men" but yet can be rejected by human beings, who also, by later "transgression," can in turn be abandoned by God.[35] Nevertheless, the Book of Mormon does include some Calvinistic-sounding verses, and Fawn Brodie even claimed the Book of Mormon accorded "Calvinism and Arminianism . . . equal status."[36]

One chapter of the Book of Mormon does make what appears to be an explicit criticism of Presbyterians and their upper-middle-class leaders. In Alma 31 (the only chapter in the Book of Mormon in which the Calvinist term "elected" is used[37]), the prophet Alma heads a mission to the heretical Zoramites, who have "a place built up in the center of their synagogue, a place for standing . . . high above the head" that "would only admit one person"—like the elevated pulpit at Western Presbyterian Church.[38] These Zoramites give repeated thanks to God that they are a "chosen and a holy people" and not like all others who are "elected to be cast by thy wrath down to hell." Furthermore, the Zoramites are "a wicked and a perverse people" whose hearts are "set upon gold, and upon silver, and upon all manner of fine goods"—like Deacon Jessup.[39]

Even more important to Smith's religious development are the messages he may have heard preached at Western Presbyterian Church between the family's arrival in New York, ca. 1816–17, and the death of his brother Alvin in 1823.[40] Unfortunately, of the three clergymen who served the church during that period, virtually nothing is known of two beyond their names.[41]

Only the Reverend Jesse Townsend (1766–1838), pastor from August 1817 to 1820 (or possibly 1821), left hints about the sort of Presbyterianism that might have stimulated the imagination of the adolescent Joseph Smith.[42] Townsend, a Yale graduate, had pastored churches in New York and Massachusetts before serving with the American Home Missionary Society in Illinois and Missouri (curiously anticipating the later moves of Joseph Smith).[43] Little remains of his considerable literary exertions, but what is extant dispels the stereotype of a dour Calvinist allowing God to work his will without lifting a finger of human assistance.[44]

Townsend was a staunch Calvinist yet fervently evangelistic in practice. In the preface to a church history abridgment, Townsend emphasizes the "progress of truth and its salutary influence on a world ruined by sin"—certainly a sentiment unsympathetic to restorationist belief in a gospel hidden since the first century.[45] Yet Townsend also evangelized under the auspices of the interdenominational American Home Missionary Society, which had offended Old School notions of denominational propriety.

In his report of a revival in a rough frontier community of the Catskills, Townsend claimed to have spoken with nearly every resident about the state of his or her soul, eventually sparking a revival that led to the organization of a new church. But Townsend also rejoiced that this backwoods congregation was "well united in Calvinistic sentiments," ascribing the change in their condition to "the sovereign grace of God." In the more settled parish of Durham, New York, Townsend registered "great rejoicing with Zion's friends" over converts young and old who had come to the Savior. But he also gave thanks that "God has most mercifully preserved us from all appearances of enthusiasm. Though the word has been like the hammer and the fire to break in pieces the rock, yet the work has not been with noise and tumult."[46]

Townsend's sentiments are made all the more striking by his account of a dream experienced during a religious awakening in Homer, New York. In a letter to a fellow pastor, Townsend elliptically noted his successful mediation of disharmony that had threatened the brethren. He recalled that while his mind was troubled by the discord, he dreamed he saw the church members "dressed in deep mourning." After the presiding clergyman publicly confessed his sins to God and the congregation, the church members did likewise "in the most solemn & impressive manner," after which the "whole assembly burst into a flood of tears." Although portions of this letter have been lost, its implication is that the events of the dream were replicated in the actual congregation.[47] In the light of such sentiments it seems Townsend's obituary writer accurately portrayed the clergyman by describing him as a member of "the *old school* of New England divines," yet one who favored whatever "measures of the day, whether *new* or *old*, as were instrumental in the salvation of souls."[48]

Superficially, Townsend's one surviving sermon, one preached at the dedication of the first Western Presbyterian Church, seems to emphasize neither Calvinistic nor Arminian themes. Rather, Townsend's sermon is a discourse in the grand style, appropriate for the most formal sort of ceremony that could be conducted at that time and place. Townsend understood what was expected of him, and he provided it. The *Palmyra Register* described the dedication as "solemn and interesting to every rational and sober mind."[49]

Townsend took as his text Luke 2:14, the message of the Christmas angels. He noted that Christ's incarnation was "preparatory for the enlargement of his church" and further argued that buildings erected for the worship of God allowed men to "unite in the angelic song" sung at Christ's birth. Townsend then launched into a long dedicatory prayer (during which the congregation remained standing) that concluded with a plea for his listeners to "truly become as individuals, a habitation of God, through the Spirit. See to it that you do this and you will be able to with the most animated delight to unite in the angelic song. 'Glory to God in the highest and on earth peace, good will toward men.' May you all do this and with one accord devoutly subjoin your sincere and cordial Amen."[50]

While there is no certainty that Smith attended this church dedication one month shy of his fourteenth birthday, the event was as much a community celebration as a sectarian religious occasion and would have engaged his imagination, tuned as it was to sonorous religious language. And the Palmyra church dedication would have been the only such event Smith could have witnessed before the dedication of the Kirtland Temple in 1836.[51]

Parallels between the two occasions are striking. Certainly an imprecatory tone about the Kirtland dedication contrasts with a plea for brotherly unity in Palmyra, and some similarities between the two ceremonies might be attributed to the limited number of ways in which religious buildings could be dedicated in early-nineteenth-century America. Yet at both Palmyra and Kirtland, the sermons refer to an angelic visitation. In Palmyra, the preacher calls the church a "temple," asks God to fill the house with his glory, and petitions that the ceremony be "a Pentecost to our souls." Townsend refers to the church as "Zion" as well as "the Israel of God" and asks congregation members to "feel their hearts burn within them"—all aspects of the Kirtland dedication as well. Three phrases in Townsend's sermon ("execute vengeance," "fallen state," and "eternal father") do not appear in the King James Version (KJV) of the Bible but do occur in the Book of Mormon. The word "delightsome" also appears once in Townsend's sermon, once in the

KJV, and eight times in the Book of Mormon. Joseph Smith concluded his prayer with two sentences that might have been exchanged with two final sentences from Townsend.[52] Both services featured hymns of nine stanzas in long meter (8.8.8.8) whose verses could been have been interchanged or substituted for one another without the notice of either congregation; and like the Palmyra dedication prayer, the final Kirtland prayer was followed by a specially commissioned hymn.[53]

Still, the most influential element of Presbyterianism for Joseph Smith's religious development was neither the early hostility of its members nor Smith's possible later reflection of its ceremony. Calvinism's most important contribution to the Restoration was as a fully developed theological system against which Smith could react. Less than a year before his death, Smith was still considering how believers might be assured of eternal security, and he instituted a "second anointing," a human ritual, to confer a benefit that in Calvinistic theology could be imparted only by the sovereign decree of God.[54]

While Calvinists worshipped a God who received the powerless inheritors of Adam's sin through his grace alone, Smith gloried in agency, the ability of an individual to choose good or evil untrammeled by any predestining power. Unlike the Presbyterians who emphasized God's sovereignty, Smith declared that God had cast down Satan precisely because he had "sought to destroy the agency of man"; the Messiah had redeemed humanity from the Fall so that humans could "become free forever, knowing good from evil," free "to act for themselves and not to be acted upon."[55]

Methodism could serve only as a way station on the road to the emphasis Smith was later to place on the exaltation of humankind. Without his exposure to Presbyterianism in half-settled but "burned over" western New York, it is doubtful that Joseph Smith could have so easily conceived such a sophisticated countersystem. Calvinism, rather than Methodism, was an elaborate theological structure that Smith found worthy of his mettle. To him, it was indeed Presbyterianism that was most importantly "not true."

NOTES

The author expresses gratitude to Richard Bushman, NEH Summer Seminar co-director, and Mark Sidwell, the author's colleague at Bob Jones University, for their valuable comments on an earlier draft of this essay.

1. Oliver Cowdery to W. W. Phelps, December 1834, "Letter III," *Latter Day Saints' Messenger and Advocate* 1 (December 1834): 42, in Dan Vogel, ed., *Early Mormon Documents* (Salt Lake City: Signature Books, 1996–2003), 2:424 (hereafter *EMD*); Joseph Smith, "Manuscript History," 2 in Vogel, *EMD*, 1:59.

2. Orsamus Turner, *History of the Pioneer Settlement of Phelps and Gorham's Purchase, and Morris' Reserve* (Rochester, N.Y.: William Alling, 1851), 214, in Vogel, *EMD*, 3:50. Since the Methodists did not acquire property on the Vienna Road until July 1821, the camp meetings were almost certainly held after that date. Wesley Walters, "A Reply to Dr. Bushman," *Dialogue* 4 (Spring 1969): 99. D. Michael Quinn argues to the contrary that a Methodist camp meeting of 1820 can be fairly interpreted as the religious revival to which Joseph Smith refers and that Methodists typically only asked permission to use property for camp meetings rather than purchase the land. D. Michael Quinn, "Joseph Smith's Experience of a Methodist 'Camp Meeting' in 1820," *Dialogue Paperless*, E-Paper #3, expanded version ("definitive"), December 20, 206, www.dialoguejournal.com/excerpts/e4.pdf (accessed March 6, 2007).

3. Joseph and Hiel Lewis, "Mormon History: A New Chapter about to Be Published," *Amboy [Illinois] Journal* 24 (April 30, 1879): 1 in Vogel, *EMD*, 4:305–306.

4. Nathan O. Hatch, *The Democratization of American Christianity* (New Haven, Conn.: Yale University Press, 1989); Richard Lyman Bushman, *Joseph Smith: Rough Stone Rolling* (New York: Alfred Knopf, 2005), 153, 251–52, 254.

5. "Joseph Smith History, 1839" in Vogel, *EMD*, 1:143.

6. George M. Marsden, *The Evangelical Mind and the New School Presbyterian Experience* (New Haven, Conn.: Yale University Press, 1970), 9; Paul K. Conkin, *Cane Ridge: America's Pentecost* (Madison: University of Wisconsin Press, 1990).

7. Sydney E. Ahlstrom, *A Religious History of the American People* (New Haven, Conn.: Yale University Press, 1972), 432–39, 444–45, 461; Marsden, *Evangelical Mind*, 59–87.

8. Philip Schaff, *America: A Sketch of Its Political, Social, and Religious Character*, 1855; rpt., Perry Miller, ed. (Cambridge, Mass.: Harvard University Press, 1961), 118.

9. Marsden, *Evangelical Mind*, 10–11.

10. Bushman, *Joseph Smith*, 11–13. Solomon Mack, Lucy's father, was a Universalist during her childhood, but in 1810–11 (when he was seventy-six), Mack said that "God did appear for me and . . . set my feet on the rock of Christ Jesus"—after which Mack rejected Universalism as "building on sand." *Narrative of the Life of Solomon Mack . . .* (Windsor, Vt.: self-published, 1811), 18–20.

11. "Miscellaneous Church Files of Palmyra," microfilm, Brigham Young University; Woman's Society of the Western Presbyterian Church, comp., *Palmyra, Wayne County, New York* (Rochester: Herald Press, 1907), microfilm, 900 no. 61, Microforms Room, Lee Library, Brigham Young University, Provo, Utah (hereafter Lee Library, BYU). This church building also served Palmyra as a town hall.

12. *One Hundred and Twenty-Five Years of the Western Presbyterian Church* (Palmyra, 1942), n.p., in "Miscellaneous Church Files on Palmyra"; *Wayne Sentinel,*

January 28, 1824, 4; "Records of the Session of the Presbyterian Church in Palmyra," microfilm, 900 no. 61, Microforms Room, Lee Library, BYU; Dan Vogel, *Joseph Smith: The Making of a Prophet* (Salt Lake City: Signature Books, 2004), 77.

13. Lorenzo Saunders interviewed by William H. Kelley, September 17, 1884, 1–18, E. L. Kelley Papers, RLDS Church Library-Archives, Independence, Missouri, in Vogel, *EMD,* 2:127.

14. Dan Vogel, "Introduction to Palmyra and Manchester, New York, Documents," in Vogel, *EMD,* 2:5; William Smith interview with E. C. Briggs, 1893, published in the *Deseret News,* January 20, 1894, in Vogel, *EMD,* 1:512–13.

15. Lucy Mack Smith, "Preliminary Manuscript" (1845), Church Archives, Salt Lake City, in Vogel, *EMD,* 1:306; for notice of the revival of 1824–25, see *Wayne Sentinel,* March 2, 1825. No membership records of the Western Presbyterian survive for this period, and the date of their membership remains controversial, but Lucy Smith strongly implied that she joined the Presbyterian Church after Alvin's death. Stockton served as pastor of Western Presbyterian Church from February 1824 until October 1827, the most likely period of the Smiths' church membership.

16. Lucy Mack Smith, "Preliminary Manuscript" (1845), in Vogel, *EMD,* 1:241–42.

17. Dean C. Jessee, ed., *Papers of Joseph Smith,* 2 vols. (Salt Lake City: Deseret Book, 1989–92), 1:270. Smith said that that he attended meetings of various denominations—including, presumably, Presbyterian—"as often as occasion would permit."

18. Ibid., 1:271.

19. It is also perhaps noteworthy that Smith accused the Presbyterians of using "all their powers of either reason or sophistry" to prove the errors of the Baptists and Methodists, while he used the word "zealous" only to describe the arguments of the latter.

20. Hatch, *Democratization of American Christianity,* 167.

21. Lucy Smith, *Biographical Sketches of Joseph Smith the Prophet, and His Progenitors for Many Generations* (Liverpool: S. W. Richards, 1853), in Vogel, *EMD,* 1:308. Henry Jessup was actually an elder rather than a deacon. A good candidate for this orphaned family is that of Enoch Saunders, who died October 10, 1825, and who had seven children at the 1820 census. Lorenzo Saunders, who recalled attending the Presbyterian Sunday School with Joseph, also remembered the Smiths as "kind neighbors in sickness." Vogel, *Joseph Smith,* 61; Lorenzo Saunders interview, 1884, in Vogel, *EMD,* 2:156. The date of Enoch Saunders's death lends further weight to a later date for Smith family membership in Western Presbyterian Church.

22. "Records of the Session of the Presbyterian Church in Palmyra," 11; records relating to the Smith family have been transcribed in Vogel, *EMD,* 3:496–501. By this date, Sophronia Smith had married and had probably transferred her church membership, and so she was not included in the notice of church discipline.

23. Eber D. Howe, *Mormonism Unvailed* (Painsville, Ohio: E. D. Howe, 1834), 261–62, in Vogel, *EMD,* 2:48–55. As Vogel notes, the "vicious habits" referred to are likely to have included drinking (49n2). Later, Alexander McIntyre (1792–1859),

another pewholder at Western Presbyterian Church, asserted that Joseph Smith, Sr., was a drunkard, liar, and thief, and "his house a perfect brothel." Vogel, *EMD*, 3:172.

24. Jesse Smith to Hyrum Smith, June 17, 1829, in Vogel, *EMD*, 1:551–52; see also 1:633; Bushman, *Joseph Smith*, 114.

25. W. W. Phelps to Oliver Cowdery, February 21, 1835, in Vogel, *EMD*, 3:32; *New York Evangelist* (1832) quoted in Vogel, *EMD*, 3:297–98.

26. Emily M. Austin, *Mormonism: or, Life among the Mormons* (Madison, Wisc.: M. J. Cantwell, 1882), 30–52, 56–58, in Vogel, *EMD*, 4:174–76; see also "Newel Knight Journal," in *Scraps of Biography: Tenth Book of the Faith-Promoting Series* (Salt Lake City: Juvenile Instructor Office, 1883), 46–69 in Vogel, *EMD*, 4:45–65. According to Knight, Sherer himself returned with the power of attorney. During the Nauvoo period, Emily Colburn Austin became disillusioned with Mormonism and left the church.

27. Bushman, *Joseph Smith*, 116–18; Vogel notes that in "Smith's zeal to place blame for his early persecutions on the Presbyterians," he may have mistaken the religious affiliation of Abram Benton, who seems to have been a Universalist. See Vogel, *EMD*, 4:94.

28. Joseph Smith Journal, February 21, 1843, 210–11 in Scott H. Faulring, ed., *The Diaries and Journals of Joseph Smith: An American Prophet's Record* (Salt Lake City: Signature Books, 1987), 311. The full quotation is more cryptic and less specifically directed against Presbyterians than the above excerpt suggests: "The pagans, Roman Catholics, Methodists, and Baptists shall have peace in Nauvoo only they must be ground in Joe Smith's mill. I have been in their mill. I was ground in Ohio and [New] York States—a Presbyterian smut machine—and [the] last machine was in Missouri and last of all I have through [the] Illinois smut machine. Those who come here must go through my smut machine and this is my tongue." On December 29, 1835, Smith discovered that there had been some Presbyterians at one of his meetings, and he rejoiced in his journal that he had "exposed their abominations in the language of the scriptures." Ibid., 93. But thereafter, Smith seemed to lump Presbyterians indifferently with Methodists, Baptists, and other Protestant denominations, perhaps because farther west, Presbyterians were a limited threat to the LDS Church.

29. "Yea, he that repenteth and exerciseth faith, and bringeth forth good works, and prayeth continually without ceasing—unto such it is given to know the mysteries of God" (Alma 26:22).

30. "Wherefore, the Lord God gave unto man that he should act for himself" (2 Nephi 2:16); "Wherefore, men are free according to the flesh; and all things are given them which are expedient unto man. And they are free to choose liberty and eternal life, through the great Mediator of all men, or to choose captivity and death, according to the captivity and power of the devil" (2 Nephi 2:27).

31. "Hath he commanded any that they should not partake of his salvation? Behold I say unto you, Nay; but he hath given it free for all men" (2 Nephi 26:27).

32. "I work not among the children of men save it be according to their faith" (2 Nephi 27:23); "Behold, I say unto you, that the good shepherd doth call you; yea, and in his own name he doth call you, which is the name of Christ; and if ye will not hearken unto the voice of the good shepherd, to the name by which ye are called, behold, ye are not the sheep of the good shepherd" (Alma 5:38).

33. "Continue in fasting and praying, and endure to the end; and as the Lord liveth ye will be saved" (Omni 1:26).

34. "Adam fell that men might be; and men are, that they might have joy" (2 Nephi 2:25).

35. "And I would that ye should remember also, that this is the name that I said I should give unto you that never should be blotted out, except it be through transgression; therefore, take heed that ye do not transgress, that the name be not blotted out of your hearts" (Mosiah 5:11).

36. "Wherefore, all mankind were in a lost and in a fallen state, and ever would be save they should rely on this Redeemer" (1 Nephi 10:6); "Remember, after ye are reconciled unto God, that it is only in and through the grace of God that ye are saved" (2 Nephi 10:24); "Behold, he changed their hearts; yea, he awakened them out of a deep sleep, and they awoke unto God" (Alma 5:7); "Now we see that Adam did fall by the partaking of the forbidden fruit, according to the word of God; and thus we see, that by his fall, all mankind became a lost and fallen people" (Alma 12:22); "Because of the fall our natures have become evil continually" (Ether 3:2). Fawn M. Brodie, *No Man Knows My History: The Life of Joseph Smith*, rev. ed. (New York: Alfred Knopf, 1971), 70. It should be noted, however, that Brodie once confessed that the theological side of Joseph Smith mostly "bores me." Brodie to Dale L. Morgan, July 13, 1944, in Newell G. Bringhurst, *Fawn McKay Brodie: A Biographer's Life* (Norman: University of Oklahoma Press, 1999), 94.

37. The Doctrine and Covenants uses the terms "elect" and "election" seven times—most memorably in referring to Emma Smith as "an elect lady" (D&C 25:3), but in all the LDS scriptures only the Zoramites are "elected."

38. Joseph Smith might also have seen such an elevated pulpit as a boy of seven or eight during the time he spent living with his uncle, the Congregationalist Jesse Smith, in Salem, Massachusetts.

39. Alma 31:13, 17, 18, 24; Grant Underwood, *The Millenarian World of Early Mormonism* (Urbana: University of Illinois Press, 1993), 105.

40. Bushman, *Joseph Smith*, 28–30, 263.

41. The three pastors of Western Presbyterian Church, 1817–1823, and the date of their entering that office, are Stephen M. Wheelock (April 1817), Jesse Townsend (August 1817), Daniel C. Hopkins, stated supply (January 1822). Benjamin B. Stockton became the pastor of the church in February 1824. "Miscellaneous Church Files of Palmyra."

42. Lorenzo Saunders interview (1884) in Vogel, *EMD*, 2:127.

43. Franklin Bowditch Dexter, *Biographical Sketches of the Graduates of Yale College* (New York: Henry Holt, 1912), 4:695–96, largely assembled from an obituary

in the *New York Observer,* September 1, 1838, 140. Townsend was born in Andover, Connecticut, ten years before the American Revolution, and he graduated from Yale College in 1790 at the then mature age of twenty-five. He was first settled as pastor of the Congregational church in Shelburne, Massachusetts (1792), and then was called to the Congregational church in Durham, New York (1798). He preached for some years in Madison, New York, and took charge of a Utica academy for a year. Returning to Palmyra from Missouri in 1826, Townsend preached in the neighboring town of Sodus and supplied vacant pulpits in the area while preparing young men for college. Townsend married the widow of another clergyman and fathered four children.

44. Townsend published a one-volume abridgment of a five-volume church history, two letters about New York revivals (1802–1803), and two unflattering letters about the "Mormonites." Also extant are four unpublished private letters and a dedication sermon preached at the Western Presbyterian Church in 1819. Jesse Townsend, *The History of the Church of Christ from the Days of the Apostles to the Year 1551 Abridged from the Five First Volumes of Milner's Church History* (Utica, N.Y.: Camp, Merrell & Camp, 1816); *Connecticut Evangelical Magazine* 2 (June 1802): 469–71; 4 (August 1803): 65–67; Townsend to Phineas Stiles (December 24, 1833) and Townsend to Elisha Camp (August 16, 1834) in Vogel, *EMD,* 3:21–27; Townsend to David Selden, November 19 [?], 1792; February 23, 1808; September 11, 1811; January 2, 1813, David Selden Correspondence, Connecticut Historical Society, Hartford; Sermon (November 28, 1819) in "Miscellaneous Church Files of Palmyra." Townsend died two months after the denominational split between Old School and New School Presbyterians in 1838.

45. Townsend, *History of the Church of Christ,* vii.

46. *Connecticut Evangelical Magazine* 4 (August 1803): 65–67; 2 (June 1802): 470–71.

47. Townsend to David Selden, January 2, 1813. It is unlikely that Townsend ever described this dream to his Palmyra congregation because he closes his account to his friend with the words, "I write this dream, brother, inter nos [between us]."

48. "Rev. Jesse Townsend," *New York Observer* 16 (September 1, 1838): 140.

49. *Palmyra Register,* December 1, 1819, 3.

50. Townsend, Sermon, November 28, 1819, in "Miscellaneous Church Files of Palmyra"; the original is owned by Western Presbyterian Church, Palmyra, New York.

51. As an argument against Smith's presence at the Palmyra dedication, Townsend's later denunciation of Joseph as a man of "questionable character" and "low cunning" implies that the preacher knew the prophet only by reputation. Townsend to Phineas Stiles, December 24, 1833, in Vogel, *EMD,* 3:20. In 1833, Townsend says that he has known of Smith for "ten years." If not a rounded figure, 1823 would put the beginning of Townsend's knowledge of Smith after his Palmyra pastorate.

52. Townsend ended his prayer by asking the congregation to "dedicate themselves, with all they have, unfeignedly and unreservedly to the God of their salva-

tion and truly become as individuals, a habitation of God, through the Spirit. See to it that you do this and you will be able with the most animated delight to unite in the angelic song, 'Glory to God in the highest and on earth peace, good will towards men.' May you all do this and with one accord devoutly subjoin your sincere and cordial Amen." Smith closed his prayer with the words: "And help us by the power of thy Spirit, that we may mingle our voices with those bright, shining seraphs around thy throne, with acclamations of praise, singing Hosanna to God and the Lamb! And let these, thine anointed ones, be clothed with salvation, and thy saints shout aloud for joy. Amen, and Amen" (Doctrine and Covenants 109:79–80).

53. The nine stanzas of Palmyra's "Dedicatory Ode" include the following:

> In Temples sacred to His name,
> His Saints assemble round his board;
> Raise their hosannahs to the Lamb,
> And taste the supper of the Lord.
>
> Their songs seraphic shall they raise,
> And Gabriel's Lyre the notes resound;
> Heaven's full toned organ join the praise,
> And world to world repeat the sound.
>
> —*Palmyra Register,* December 1, 1819, 3.

The nine stanzas sung at Kirtland, written by Parley Pratt, include the following:

> Celestial crowns we shall receive,
> And glories great our God shall give,
> While loud hosannas we'll proclaim,
> And sound aloud the Savior's name.
>
> Our hearts and tongues all joined in one,
> A loud hosanna to proclaim,
> While all the heav'ns shall shout again,
> And all creation say, Amen.
>
> —*Latter Day Saints' Messenger and Advocate* 2:6 (March 1836): 274–75.

54. Bushman, *Joseph Smith,* 497–98; John L. Brooke, *The Refiner's Fire: The Making of Mormon Cosmology, 1644–1844* (Cambridge: Cambridge University Press, 1996), 259–60.

55. Moses 4: 3; 2 Nephi 2: 26; Douglas J. Davies, *An Introduction to Mormonism* (Cambridge: Cambridge University Press, 2003), 89, 174.

4

What Has Pentecostalism to Do with Mormonism?

THE CASE OF JOHN ALEXANDER DOWIE

D. William Faupel

"What has Athens to do with Jerusalem?" So asked Tertullian centuries ago. For him the answer was fairly obvious: "Not much." And to the extent that they did share things in common, he thought it was probably dangerous, especially for "Jerusalem," symbolizing the church. The initial response to my essay title could well be similar to any thoughtful member of the Church of Jesus Christ of Latter-day Saints. Several images may come to mind: Oral Roberts revealing his vision of a nine-hundred-foot Jesus commanding him to build the "City of Faith"; Jim and Tammy Bakker proclaiming a "Prosperity Gospel"; or Jimmy Swaggart tearfully confessing to his television audience that he had had sexual relations with "that woman," begging their forgiveness and God's. Although admittedly these are extreme examples, a religious movement that appeals so strongly to a person's emotions could set off alarm bells if one were to suggest the possibility of its close relationship to Mormonism.

John Alexander Dowie, my test case, serves to epitomize the image of Pentecostalism and suggests that this movement came by its flamboyant, emotionally charged practices quite naturally. Colorful, and always controversial, at the height of his popularity Dowie made national headlines almost daily. Although Dowie himself never became Pentecostal, thousands of his followers—including hundreds in leadership roles—would leave his organization to join the emerging Pentecostal movement. Today, many Pentecostal churches in North America, Europe, New Zealand, Australia, and especially South Africa trace their origins to this enigmatic man.[1] What most of their congregants do not know is how deeply Dowie drew on Mormon faith and practice during the latter half of his ministry.

Dowie's Life

Dowie was born in Edinburgh, Scotland, in 1847. He immigrated with his parents to Australia at age fourteen. Feeling the call of God to the ministry, he returned to Edinburgh at age twenty-one, spending three years at New College. He returned to Australia in 1872 to become a Congregational minister. Dowie quickly climbed the ecclesiastical ladder, holding a succession of pastorates. Within four years of his ordination, he was called to the prestigious Collegiate Church in Newton, a suburb of Sydney, where the church grew by 70 percent the first year. As he entered his third year of this pastorate, Dowie abruptly resigned in 1878, announcing that he was leaving his denomination to devote himself to independent evangelistic work.[2]

Determining to make divine healing the central focus of his ministry, Dowie, after an initial period of struggle, experienced success in 1883. Crowds came in droves to hear his message. Testimonies of miraculous healing were received daily. Finances to fund an expanding operation began to flow. He established the Free Christian Church in Melbourne, and from this base, he conducted healing missions throughout Australia and New Zealand. It was during this period that he first encountered Mormonism. A husband-and-wife missionary team who had recently arrived from Salt Lake City had met sustained hostility from an Australian Protestantism determined to prevent a beachhead of Mormonism from being established on the continent's shores. Having recently experienced growing hostility from establishment Christianity himself, Dowie felt instant empathy for this couple, inviting them to spend a period of time in his home while he was on break from his evangelistic activities. He became deeply impressed with their sincerity and was intrigued with their theological understanding. He determined to learn more and accepted their invitation to visit them someday in Salt Lake City when they returned to the United States.[3]

Influenced in part by this Mormon encounter, Dowie began to think in terms of worldwide ministry. He decided to visit England, where he had many contacts. With London as a center, he reasoned that he would be able to develop a following throughout the British Empire. To this end he set sail in March 1888, going by way of the United States.[4] He received such a tremendous response to his ministry in North America that he never left. For two years he traveled up and down the Pacific Coast holding crusades before heading across the continent.[5]

In 1890, after concluding his two-year West Coast evangelistic tour, Dowie headed east. Traveling by train from San Francisco, Dowie and his family spent several days in Salt Lake City, staying with their Mormon missionary friends who had since returned from Australia. They arranged for Dowie to meet with the Quorum of the Twelve, followed by a private meeting with President Wilford Woodruff.[6] Arthur Newcomb, longtime managing editor of *Leaves of Healing,* quotes Dowie as he recounted part of his conversation with President Woodruff years later: "I remember so well, several years ago, I visited the president of the Mormon Church in Salt Lake City. While I was in his office a fine handsome young man came in, affectionately kissed the president, and was introduced to me as his son. His love and respect for his father were beautiful to see. When he had gone out, I congratulated the president upon his son. He thanked me and said, 'God has blessed me with twenty-five more like him.' 'And I,' I thought sorrowfully, 'have only one!'"[7]

Unfortunately, to date no written documentation has been found to disclose what else was discussed. Oral tradition that has been passed down by some of Dowie's adherents suggests that Dowie proposed merging his movement with the Mormons on the condition that he be appointed to the Quorum. According to this tradition, the proposal was rejected, and Dowie went on to found Zion City in Illinois.[8]

Nonetheless, Dowie left Salt Lake City impressed. Nine years later he would state that he found the Church of Jesus Christ of Latter-day Saints to be "the best organized and most clearly scripturally organized of all churches. . . . [T]he Mormons have kept closely to the Apostolic model." He continued: "I studied that church . . . I saw that by their industry and frugality they had made the land around Salt Lake a wonderful garden. . . . When I visited Salt Lake, they treated me as if I had been a prince of the church, and I was enabled to learn a great many things concerning the internal organization."[9]

He then traveled to Chicago, the second-largest city in the United States, where he decided to establish his headquarters. From this base he held crusades throughout the United States. By 1895 he had established vital branches of his International Divine Healing Association in every major city in America.[10]

The World's Fair opened in Chicago in 1893, providing Dowie with further opportunities. Always a strategic planner, he set up a tabernacle just outside the fairgrounds' entrance, hoping to attract people from throughout the world. This effort paid off handsomely; ever-increasing crowds attended, forcing him to relocate to a succession of larger meeting places.[11] The period following the World's Fair was filled with controversy, decisive action, and huge success. The press, medical community, clergy, and politicians all sought to put him out of business, but Dowie was able to turn this free publicity to his advantage. By this time Dowie had recognized that he had completely alienated the religious establishment. He therefore disbanded the International Divine Healing Association in November 1895, announcing that his followers would no longer be able to retain membership in their old denominations. Instead they must join the Christian Catholic Church, which he formally established in February 1896.[12]

Events moved with dizzying speed following the creation of his new denomination. On New Year's Eve 1899, Dowie announced plans to build Zion, a utopian community, forty miles north of Chicago. By 1901, Zion became a bustling city of eight thousand residents with plans to grow to two hundred thousand. Building was going on everywhere—homes, stores, even a large hotel for persons coming from great distances to attend the healing meetings. An educational system from elementary school through college was established. A huge tabernacle holding fifty-two hundred people was constructed in the heart of Zion, and plans called for a temple with a seating capacity of twenty-five thousand on an adjacent block. Zion was the first and largest of several communities that Dowie planned to establish around the world; a large farming development, planned for Mexico, was next on the agenda.[13] The ideas for the design of Zion City (not to mention its name) and the structure of his church were clearly borrowed from what Dowie had learned from the Mormons.[14] The press in Salt Lake City, which had kept tabs on Dowie's growing influence, complained bitterly that all that "is good in Dowieism is clearly borrowed from the doctrines of the Church. It is clearly plagiarism."[15]

Dowie's expanding empire was paralleled by the elevation of his ecclesiastical status. He had named himself General Overseer of the Christian

Catholic Church upon its formation in 1896. In 1899, he proclaimed that he was the "Messenger of the Covenant." Then, in June 1901, he declared himself to be Elijah, who was to be "The Restorer of All Things." Finally, in September 1904, he consecrated himself First Apostle of a worldwide church.[16]

Dowie's Message

Dowie's message was clearly rooted in the perfectionist and evangelical theology of his era. But he quickly developed distinctive characteristics with Mormon overtones. He summed up his theology by stating: "Zion stands for Salvation, Healing and Holy Living," which he referred to as the "Full Gospel."[17] Included in this summation was the understanding that Christ's atonement had a threefold dimension: Jesus as Savior, Healer, and Sanctifier.

The Full Gospel

Dowie found scriptural support for his threefold emphasis in Isaiah 35:4–10 (KJV): "Be strong, fear not: behold, your God will come . . . he will come and save you. Then the eyes of the blind shall be opened, and the ears of the deaf shall be unstopped. Then shall the lame man leap as an hart, and the tongue of the dumb sing: . . . And an highway shall be there . . . and it shall be called The way of holiness; the unclean shall not pass over it; . . . but the redeemed shall walk there: And the ransomed of the LORD shall return, and come to Zion with songs and everlasting joy."

Of the three emphases, Dowie gave least attention to the first: Jesus as Savior. One possible reason for this, as his critics were quick to point out, is that most of his adherents came from other denominations rather than as new converts to the Christian faith.[18] When he did speak on this theme, his message was similar to other Protestant clergy of his day, teaching that salvation came through faith in Jesus whose death and resurrection provided pardon from one's sins.

Like his doctrine of salvation, Dowie's understanding of divine healing was grounded in the atoning work of Christ. Healing is obtained through faith. Just as Christ breaks the power of sin, he breaks the power of disease.

Using the ministry of Jesus as his model, Dowie taught that healing was the third order of things. First Jesus taught, then he preached, finally he healed. Dowie interpreted this to mean that the candidate for healing must receive correct teaching and hear correct preaching before expecting to be healed.

The reason sickness had such a grip on the church, Dowie maintained, stemmed from the incorrect teaching that the source of disease was God, either as divine judgment for sin or as an instrument for perfecting the human spirit. Dowie argued that this was a lie from Satan to keep the church in bondage. In Christ's resurrection, God demonstrated his power over sickness and death. This power, Dowie asserted, must now be appropriated by faith.

Preaching preceded healing in Dowie's view, so that the power of the Gospel could convict the listener of sin and elicit faith. Healing would not come to an impure heart. Indeed, sickness in the life of a Christian was evidence that there was "sin in the camp."[19]

Despite the fact that Dowie is most well known for his healing ministry, his adherents claimed that his emphasis on "holy living," the final component of his threefold gospel, was the most significant part of his message. For him, holiness was not a goal to be achieved but a way of life to be lived. Dowie was convinced that salvation brought not only pardon for the guilt of sin, but deliverance from its power as well. Visitors to Zion would often remark with surprise about the practical nature of Dowie's messages to the community, helping them to find ways of dealing with problems arising within family and communal life.[20]

Dowie's concern for holy living included both personal and social dimensions. His lists of guidelines to regulate individual behavior were endless. But he recognized that such behavior modification could best take place in a social context. This was the major reason for establishing the city of Zion. All life within the city was structured in ways to encourage the desired behavior. Land leases could be revoked if a family member was caught violating one of the codes. The city was divided into small sections for the purpose of weekly cottage prayer meetings; these occasions included exhortation and prayer, as well as time for sharing personal struggles and victories.[21]

Dowie's hope to lead his flock in the way of perfection was especially apparent in Zion's educational system. Adherents recognized that worldly influences and their association with "apostate denominationalism" had hindered their own spiritual progress. In their children, they saw the possibility for greater advancement in the way of holiness. Everything possible was provided to ensure their progeny would be a "royal generation."

Dowie's concern for holy living took on a social dimension as well. He tried to instill in every convert the conviction that God is the Father of all and that all peoples are brothers and sisters. Mutual respect for all was taught. Policies were formed to discourage a multiclass society. Concern for Jews and African Americans was stressed. One visitor, observing the conditions of his fellow African Americans, stated that Dr. Dowie must be the most courageous man in the nation.[22] Dowie defended miscegenation as a means to regain the purity and strength of the human race. Respect for fellow humans caused Dowie to advocate a pacifist position. Because he believed nation-states created jealousy, Dowie defended the concept of world government. He devised a welfare system to provide for the needs of the less fortunate and established an orphanage, a hospice for "fallen women," and a retirement home for the elderly.[23]

Thus, the implications of Dowie's doctrine of holy living reached far beyond his subculture and became part of his evangelistic effort. Dowie envisioned establishing other such communities throughout the world. He believed that his movement would eventually transform society, thus preparing the way for Christ to return to rule as head of theocratic government. For him, the way of holiness was truly through the gates of Zion.[24]

The Restoration of All Things

Although he believed Christ's return was imminent, Dowie did not include this as a fourth point in his Full Gospel. Rather, it became the backdrop of all his activity and preaching. On one occasion he stated: "That is all my message, I have no other."[25] However, despite the fact that most of his adherents were drawn from the premillenialist camp, Rolvix Harlan, Dowie's first biographer, correctly observed that Dowie offered "no official program of the future of an apocalyptical nature."[26] Instead of looking to external events to show evidence of Christ's impending return, Dowie was content to incarnate the end-time events in his own person and movement. At its theological center, Dowie's message was eschatological, declaring "the restoration of all things."[27] Gordon Lindsay, his most sympathetic biographer, summed up his conviction: "He utterly believed that as a fulfillment of prophecy, God raised him up to bring about a restoration of worldwide extent, of all things spoken by the prophets. This if true actually involved and anticipated nothing more nor less than a dispensational change in God's dealings with the human race. John Alexander Dowie so regarded it. He believed that the ministry of his office, and the ministry of his Restoration Host would affect [*sic*] world changes prophetically incident to the ushering in of the Millennium and the Return of Christ."[28]

To grasp this coherent center of Dowie's message and to gain insight into how he came to understand his own role in this scheme of things, it is necessary first to place his "Full Gospel" in the context of his worldview and to interpret his self-pronouncements in the light of the events of his ministry. Dowie first articulated his worldview in a sermon entitled, "Satan, the Defiler." In this sermon, he stated his conviction that Satan and his demonic hosts had once inhabited the earth as a pre-Adamic race. As a judgment for disobedience, God cast them into hell where they were to continue existence for eternity in the form of disembodied spirits. Refusing to accept this penalty, they determined to repossess the earth for themselves. They seduced the angelic hosts who were sent to keep watch over the earth, thus penetrating God's defenses. As a result, they deceived God's new creation. Satan, therefore, became the author of humankind's destruction, the cause of their sickness, death, and judgment.[29]

The purpose of Christ's first coming, as Dowie understood it, was to declare war on Satan and his legions. The decisive battle was waged at Calvary. Victorious in death and vindicated by resurrection, the risen Lord returned to heaven to await the final triumph of God. The church was called into existence to bear witness to Christ's victory and empowered by the Holy Spirit to establish and extend Christ's kingdom over all the earth. But like Israel before it, the church failed in its mission. Even in the apostolic era, unbelief and apostasy hampered the mission and rendered the church powerless. Many had since responded to the call of God, but they failed to grasp the Full Gospel.[30]

However, the victory Christ had achieved at Calvary was "without repentance." The benefits he had won were not changed "by the unbelief of men." They were "a permanent possession." They simply had lain dormant. If unbelief were replaced with faith, and apostasy supplanted by obedience, the church would be restored and once again be empowered to accomplish

God's will on earth. The culmination of the present age would come when a person or a movement stepped forward in perfect obedience to say "yes" to God's call. Dowie determined to be that man.[31]

From the outset, Dowie understood his healing ministry in eschatological terms. The outline of his vision was clear by the time he founded the International Divine Healing Association and set out on his initial world tour in 1888. He thought that men and women would be awakened to the claims of primitive Christianity through the confirming sign of healing.[32]

In his opening sermon, following the formation of the Christian Catholic Apostolic Church in Zion, he spelled out his understanding of the role it would play in the end-time events. "The Church of God shall be the Divine agency in the building up of the family, the home, the city, the state, the world, the Church of God, until God's work is completed." This was not just "a mere question of Chicago." Branches would be established in Joliet and Rockford, Illinois, and in Ohio, Iowa, Canada, England, Ireland, Scotland, and Australia. Implicit was his vision for a worldwide network of theocratic communities seeking to extend the Kingdom of God on earth.[33]

More explicit in the sermon was the role that Dowie was ordained to play in this work. The major thrust of his address was to demonstrate that God had intended the apostolic office to be perpetual and that it was the Almighty's desire to restore this office to the church today.[34] He intended to add others to the Apostolate in July 1906.[35]

Dowie's Demise

By the end of 1903, Dowie had reached the pinnacle of his power. As noted earlier, through his crusades he had established thriving churches in every major city in the United States. Dozens of smaller churches grew up in the surrounding towns and villages. His work in Australia and New Zealand continued to prosper under the leadership of loyal lieutenants that he had left behind. As ministers and Christian workers converted to his movement, he would bring them to Zion for a period of training and then send them forth as missionaries in foreign lands. His weekly periodical, *Leaves of Healing*, gave glowing accounts of the success they were experiencing in thirty-nine different countries on five continents. He claimed that his church now boasted a membership of five hundred thousand. He decided it was time for him to conduct a world tour, visiting many of his missions and consolidating his gains.[36]

The tour began with a three-week crusade in Madison Square Garden in October 1903, for which he brought three thousand adherents along to conduct door-to-door evangelism during the day. Then Dowie set out to "strengthen his growing church" in Great Britain, Europe, Africa, Asia, Australia, and New Zealand. His periodical claimed that everywhere he went he was met with great hostility by the establishment, but great success among the masses.[37]

Upon his return from this global trip, Dowie planned a crusade in Salt Lake City. He had first visited that city quietly, but hoping to play a leading role in the Mormon mission. Rebuffed then, this time he determined to return in triumph. For months he had been discussing this with his leadership in Zion City. He had made his intention public in a sermon on September 1, 1903, one month before he embarked on his global tour. The following day a reporter from the *Chicago Record-Herald,* who had been present at the service, broke the story under a headline titled, "Dowie Is Coming," declaring that "Dr. Alexander Dowie" intends "to come to Utah with an immense following in order to convert the 'Mormons.'" He quoted one of Dowie's deacons as stating, "'The restoration hosts will assuredly crusade to Utah in 1904. From Chicago and the neighboring states we will move 3,000 or 4,000 strong. In the West Zion has many followers and they will be expected to join the army.' . . . No secret has been made by Dr. Dowie of his longing to contrive a conversion of the Mormons, and the deeds that they hope to do in the Utah stronghold are constantly being discussed by the citizens of Zion."[38]

By this time in Dowie's career his former praise of the Mormon Church had long ceased. When he was accused of having Mormon sympathies by the evangelical Christian community, he would bitterly denounce the LDS Church in the same vitriolic terms that he heaped upon most Protestant denominations. The Mormon press, which had been reporting on Dowie's activities since he had established himself in Chicago, responded to the challenge: "The Chicago 'doctor' may count on full houses for a couple of performances or more. He may even secure a few converts. Nearly everything that comes along, from Christian Science to the most palpable humbug, obtains a following among people who are groping in the dark and unable to judge for themselves about truth and error. But he will not make any inroad upon the members of the Church."[39] This journalist went on to say: "Much of what is good in Dowieism is clearly borrowed from the doctrines of the Church. It is clearly plagiarism. The distinctive Dowie features are almost repulsive. Such a system can make no lasting impression upon a people that lives in the light of truth. . . . There are, however, a great many sectarians in Utah. Some of these may find in Dowieism something to suit them."[40]

Two months later, the *Deseret Evening News* was still smarting over the pending "invasion." In an article entitled, "Totally Dissimilar," the writer stated that "although there is little if any doubt that Dowie once made a study of 'Mormonism,' and endeavored to adopt some of its ideas and discipline in his own system. . . . [he did so] without really understanding either the principles or the organization of the Church which he attempted to plagiarize." After highlighting differences in Dowie's theology and practice from the those of the Saints, the writer concluded: "The doctrines, the Church organization, the ordinances, the gifts, the spirit, the orders of the Priesthood, the methods, the services, the missionary work, the entire system, aims, effects and position of 'Mormonism' are as different from Dowie's . . . as the mighty Rockies in their mountain grandeur are from the hills thrown up by the moles of the plains."[41]

In February 1904, while on his world tour, Dowie had sent three representatives to Salt Lake City to begin preparations for the crusade now planned for sometime in 1905.[42] The Salt Lake City press remained confident that Dowie would make little impact on the Mormon community. But Dowie planned to play a trump card that the press had not anticipated: upon his arrival, Dowie would announce that he had received a revelation from God that had earlier been given to Joseph Smith. He planned to declare that he would reinstitute plural marriage as part of God's end-time program in preparation for Christ's return to reign on earth for a thousand years. Since, thanks largely to the Mormons, polygamy was illegal in the United States, he would institute this practice on his new plantation in Mexico. The Saints would be invited to join his community and become part of the Christian Catholic Apostolic Church in Zion.[43]

However, Dowie's planned crusade to Salt Lake City never materialized. Early in 1905 he went to Mexico for a final inspection of the lands he planned to purchase. While there he suffered a slight stroke, undoubtedly caused in part by the strenuous schedule he had imposed upon himself. Equally important was the growing conflict he experienced with the leadership he placed in charge of Zion City. His financial resources had been outstripped by his ever-expanding vision. The cost of his New York City crusade and world tour had far exceeded funds he had raised for those purposes. Now, with Zion City still less than half developed, he was contemplating the purchase of 2 million acres in Mexico and was calling for his following from around the world to resettle there rather than in Illinois.

No longer trusting his leadership team to carry out his will in his absence, Dowie recalled Wilbur Glenn Voliva, his overseer for Australia and New Zealand. Named deputy general overseer, Voliva was given power of attorney. Shortly after his arrival in Zion City, Voliva joined the existing leadership in revolt against Dowie, claiming mismanagement of funds and immorality. They based these charges on private conversations Dowie had with them in which he spoke of the policies he planned to enact in Mexico. They especially reacted to his intention to introduce polygamy into the movement.[44]

Arthur Newcomb related two of those private conversations (here in sermonic form) as Dowie was departing on his 1904 world tour:

> We have been reading . . . of the Great and Dreadful Day of the Lord, now so close at hand, and of the glorious Millennium which will follow that Day. It is clear that those of us who are alive when the Millennium is ushered in, those who share in the First Resurrection at that time, will all wear the "glorified," "incorruptible" body which St. Paul mentions. That body could be only our present, human body, created in the image of God, but freed from its weaknesses, its imperfections, its liability to disease and death, and its bondage to old age—a body of wondrous beauty, symmetry, strength, vigor, and inexhaustible youth. And can you conceive such a body without full sexual powers and passions?
>
> Think well what this means. Throughout the Millennium we shall be the fathers of children—the offspring of clean, pure, healthy, vigorous youth. They will be beautiful, perfect children, a race such as this earth has never before seen. . . .

> I call your attention to a further fact. All through the ages, and even to-day, there have been and are more women than good men. So we shall find more women among the redeemed, those of the first resurrection. These women, with their strong, beautiful, youthful bodies will all be entitled to love. They will have the pure but strong passions of healthy young women. And there will not be enough men so that each can have a husband.[45]

Upon learning of the coup, Dowie suffered his stroke. Nonetheless, he rushed home from Mexico in an effort to regain control of Zion City. While he was en route, a rumor spread throughout the United States that he had sold the city to the Mormons to keep it out of the hands of the rebel leaders.[46] This was quickly denied by all parties and was soon proven false.

But the reports of Dowie's views on plural marriage discredited him in the eyes of the majority of his faith community. Whatever the source(s) of his initial vision, his followers came to view him as a tragic figure, consumed with his own importance and deluded with regard to his role in salvation history. Only a few remained faithful to his memory under the leadership of John Lewis, who had been given charge to develop the Mexico plantation. Voliva gained control of Zion City and the Christian Catholic Apostolic Church. The church continues to this day, having become a small but respectable denomination affiliated with the National Association of Evangelicals.

The majority of Dowie's followers, however, would join the ranks of the emerging Pentecostal movement. That this shift would occur is not surprising. Like Dowie's adherents, early Pentecostals were drawn primarily from the ranks of the Wesley Holiness and Keswick traditions. Like Dowie, they fervently believed that Christ would soon return, but that just prior to his appearance there would be a great outpouring of the gifts of the Spirit that would result in a worldwide revival. The gifts would be restored to the church and apostolic authority would be manifested through mighty signs and wonders.[47] Dowie himself was allowed to live in his home in Zion City until his death in March 1907. Thus Dowie's legacy was manifested in a different sort of restorationist movement from the one that had inspired—and rejected—him so many years earlier.

NOTES

1. E. L. Blumhofer, "A Pentecostal Branch Grows in Dowie's Zion," *Assemblies of God Heritage,* Fall 1986, 3–5; W. J. Hollenweger, *The Pentecostals* (Minneapolis: Augsburg Press, 1972), 65, 120–21.

2. G. Lindsay. *The Life of John Alexander Dowie* (Shreveport, La.: Voice of Healing Publishing Company, 1951), 11–26; J. Swain, "John Alexander Dowie: The Prophet and His Profits," *Century Magazine* 64 (October 1902): 934.

3. A. W. Newcomb, "A Voice to Zion and God's People in Every Land," *Leaves of Healing* 8, no. 5 (November 24, 1900): 144.

4. Lindsay, *Life,* 72–75; Swain, "John Alexander Dowie," 936.

5. Rolvix Harlan, *John Alexander Dowie and the Christian Catholic Apostolic Church in Zion* (Evansville, Wisc.: R. M. Antes, 1906), 34; Swain, "John Alexander Dowie," 937; Lindsay, *Life,* 90, 93–94.

6. Newcomb, "Voice to Zion," 144.

7. Arthur Newcomb, *Dowie: Anointed of the Lord* (New York: Century, 1930), 282. Although this is a fictionalized account of Dowie's life, the author states in the preface, "The attempt here is to present an accurate—although abridged—account of the personality, words, acts, and experiences of John Alexander Dowie, and a true picture of his human and material environment." In my research thus far I have found nothing in his work that is contradicted by historical evidence.

8. I first learned of this tradition from David Paulsen while attending the NEH Summer Seminar at Brigham Young University in 2005. Paulsen, then professor of philosophy at the university, spent his missionary years at Zion, Illinois, in 1957–58. While in Zion, Paulsen learned from Dowie's followers much of what I have subsequently discovered in Dowie's publications. Author interview with David Paulsen, June 22, 2005. Subsequent research confirms from Mormon sources that Dowie did visit Salt Lake City. To date, however, I have been unable to confirm from Mormon sources that he had a visit with the Quorum of the Twelve or with President Woodruff.

9. "Opening of Zion's Hall of Seventies," *Leaves of Healing* 9, no. 14 (January 28, 1899): 255. Later he would elaborate: "The Mormons taught what the Word of God distinctly teaches: that the apostolic, prophetic, and teaching offices are perpetual in the Church, according to I Corinthians 12:28. They taught the perpetual organization of the Church and the Gifts of the Spirit as the 12th [chapter of 1] Corinthians teaches it. They taught tithing as God's Word has taught it from the far-distant age of Melchizedek, King of Salem, and high priest of God, when Abraham paid tithes to him. The 'word of wisdom' of Joseph Smith contains excellent provisions for the good of the people." J. A. Dowie, "Elijah the Restorer," *Leaves of Healing,* 13, no. 20 (September 12: 1903): 662.

10. Harlan, *John Alexander Dowie,* 34; Swain, "John Alexander Dowie," 937; Lindsay, *Life,* 94.

11. Swain, "John Alexander Dowie," 937; Lindsay, *Life,* 134.

12. Lindsay, *Life*, 161; Harlan, *John Alexander Dowie*, 34–37.

13. P. L. Cook, *Zion City, Illinois: Twentieth Century Utopia* (Syracuse, N.Y.: Syracuse University Press, 1996), 31–32, 55, 61–67, 71–77, 169.

14. For example, a careful study will show that Zion City was organized on the same basis as Joseph Smith organized Nauvoo, Illinois, several years earlier. Both headquarters cities were initially to serve as model communities for others that would be established throughout the world. These communities, in their life and practice, were to model as closely as possible what life would be like in the coming millennium. From these communities, the ministry of the "Seventy" would be sent forth to evangelize the surrounding countryside. For both, the temple stood at the center of the city, symbolizing the centrality of liturgical life as well as the center of the respective movement's theological system. Like Joseph Smith, Dowie claimed for himself the office of Prophet, First Apostle and High Priest, as well as chief officer governing the temporal affairs of the community. Like Smith, Dowie would run for president of the United States. Like Smith, Dowie expected the recovery of ancient texts that would be regarded on a par with the Old and New Testaments as sacred scripture. As an example, he pointed to the recently discovered apocryphal book, *Enoch*, which he believed was a revealed account of Satan's physical pre-existence. While he acknowledged the manuscript that had been discovered was corrupted through transmission, he predicted the original copy, written by Enoch himself, would soon be found and accepted by Christianity as the oldest book of the Bible. This would be but one of several new biblical texts that had been preserved by God, which would now come to light since the power of the British Empire (which along with the United States was the restored ten Lost Tribes of Israel) had extended its control over the Middle East. Such discoveries, he maintained, demonstrated that the beginning of "the restitution of all things" was now unfolding. Finally, like Smith, he believed that God was imparting new revelation through him that was consistent with, further explained, and fulfilled earlier prophesies of the Old and New Testaments. A. Dowie, *Satan the Defiler: A Sermon* (Chicago: Zion Publishing House, 1899), 8–9.

15. "Dowie Is Coming," *Chicago Record-Herald*, found in *The Journal History Project*, September 2, 1903, 2.

16. Harlan, *John Alexander Dowie*, 36–39.

17. E. L. Blumhofer, "The Christian Catholic Church and the Apostolic Faith: A Study in the 1906 Pentecostal Revival," in M. Cecil Robeck, Jr., ed., *Charismatic Experiences in History* (Peabody, Mass.: Hendrickson, 1985), 131.

18. Harlan, *John Alexander Dowie*, 162.

19. Lindsay, *Life*, 214–19.

20. Cook, *Zion City*, 217; W. M. Hundley, "The Flag of the Salvation Army Eclipsed by the Standard of Zion City," *Physical Culture* 21 (January 1901): 226.

21. Cook, *Zion City*, 216, 220, 251.

22. Ibid., 235.

23. Ibid., 221, 229–35; 244–46.

24. Lindsay, *Life,* 208–209.

25. Harlan, *John Alexander Dowie,* 155.

26. Ibid., 155–56.

27. Blumhofer, "Christian Catholic Church," 131.

28. Lindsay, *Life,* 208–209.

29. J. A. Dowie, *Satan, The Defiler* (Chicago: Zion Publishing House, 1899), 8–9.

30. Ibid., 12.

31. J. A. Dowie, *Talks with Ministers on Divine Healing* (Chicago: Zion Publishing House, 1897), 19.

32. Lindsay, *Life,* 84–89.

33. J. A. Dowie, "The Ministry of an Apostle—Is It for Today?" reprinted in G. Lindsay, ed. *The Sermons of John Alexander Dowie: Champion of the Faith* (Dallas: Christ for the Nations, 1982), 113–14.

34. Ibid., 124–25.

35. Cook, *Zion City,* 106–107.

36. Harlan, *John Alexander Dowie,* 36–39.

37. Ibid.

38. "Dowie Is Coming," unnamed Salt Lake paper [*Deseret News,* September 2, 1903, 4] citing *Chicago Record-Herald,* in *The Journal History Project,* September 2, 1903, 2.

39. *Journal History Project,* September 2, 1903, 2.

40. Ibid.

41. *Deseret Evening News,* in *Journal History Project,* November 7, 1903, 1.

42. "Dowieites to Invade Utah," *Salt Lake Herald,* in *The Journal History Project,* 10 February 1904, 2. For an analysis of Dowie's world missionary tour, see my article, "The Missionary Strategy of John Alexander Dowie," *Wesleyan Theological Journal* 42, no. 1 (Spring 2007): 199–214.

43. I provide a complete analysis of the Mexico project in my unpublished paper, "The Place of Mexico in the Eschatological Vision of John Alexander Dowie," presented at Fuller Theological Seminary on February 11, 2006.

44. Cook, *Zion City,* 191–200.

45. Newcomb, *Dowie,* 279–81.

46. "Dowie and the 'Mormons,'" *Deseret Evening News,* April 13, 1905, 4.

47. For an account of the shift to Pentecostalism, see Blumhofer, "Christian Catholic Church," 126–46.

5

The Prophetic Legacy in Islam and Mormonism

SOME COMPARATIVE OBSERVATIONS

Grant Underwood

The ink was barely dry on the pages of the Book of Mormon before comparisons between Joseph Smith (1805–44) and Muhammad (ca. 570–632) began to appear. The similarities seemed irresistible. Both men founded a new religion, produced new scripture, gathered a body of loyal followers, blended temporal and spiritual, and later—embracing a practice particularly scandalous to Victorian Americans—had more than one wife. Early comparisons were superficial at best and often based on inaccurate information. Most problematically, they were placed in the service of a traditional Christian polemic intent on discrediting both Muhammad and Joseph Smith. Blatant bias bedeviled even learned observers like Sir Richard Burton, who actually spent time with both Muslims and Mormons. In the later 1800s and early 1900s, with the rise of more academic approaches like the phenomenology of religion that called for the "bracketing" of bias and application of empathy, comparative religious studies became less overtly judgmental. Yet, for a variety of reasons, the public analysis of Mormonism rarely reflected such developments.

The work of prominent commentators Eduard Meyer and Hans Thimme a generation later was still being driven by ideology—Thimme's by theology and Meyer's by Hegelianism—and their analyses consistently reflected the old tendency to compare in order to demonstrate superiority. This proclivity eventually helped bring the entire comparative method into disrepute for a time. Meyer also took up the study of historically accessible Mormonism in hopes of understanding the rise of historically distant Islam. This paralleled the extrapolative methodology of anthropologists and scholars of religion who studied so-called contemporary primitive societies (such as certain aboriginal peoples in Australia) in order to understand the prehistoric origins of religion. Comparativists continued to examine the world's great religions with varying degrees of subtlety and sophistication as the century wore on, but Mormonism was rarely included in their studies. Such was the paucity of quality comparative analyses of Mormonism and Islam that as recently as 1971, two Islamic studies Ph.D. students at UCLA who surveyed the field were compelled to conclude that thus far comparative study had "contributed little to an understanding of either religion."[1]

Since then, additional studies have been published, but they are few in number and generally lack either methodological rigor or conceptual depth. Thus, the comparative study of Mormonism cries out for a sustained and substantive engagement with Islam.[2] Among the many comparisons possible, this chapter offers a close examination of Joseph Smith and Muhammad.[3] In particular, it focuses on how their respective followers came to define the role of prophet, how they assessed the relative authoritativeness of the prophet's words (ranging from canonical scripture to pious advice), and how community memory of the prophet's life influenced in various ways both religious precept and praxis.

Let us be clear at the outset. Not only is there no single Islam—only Islams, manifest in different sects and schools of thought—but each of these has its own unique history and regional variations. Likewise, it is inappropriate to speak of Mormonism as if it were a monolith. Not all of Joseph Smith's followers went west to Utah with the Church of Jesus Christ of Latter-day Saints. Divergent groups bearing different names and smaller constituencies exist to this day.[4] Even within the Church of Jesus Christ of Latter-day Saints, which is the focus of this chapter's comparison, historical and geographical variation, differences between popular and official theology, and the impact of that crucial triumvirate of race, class, and gender make it difficult to speak in universals. And yet, there are perceived commonalities that bind believers together and enable them to call themselves, broadly, "Muslim" or "Mormon."

In addition to definitional clarifications, a word about methodological convictions is in order. First, similarity is not identity. No matter how similar certain ideas or practices may seem, they are never identical. They grow out of different contexts and carry different connotations. Differences may be slight, but, upon close examination, they are always present. Second, parallels do not prove provenance. The fact that doctrines or practices may be similar does not prove that one religion borrowed from the other, as Richard Burton assumed Joseph Smith had done from Muhammad, or that both drew from yet another source, even when that source is proximate in time and space. Conversely, uniqueness does not prove divine origin. It is a common tendency among believers to assume that because their religion seems to offer unique understandings and insights that these are proof of its divinity. Similarity and difference are descriptive evaluations; they say nothing necessarily about origin. Assessing a religion's divine origin is an endeavor that falls outside the realm of the academic study of religion. Third, at the level of the particular, comparisons can make aspects and tendencies in one religion that might otherwise be overlooked stand out in bold relief. What is more, human comprehension requires some degree of generalization and comparison. In the words of cognitive scientist Douglas Hofstadter, "analogy [is] the core of cognition."[5]

Role of the Prophet

Founders are almost always revered, and often their lives take on a paradigmatic quality for their followers. It has been so both in Muslim and Mormon communities, though to varying degrees. Early on, a body of tradition emerged that recalled the words and deeds of the founding prophet in ways that were meaningful to each believing community. During the first two centuries after Muhammad, those traditions (*ahadith;* literally, "reports," "accounts") were recovered and eventually compiled into large, authoritative collections known as the Hadith. The thousands of recollections of what Muhammad said and did, approved and disapproved, collectively constituted his *Sunna* (way of life, words and deeds) that would interpret the Qur'an and help Muslim jurists determine proper codes of conduct for the *umma* (believing community). A similar literature arose within Mormonism about Joseph Smith, though on a much smaller scale and in a less formalized manner.[6] Those literatures will be discussed later, but first some comparative observations about the founding prophets and the scripture they recorded are necessary.

In terms of scripture, the closest parallel in Mormonism to the Qur'an is not, as some have assumed, the Book of Mormon. The Book of Mormon, more like the Bible, is a loosely chronological narrative set in ancient America and interwoven with prophecies and sermons from its protagonists. The LDS Doctrine and Covenants, on the other hand, is a collection of over 130 separate revelations called "sections" given to Joseph Smith during his twenty-four-year ministry, just as the Qur'an contains 114 *Suras* (chapters, sections) given to Muhammad during the twenty-two years he was in revelatory relationship with Allah.[7]

For Muslims, the *i'jaz al-Qur'an* (miraculous, inimitable nature of the Qur'an) makes clear that, though the divine recitations conveyed by the angel Gabriel that constitute the Qur'an were in a known human language (Arabic), the choice of words was God's, not Muhammad's. Among Latter-day Saints, however, there is some ambiguity about whether scripture contains the very words of God. No official Mormon statement defines the precise relationship between the human and the divine in the genesis of scripture. However, suggestive comments have occasionally been made by church leaders. For instance, the nineteenth-century apostle Orson Pratt offered this explanation: "Joseph the Prophet in writing the Doctrine and Covenants, received the ideas from God, but clothed those ideas with such words as came to his mind—but in translating the book of Mormon by the use of the Urim and Thummim [a divine object], God not only revealed the ideas but the words also."[8] Pratt's description of the sections of the Doctrine and Covenants resembles the way Muslims explain a *hadith qudsi* (sacred saying). In this special type of hadith, the meaning comes directly from God but the wording is the Prophet's.[9]

There is no record of Joseph Smith himself ever having claimed a conscious role in wording the revelations, but the revelation texts themselves hint that he heard the voice of God spiritually rather than audibly, as Muhammad heard Gabriel's Qur'anic recitations. "I speak unto you with my voice, even the voice of my Spirit," declared God in one revelation (Doctrine and Covenants 97:1). In another: "I will tell you in your mind and in your heart by the Holy Ghost. . . . Behold, this is the spirit of revelation" (Doctrine and Covenants 8:2–3). In the first section of the Doctrine and Covenants, the self-designated "preface" to the compilation, God explains that the book's revelations were "given unto my servants in their weakness, after the manner of their language that they might come to understanding" (Doctrine and Covenants 1:24). Mormon thinkers have variously interpreted this to mean that the infinite can never properly be expressed in finite language, or that God chose to speak to Joseph Smith in the religious dialect of nineteenth-century New York, or that, as one early church leader explained, the Mormon prophet expressed the revelations "in such language as [he] could command, in such phraseology as he was master of and [was] common to the time and locality where he lived; modified, of course, by . . . the inspiration of God that was upon him."[10]

However Mormons have interpreted the divine-human mix in the articulation of scripture, even the highest view falls short of the *i'jaz al-Qur'an* and the understanding (by the third Islamic century) that the words of the Qur'an were wholly transcendent, uncreated, and eternal in nature. Part of what restrains such elevated perceptions among Latter-day Saints is that, in contrast to the Qur'an, a sizeable number of manuscript copies of Joseph Smith's revelations have survived. These prepublication copies allow a level of textual and redaction criticism impossible in Qur'anic studies. What such criticism shows is that the Mormon prophet occasionally revised his revelations to clarify meaning or adjust tone, or he modified them to keep pace with the emerging polity and doctrine of the church. In all, around 5 percent of the total text of the Doctrine and Covenants was revised prior to the volume's publication.[11]

Ultimately, despite the significantly different origins of their foundational scriptures, most Mormons and Muslims end up affirming the complete reliability of the sacred texts produced by their prophets. This is so particularly at a popular level. Rank-and-file Latter-day Saints generally do not hold the nuanced views discussed above and merely assume not only that God revealed the Book of Mormon to Joseph Smith word-for-word but that he also dictated the revelations of the Doctrine and Covenants verbatim. Thus, similar to the orthodox Muslim position, scripture is viewed as unaffected in any way by the human messenger. As with Muslim perceptions of Muhammad and the Qur'an, Latter-day Saints discern little of Joseph Smith, the man, in the scriptural texts he dictated. This notion is suggested by the popular LDS synonymous reference to their prophet as God's "Mouthpiece." In short, for most Mormons and for most Muslims, the transmission of God's Word is thought to be impervious to human influence and effect.

Such an understanding of scripture reinforces and is reinforced by the common tendency over time to hallow the founder, though this occurs somewhat differently in Mormonism than in Islam. In the Mormon case, the weight of documentary history again acts to restrain the apotheosis of Joseph Smith. The Mormon prophet has not reached the heights of adulation and imitation that Muhammad attained among many of his followers. Even the most flattering hymns and poetic tributes to the Mormon prophet cannot match, for instance, the rhapsodies of the "Mantle Ode" composed by the thirteenth-century Egyptian poet al-Busiri.[12] Mormon constructions of their prophet take cognizance of, even if they ultimately justify, the fact that he was chastened for his sins in several Doctrine and Covenants revelations, that he repeatedly acknowledged his imperfect human nature, and that he lost a fair number of followers over the course of his life because his perceived shortcomings led the disaffected to consider him a "fallen prophet."[13] Still, Mormons share with most Muslims something of a doctrine of *isma* (protection, immunity from error), which in Joseph Smith's case at least ensures the purity of LDS scripture. "I never told you I was perfect," Joseph Smith reportedly declared, "but there is no error in the revelations which I have taught."[14]

But how far does prophetic isma extend beyond scripture in both Mormonism and Islam? To what degree is the Prophet's Sunna, as preserved in the Hadith, protected from error? In Islam, despite the minority view of the early *ahl al-kalam* (a group of dialectical theologians) that only the Qur'an was *wahy* (divine revelation), the classical position articulated most forcefully by the famous ninth-century scholar of religious law, al-Shafi'i (d. 820), was that the Sunna also was to be accepted as revelation. "The Prophet of God proferred nothing that was not *wahy*," wrote al-Shafi'i in *Kitab al-Umm*, "for *wahy* includes [both] that which is recited [the Qur'an] and also *wahy* by which the Prophet established sunna."[15] In the words of the later Ibn Hazm (d. 1064): "God distributed two kinds of *wahy* to Muhammad: The first is *wahy matlu* [recited revelation], recorded verbatim by miraculous arrangement; this is the Qur'an. The second is the *wahy* of tradition (sunna in the Hadith), which is not verbatim, is not inimitable, and is not ritually recited . . . [but] we find that God requires obedience to this second type of *wahy* in the same way that he requires obedience to the Qur'an."[16] Although there were subtle differences among the four great Sunni schools of jurisprudence on the status of the Sunna as a normative source of Islamic law, even when a distinction was made between the Qur'an as revealed and the Sunna as inspired, both were considered foundational for the elaboration of Islamic law.

Distinct from Sunni Muslims, the Shi'a, who espouse a hereditary rather than elected caliphate (Muhammad's successors), add yet another source of normative guidance—the Sunna of the *imams* (literally, leaders), whom they view as the legitimate leaders of the Islamic *umma* after 'Ali bin Abi Talib, the Prophet's cousin and son-in-law. "For the Sunnis," explains Mohammed Kamali, "the possibility of divine revelation (*wahy*) ended with the death of the Prophet. For the Shiites, however, divine revelation continued to be transmitted after the Prophet's death through the line of their recognized leaders or Imams."[17] Because the Shi'a imam was viewed as the authoritative *wasi* (legatee) of the Prophet, the Shi'i Sunna includes the words and deeds not only of the Prophet but also of successor imams such as 'Ali or Ja'far al-Sadiq, a later, especially influential imam.

After the last of the imams (and the number varies depending on the particular branch of Shi'ism), ordinary legal scholars functioned as the authoritative interpreters of the Qur'an and Sunna, just as the *ulama* (scholars) did in Sunni Islam. Initially this interpretation was accomplished through the practice of *ijtihad*, or "striving" through independent reasoning to deduce from the normative sources rulings on particular issues. Approaches to ijtihad varied among the ulama, but in time their reasoned application of the Sunna and Qur'an to myriad specific situations carried the same force of normative law as did the Talmud in Judaism. Eventually, such creative legal elaboration became less common, and later clerics claimed that the "gates of *ijtihad*" had closed. Thereafter, for most Muslim jurists, analysis of precedent and the explanation and application of extant rulings rather than the generation of new norms became the established practice.[18]

All of this plays out a bit differently in Mormonism where belief in successor prophets and current revelation provides for a kind of ongoing prophetic ijtihad believed to be guided more by inspiration than mere human reasoning. Enthusiasm for this ongoing divine guidance tends to lead Latter-day Saints to focus on the present. "The most important prophet, so far as you and I are concerned," explained a senior official, "is the one living in our day and age to whom the Lord is currently revealing His will for us."[19] This should not be taken to mean, however, that Mormon scripture is constantly being expanded. Latter-day Saints recognize four books as scripture—the Bible, the Book of Mormon, the Pearl of Great Price, and the Doctrine and Covenants. The content of the first three is fixed, and newly canonized revelations are added only to the Doctrine and Covenants. Yet, this has happened very infrequently since the death of Joseph Smith. Of the volume's 138 sections and two "official declarations," only four are from prophets who succeeded Joseph Smith. Thus, while an open canon is proclaimed, in practice what sociologists of religion call the "routinization of charisma" prevails. The inspiration of successor prophets may be vigorously affirmed but it is recognized primarily in their sermons and institutional decisions rather than in new, canonical revelations. And while in theory the current Mormon prophet need invoke no authority other than his own inspiration when teaching, he typically tethers his messages quite tightly to the scriptures and occasionally to the words and deeds of predecessor prophets.

Though neither of the two major divisions within Islam embraces even the possibility of post-Muhammadan canonical revelation, the special charisma accorded the imams by the Shi'a would seem to make them the closer parallel to the major religious groups linked to Joseph Smith. Because until the 1990s all prophets in the Reorganized Church of Jesus Christ of Latter Day Saints (now called the Community of Christ) were descendants of Joseph Smith, it has been common to observe that the RLDS were like the Shi'a and the Mormons like the Sunni.[20] Actually, on the crucial matter of the authoritative status of successor prophets, *both* groups are closer to the Shi'a and diverge noticeably from the Sunni. The method of succession is a red herring that obscures attention to the substantive similarities on this point between Shi'a Islam and the two major traditions tracing their roots to Joseph Smith. Neither tradition is yet two hundred years old. At a similar point in Islamic history, Shi'a Muslims could still look to a living imam for special guidance, though that guidance did not come in the form of additions to the Qur'an. Yet, because Joseph Smith's LDS successors (and here comparison with Shi'a Islam veers closer to the LDS than the RLDS) have almost never presented new canonical revelations either, the outcome for both groups ends up being similar—the veneration of the routine teachings of their leaders.

A further similarity to the period of the imams is that Mormon prophets today are careful to confine themselves to religious and moral matters rather than wield the religious *and* temporal power they did in nineteenth-century Utah.[21] This parallels the way in which the early imams, in the face of failed Shi'a revolts against the dominant Abbasid regime and the increased surveillance they produced, began to focus on expounding the *shari'a* ("way" or law) rather than also seeking to exercise political control as Muhammad had done. As one scholar has noted, "The depoliticization of the imamate and the imams' recoil from political activities enabled them to devote themselves to the explication of various juridical and doctrinal topics, founding in the process alternative legal and theological schools and accentuating their religious rather than political authority."[22]

If, from one vantage point, the Shi'a imams are a closer parallel to Mormon prophets than are the Sunni ulama, from another perspective, whether Muhammad alone is seen to be the source of normative sunna, or whether his companions or subsequent caliphs or imams may also serve as authentic sources, or even if the juridical rulings of the classical era are considered legitimate sources, all must be interpreted and properly applied to present circumstances. No texts are self-interpreting. "The real basis for [religious] practice," notes one scholar, "rested primarily upon the foundation of *ijma* [interpretive consensus] rather than on sunna, for it was by ijma that decisions about the authenticity of sunna itself, and its interpretation, were validated."[23] Regardless of how highly lauded foundational texts and personalities may be, in the end, they serve as the legitimating means by which the current meaning-makers in any believing community shape doctrine and practice according to their own insights.

Prophetic Hadith

Turning to the Hadith, the question may be posed, is there a Mormon equivalent? Strictly speaking, the answer is "no." There is nothing comparable to the great collections by Muslim (d. 875) or al-Bukhari (d. 870), in part because the presence of a living prophet, the theoretical equivalent of Joseph Smith, means that there is less need to rely exclusively on the founding prophet's words and deeds. Yet, reports of Joseph Smith's teachings and behavior can be found in many nineteenth-century documents, ranging from private diaries and letters to public speeches and published articles.

In this sense, then, there are many "hadiths" of Joseph Smith's "sunna."[24] A well-known and influential example is an account preserved by the Prophet's close companion, John Taylor. "Some years ago in Nauvoo," reported Taylor, "a gentleman in my hearing, a member of the Legislature, asked Joseph Smith how it was that he was enabled to govern so many people, and to preserve such perfect order." Replied the Prophet: "I teach them correct principles and they govern themselves."[25] This report is not unlike what one finds in the great Islamic collections, and this Mormon "hadith," like the thousands in the Muslim Hadith, has been invoked in similarly influential ways, often in teaching leadership skills to the Mormon ministry.

Although Mormonism does not legislate appropriate behavior to the degree common in certain Islamic schools of thought and does not, in any case, tend to ground it in the sunna of its founding prophet, it does offer "counsel" in many aspects of life. That counsel, particularly in the early years of its history, drew on stories about the prophet Joseph Smith to lend legitimacy to the behavior being encouraged. As with Muhammad, Smith was held up as the paragon of piety. By the early twentieth century, a compilation of popular remembrances of the prophet had been published entitled *Stories about Joseph Smith.* The stories were organized under such headings as "Caring for the Helpless," "His Forgiving Nature," "A Lover of Children," and "Prophet's Consideration for Animals."[26] Even today many Joseph Smith stories appear in LDS sermons and denominational literature and have a similar modeling intent. Thus, these accounts exercise a function parallel to those found in the Hadith, where the prophet Muhammad is remembered as the model Muslim, even the model human in every aspect of life.[27]

Profound respect for the founding prophets in both Islam and Mormonism also spilled over into accounts of the founders' miraculous powers. On one occasion, the prophet Joseph Smith and his traveling party were compelled to camp for the night far from a source of water. One report recounted: Joseph "called for a spade . . . and selected a spot, the most convenient in the camp for men and teams to get water. Then he dug a shallow well and immediately the water came bubbling up into it and filled it, so that the horses and mules could stand upon the brink and drink from it. While the camp stayed there the well remained full, despite the fact that about two hundred men and scores of horses and mules were supplied."[28] Muhammad's companion Anas Ibn Malik reported a similar episode: "One of the

Prophet's expeditions found us, when the time came for prayer, without water for the ritual ablution. The Prophet was brought a small dish with some water in it and he ordered the troops to perform their ablution from the dish. I could see the water gushing up from under his fingers until the entire force had performed their ablution. They totaled some seventy men."[29] Such accounts not only demonstrate the founders' miraculous powers, they also illustrate their compassionate concern for their followers' needs. Ordinary Muslims are exposed to a great deal more pious detail about the life of Muhammad, including such seemingly minor matters as how he cared for his fingernails, than Latter-day Saints know about Joseph Smith. Still, the tendency to venerate and emulate has been present in Mormonism, especially in earlier generations

Another example of how stories of Joseph Smith function in a way similar to the Hadith is in providing historical settings for sections of the Doctrine and Covenants in the same way that *asbab nuzul al-Qur'an* ("occasions for revelation") provide background for the Suras or for particular verses within them. An oft-recited account recalls the setting for section 89, the Mormon health code. "Over the Prophet Joseph's kitchen," reported his companion and successor Brigham Young, "was situated the room in which the Prophet received Revelation and in which he instructed his brethren. . . . When they assembled together in this room after breakfast, the first (thing) they did was to light their pipes, and while smoking, talk about the great things of the kingdom, and spit all over the room, and as soon as the pipe was out of their mouths a large chew of tobacco would then be taken. Often when the Prophet entered the room to give the school instructions he would find himself in a cloud of tobacco smoke. This, and the complaints of his wife at having to clean so filthy a floor, made the Prophet think upon the matter, and he inquired of the Lord relating to the conduct of the Elders in using tobacco, and the Revelation known as the Word of Wisdom was the result of his inquiry."[30] The background to Sura 93 is found in a hadith from al-Bukhari's collection: "The messenger of God was not feeling well, and for two or three nights he did not get up. A woman came to him and said, 'O Muhammad, I am afraid that your familiar spirit has abandoned you. I have not seen it near you for two or three nights.' Then God revealed, 'By the morning light and by the night when it is calm, your Lord has not left you, nor has He despised you'" (Qur'an 93:1–3).[31] Hadiths like these that provide the background or setting for individual Suras or sections offer hearers a glimpse of what prompted the revelations and how the divine communications resolve the question or concern facing the prophet.

In addition to the great Hadith collections, Muhammad's sunna is also preserved in the *sira* (biographical) literature. Here a Mormon counterpart is the volume entitled *Biographical Sketches of Joseph Smith.* This is a series of stories recounted shortly after Joseph Smith's death by his mother, Lucy Mack Smith, and arranged by an editor into a sira-like format.[32] Just as Muhammad's wife A'isha was the source of numerous hadiths about him, so Joseph's mother, Lucy, is the primary source for much of what is known about the early life of the Mormon prophet.

Another important source that bears some resemblance to both the sira literature and the Hadith is a lengthy manuscript entitled "History of Joseph Smith," composed between 1838 and 1856 and published serially at first and eventually, in the early 1900s, as the six-volume *History of the Church.* Just as the earliest history of Islam is essentially the *sirat rasul Allah* (the "life of God's messenger" [Muhammad]), so the "History" revolves around the words and deeds of the Joseph Smith. A significant contrast that reflects the dramatic difference between seventh-century Arabia and nineteenth-century America is the fact that "History of Joseph Smith" is based on sources written during the lifetime of the Mormon prophet—diaries, letters, etc., and even includes a few items from his own hand. Such documents simply do not exist for Muhammad.

Still, because most Joseph Smith documents are in the handwriting of his scribes, and a good number, including entries in his diaries, were composed by them, there is a limited resemblance to the Hadith literature. To be sure, there is evidence that Joseph Smith reviewed his "History" at points, but it is not clear how much he actually dictated, despite it being written in first person. Moreover, much of it was composed after his death. This included his years in Nauvoo, Illinois, where he delivered most of his sermons. Typically, one or more of his clerks took notes while he spoke, sometimes fleshing them out later. Subsequently, church historians took these reconstituted sermon notes and combined them into a single, flowing record. Where they felt there were gaps or incomplete thoughts, they created content to round out the sermon. Readers unaware of all this may assume that the first-person "History of Joseph Smith" contains the Prophet's actual words. It rarely does. Because he lived before the advent of accurate recording devices and even before a reliable form of shorthand had been developed, his discourses—as remembered and reconstituted for his "History" in the fashion just described—are not verbatim transcripts. Instead, they are recollections, not entirely unlike accounts of Muhammad's words preserved in the Hadith. This is so especially if one credits the view of scholars like Muhammad al-Azami, Nabia Abbot, and Gregor Shoeler who, in arguing that hadiths were continuously transmitted from the earliest years rather than late compositions, point to reports of written hadiths during Muhammad's lifetime; they even posit the existence of "lecture notes" from early teachers who preserved his words and deeds.[33]

Though in comparison with reports of Joseph Smith's words, a much greater time gap exists between Muhammad and most hadiths, still cognitive scientists and memory scholars have shown that memories even only a few hours old partake of some of the same filtering and distortion that impact memories from years later. As one scholar has written, "every retrieval of memory is a reassembly of memory" and is affected by the attitudes and circumstances of the rememberer at the time of retrieval.[34] The point is that while there clearly are significant differences between the reconstituted words of Joseph Smith's sermons in his "History" and the remembered words of Muhammad in the Hadith, both are influenced to one degree or another by memory. Thus, collections like the influential and oft-cited *Teachings of the Prophet Joseph Smith* that excerpt reconstituted sermons from his "History" have something in common with the Hadith. They may not be as far along the trajectory of memory's impact as many hadiths, but they are on the trajectory nonetheless.[35]

Islam is renowned for its exacting "science" of hadith evaluation and authentication that developed toward the end of its second century. Each hadith was carefully evaluated in terms of the reliability of its *isnad* (chain of transmitters) as well as its *matn* (text), and it received a classification of trustworthiness along a graded scale from *sahih* (sound) to *da'if* (weak).[36] Nothing like this rigorous *ilm al-rijal* (lit., "science of men," transmitter criticism) developed in Mormonism, but there was a concern to monitor the legitimacy of the numerous accounts of alleged Joseph Smith sayings and stories that circulated in the several generations following his death. "We fear that many things that are reported as coming from the Prophet Joseph," wrote a member of the church's governing First Presidency in 1898, "by not being carefully recorded or told with strict regard for accuracy, have lost something of their value . . . and unwarranted additions have sometimes been made to the original facts, until it is difficult to determine just how far some of the traditions which have come to us may be accepted as reliable representations of what was said or what was done."[37]

Even the semiofficial "History" was carefully reviewed prior to republication in the early twentieth century. This review was no sahih movement, and editor B. H. Roberts was no al-Bukhari, but with the approval of the current prophet, Roberts made a number of judgments about accounts of Joseph's words or deeds that seemed inconsistent, unsupported, and even undignified, in short da'if, if not "wholly apocryphal," and deleted them from the *History of the Church.* Roberts determined that an article on the "signs" of the "second coming" of Jesus Christ and one on "Election and Reprobation" could not have been authored by Joseph Smith and deleted them from the *History.* He similarly challenged the authorship of some letters alleged to have been dictated by Smith, such as one written to the prominent American politician Henry Clay. And he questioned a variety of other supposed Smith expressions, such as identifying the etymology of the word "Mormon" as meaning "more good."[38]

Conclusion

The comparative analysis essayed in this chapter brings into sharper focus how Mormons over time have viewed Joseph Smith, his role as prophet, the scripture he produced, and the legacy he left. Despite the popular and superficial equation of Joseph Smith with Muhammad, close examination has provided a more nuanced picture. Unlike Muhammad, Joseph Smith is revered rather than reverenced, his authoritative status, while foundational, is also as that of one prophet among others, rather than the unique "seal of the prophets," and the scriptures Smith produced are considered the word of God rather than the very words of God. In probing his prophetic legacy, we have seen that something like the Hadith emerged in early Mormonism, though on a much smaller scale and functioning in a less formal, doctrinally normative fashion. Still, comparison with the Muslim experience draws attention to the ways in which Mormon memory of the words and deeds of Joseph Smith have been influential in the LDS community. Hagiography is often didactic, and stories of Smith's life tended to serve devotional purposes. Even the preservation of his words reflected some of the same tendencies apparent in collecting hadiths about Muhammad, thus drawing attention to the degree to which key sources used to reconstruct the history of Joseph Smith and early Mormonism are rooted in recollection and reflect the values and intentions of their creators.

Although this essay barely scratches the surface of Mormon-Muslim comparison, it does illuminate a number of substantive similarities as well as significant differences between Mormonism and Sunni and Shi'a Islam. When the caveat is remembered that comparisons are approximations, not equations, designed to offer a different angle of vision, then the heuristic value of comparative studies like this can be appreciated and fresh perspective gained. Generations of scholars who have done extensive study of either Mormonism or Islam have laid a firm foundation for further comparative analysis. What Mormon studies, in particular, needs in the twenty-first century is a sustained and systematic engagement with comparative religious studies. Such work should be aggressively interdisciplinary and international in orientation. And it should draw strength from, and contribute to, the impressive depth and breadth of the best comparative work being done in associated disciplines. In pursuing such an agenda, new and exciting vistas will be opened onto the world that is Mormonism.

NOTES

1. Arnold H. Green and Lawrence P. Goldrup, "Joseph Smith, an American Muhammad? An Essay on the Perils of Historical Analogy," *Dialogue: A Journal of Mormon Thought* 6 (Spring 1971): 46–58.

2. Over fifteen thousand scholarly items are referenced in James B. Allen, Ronald W. Walker, and David J. Whittaker, eds., *Studies in Mormon History, 1830–1997: An Indexed Bibliography* (Urbana: University of Illinois Press, 2000). Only thirteen, or less than 1/10 of 1 percent, offer any kind of comparison between Mormonism and Islam or Joseph Smith and Muhammad. Since publication of this bibliography, a special issue of *BYU Studies* and several other publications have been devoted to the subject.

3. A recent, prize-winning article of related interest to this study is J. Spencer Fluhman, "An 'American Mahomet': Joseph Smith, Muhammad, and the Problem of Prophets in Antebellum America," *Journal of Mormon History* 34 (Summer 2008): 23–45.

4. For an introduction to these groups, see Steven L. Shields, *Divergent Paths of the Restoration,* 4th ed. (Los Angeles: Restoration Research, 1990); and Newell G. Bringhurst and John C. Hamer, *Scattering of the Saints: Schism within Mormonism* (Independence, Mo.: John Whitmer Books, 2007).

5. Douglas R. Hofstadter, "Analogy as the Core of Cognition," in Dedre Gentner, Keith J. Holyoak, and Boicho N. Kokinov, eds., *The Analogical Mind: Perspectives from Cognitive Science* (Cambridge, Mass.: MIT Press, 2001), 499–538.

6. I recognize that the Hadith is unique and, to the umma, sacred. To illuminate certain developments in Mormon history, however, I shall discuss it comparatively.

7. First issued in 1835, the *Doctrine and Covenants of the Church of the Latter Day Saints, Carefully Selected from the Revelations of God* (Kirtland, Ohio: F. G. Williams, 1835) has gone through numerous editions. Revelations were added after 1835, and the numbering and versification of Doctrine and Covenants revelations have been modified over the years. The citations in this chapter are from the most recent (1981) LDS edition. Earlier observers who noted that the Doctrine and Covenants was the better LDS analogue to the Qur'an include Henri Bousquet and George Arbaugh (Green and Goldrup, "Joseph Smith," 50).

8. Orson Pratt, as reported in "Minutes of the School of the Prophets, Salt Lake Stake, 9 December 1872," and cited in Robert J. Woodford, "The Historical Development of the Doctrine and Covenants," 3 vols. (Ph.D. dissertation, Brigham Young University, 1974), 1:9.

9. See William A. Graham, *Divine Word and Prophetic Word in Early Islam: A Reconsideration of the Sources, with Special Reference to the Divine Saying or Hadith Qudsi* (Hague: Mouton, 1977).

10. B. H. Roberts, *A Comprehensive History of The Church of Jesus Christ of Latter-day Saints*, 6 vols. (Salt Lake City: Deseret News Press, 1930), 1:133.

11. Grant Underwood, "Revelation, Text, and Revision: Insight from the Book of Commandments and Revelations," *BYU Studies* 48 (2009): 67–84. The Book of Mormon, too, has its own unique history of revision, primarily grammatical in nature.

12. Syed Mohiuddin Qadri, ed., *Qasidat al-Burdah: The Poem of the Mantle*, chapter 3, accessed at www.qasidaburdah.com/Qasidat_al-Burda.pdf.

> For he is the one with whom, ended all outward and inward perfection
> And then the creator of all creation chose him as (His) most beloved
> He has no equal in his magnificence . . .
> . . . say what you wish in praise of him [Messenger of Allah] . . .
> And attribute towards his personality whatever you wish of excellence
> And attribute to his dignified status as much greatness as you wish
> For verily the excellence of the Messenger of Allah has no (limits).

13. A sampling of the divine chastening embedded in the revelations is Doctrine and Covenants 3:6, "how oft you have transgressed the commandments and laws of God, and have gone on in the persuasions of men"; and Doctrine and Covenants 93:47, "verily I say unto Joseph Smith, Jun.—You have not kept the commandments and must needs stand rebuked before the Lord." Regarding Joseph Smith's

acknowledgements of his own shortcomings and the dissension that their observation by followers sometimes produced, see Richard Lyman Bushman, *Joseph Smith: Rough Stone Rolling* (New York: Knopf, 2005), 43, 331–38, 346–49, 368–70, 466–68, 527–31.

14. Andrew F. Ehat and Lyndon W. Cook, eds., *The Words of Joseph Smith: The Contemporary Accounts of the Nauvoo Discourses of the Prophet Joseph* (Provo, Utah: BYU Religious Studies Center, 1980), 369 (May 12, 1844).

15. Cited in Daniel W. Brown, *Rethinking Tradition in Modern Islamic Thought* (Cambridge: Cambridge University Press, 1996), 16.

16. Ibid., 51.

17. Mohammad Hashim Kamali, "Law and Society: The Interplay of Revelation and Reason in the Shariah," in John Esposito, ed., *The Oxford History of Islam* (New York: Oxford University Press, 1999), 121.

18. This "closure" is disputed by some modern Islamic scholars and reformers who argue that there is an ongoing need for ijtihad.

19. Ezra Taft Benson, "Fourteen Fundamentals in Following the Prophet," *1980 Devotional Speeches of the Year* (Provo, Utah: BYU Press, 1981), 27.

20. Over the years, in an effort to distinguish itself from the numerically dominant and better-known Church of Jesus Christ of Latter-day Saints, the RLDS church avoided using the term "Mormon" to refer to itself. The move toward terminological differentiation culminated in their April 2000 decision to change the church's name to the Community of Christ. Consistent with these preferences, here and elsewhere "Mormon" and "Mormonism" are used primarily to refer to the Church of Jesus Christ of Latter-day Saints.

21. A notable, fairly recent exception to this might be the church's support of Proposition 8 in California (a ballot initiative in 2008 banning marriage between persons of the same gender), although church leaders were careful to maintain that rather than a political matter they considered Prop 8 a "moral issue" about which they reserved the right to wield public influence.

22. Liyakat N. Takim, *The Heirs of the Prophets: Charisma and Religious Authority in Shi'ite Islam* (Albany, N.Y.: SUNY Press, 2006), 79, 80.

23. Brown, *Rethinking Tradition*, 26.

24. For an introduction and convenient sampling, see Davis Bitton, "Joseph Smith in the Mormon Folk Memory," in Maurice L. Draper and Clare D. Vlahos, eds., *Restoration Studies 1* (Independence, Mo.: Herald Publishing House, 1980), 75–94.

25. John Taylor, "The Organization of the Church," *Millennial Star* 13 (November 15, 1851): 339. Taylor's first biographer also affirms that Taylor heard these words from the prophet: "Teach men correct principles and let them govern themselves, was a doctrine he learned in his early manhood from the Prophet Joseph." B. H. Roberts, *The Life of John Taylor, Third President of the Church of Jesus Christ of Latter-day Saints* (Salt Lake City: G. Q. Cannon, 1892), 344.

26. Edwin F. Parry, *Stories about Joseph Smith the Prophet: A Collection of Incidents Related by Friends Who Knew Him* (Salt Lake City: Deseret News Press, 1934).

27. Annemarie Schimmel, *And Muhammad Is His Messenger: The Veneration of the Prophet in Islamic Piety* (Chapel Hill: University of North Carolina, 1985). To what degree and in what ways Joseph Smith functions as a model for Latter-day Saint women is a matter that deserves further study.

28. Parry, *Stories about Joseph Smith*, 29–30.

29. Cited in John Burton, *An Introduction to Hadith* (Edinburgh: Edinburgh University Press, 1994), 98.

30. Brigham Young, February 8, 1868, in *Journal of Discourses*, 26 vols. (London: Latter-day Saints' Book Dept., 1855–86), 12:158.

31. Cited in R. Marston Speight, "The Function of *Hadith* as Commentary on the Qur'an, as Seen in Six Authoritative Collections," in Andrew Rippin, ed., *Approaches to the History of the Interpretation of the Qur'an* (Oxford: Clarendon Press, 1988), 68.

32. Lucy Mack Smith, *Biographical Sketches of Joseph Smith and His Progenitors for Many Generations* (Liverpool: S. W. Richards, 1853). A brief history of the work can be found in Bushman, *Joseph Smith*, 8–9, 565n3. For an assessment of its "accuracy" from the standpoint of western scholarship, see Richard L. Anderson, "The Reliability of the Early History of Lucy and Joseph Smith," *Dialogue: A Journal of Mormon Thought* 4 (Summer 1969): 13–28.

33. Harald Motzki, ed., *Hadith: Origins and Development* (Burlington, Vt.: Ashgate, 2004), passim.

34. Cited in Robert E. McGlone, "Deciphering Memory: John Adams and the Authorship of the Declaration of Independence," *Journal of American History* 85 (September 1998): 411–12.

35. For detailed discussion of the "History of Joseph Smith," see Dean C. Jessee, "The Writing of Joseph Smith's History," *BYU Studies* 11 (Summer 1971): 439–73; Dean C. Jessee, "The Reliability of Joseph Smith's History," *Journal of Mormon History* 3 (1976): 23–46; Howard C. Searle, "Authorship of the History of Joseph Smith: A Review Essay," *BYU Studies* 21 (Winter 1981): 101–22; and Davis Bitton and Leonard J. Arrington, *Mormons and Their Historians* (Salt Lake City: University of Utah Press, 1988).

36. See Jonathan Brown, *Canonization of al-Bukhari and Muslim: The Formation and Function of the Sunni Hadith Canon* (Leiden: Brill, 2007).

37. Joseph F. Smith, "Editor's Table," *Improvement Era* 1 (March 1898): 372.

38. Jessee, "Reliability," 41–44; Truman G. Madsen, *Defender of the Faith: The B. H. Roberts Story* (Salt Lake City: Bookcraft, 1980), 290–93.

6

The Ex Factor

CONSTRUCTING A RELIGIOUS MISSION IN THE EX-MORMONS FOR JESUS/SAINTS ALIVE IN JESUS, 1975–1990

Sara M. Patterson

In 1979, Ed Decker visited a church in Washington State to speak to the congregation about the dangers of the Church of Jesus Christ of Latter-day Saints (LDS). While listening to the choir sing, he meditated on the fact that Ex-Mormons for Jesus (EMFJ), a group to which he had dedicated his life, needed a new name. The group, begun just a few years earlier in 1975, was struggling with its mission to Mormons in Utah. Some in the group believed that they were less successful than they could be because the "Ex-Mormons for Jesus" name was off-putting, hindering their mission to Mormons before it had even begun. As the choir sang, Decker came up with a new name—Saints Alive in Jesus (or, as the group's current website states, "Latter-day Saints [now] alive in Jesus")—a name intended to communicate a more positive message to those who were affiliated with the LDS Church.[1] Decker believed that Mormons, familiar with calling themselves "Saints," would be able to see the connections between Saints Alive in Jesus (SAIJ) and their own faith without feeling threatened by the "ex" in Ex-Mormons for Jesus. Decker immediately wrote the name down in his Bible, and it has been a part of the organization's identity ever since.

Decker's inspiration for a new name did not result in a name change for the entire organization. Rather, it was used initially alongside the existing name, which resulted in a complicated network of chapters with differing names, all claiming to be part of one organization. For most of its history, the official legal name of the corporation has been "Ex-Mormons for Jesus Evangelistic Association, Inc." Under that legal umbrella, local chapters could either continue to call themselves Ex-Mormons for Jesus or embrace the new Saints Alive in Jesus name.[2]

The disagreements over the two names for the organization reflect the tensions about the primary purpose of the group. A 1976 newsletter stated that the mission of the group was twofold. First, the group had a mission to other Mormons "to bring the knowledge of the true God and His gospel to our brothers and sisters still blinded by the craftiness of false doctrines." Second, it had a mission to other Christians "to warn as many other people as possible of the truth about the Mormon gospel."[3] These two goals, though not official national goals, represent the conflicting ideals of the organization. Just how these missions have played out for the EMFJ/SAIJ will be the primary focus of the following analysis.[4] While the initial intention of the EMFJ/SAIJ was to focus on its mission to other Mormons, providing them with a supportive community to enter as they left Mormonism, the second goal quickly became the focus of the group after Ed Decker took over its leadership in 1979. This second goal of "warning" other Christians has led many Mormons to the conclusion that the group is simply a part of the evangelical anticult movement. This goal dominated as Ed Decker centralized the movement and it became abundantly apparent that funding and membership came not from ex-Mormons but from evangelicals who had never been Mormon. For this reason, the group often came across to outsiders as *anti-* rather than *ex-*Mormon.

This essay is an examination of the first fifteen years of the EMFJ/SAIJ organization. As such, it analyzes how this group developed its foundational practices, many of which are still utilized today. At first glance, it may seem odd to consider EMFJ/SAIJ when examining issues of Mormon history and identity, but to understand Mormonism fully it is imperative to analyze those who crossed the boundary of the church body and moved from being "insiders" to "outsiders." It is precisely at this boundary that we can learn about the construction of religious identity. What we find at that boundary is a complex space created by members of EMFJ/SAIJ that supported their understanding of self and identity as they took leave of a religious community that had defined their sense of self. To become a missionary to the people with whom one used to share religious fellowship maintains a relationship, a connection EMFJ/SAIJ members portrayed as part of a larger divine plan. It is this space and this identity that I will use to trouble the traditional categories sociologists of religion use to describe religious leave-takers. Lay members of EMFJ/SAIJ demonstrate that a more nuanced and complex understanding of religious leave-taking will help us to better understand Mormonism *and* religious leave-taking more generally.

Background

The impulse to embrace the first goal began in 1975 when the first EMFJ/SAIJ chapter was founded "with one member, a P. O. box and a desire to witness for Jesus."[5] Bob Witte, that one member, decided to join forces with two other ex-Mormons, Roger and Melanie Layton, to create the group. Initially they were headquartered in Wheeling, Illinois, but shortly after founding the group, Witte moved to Arizona, and later to Florida, founding new chapters of the EMFJ/SAIJ network in each place. The founders' intention for EMFJ/SAIJ was that there would be no central headquarters but that independent chapters would form throughout the nation and be organized in a democratic fashion.[6]

The founders of EMFJ/SAIJ envisioned the organization as "a system of affiliated former Mormons who have come to a saving knowledge of Jesus Christ as the Lord and Savior of their lives."[7] Later publications included more specific articulations of their mission. They believed they carried an immense burden: "As once deceived, escaped victims ourselves, we must publicly expose and answer the attack of Mormon doctrine, lest our silence be thought of as approval!" They approached their stated mission to enlighten current Mormons with an evangelistic fervor, convinced that they had "NO choice" but to engage in such ministry.[8] This group considered and still considers itself "trans-denominational," and therefore held only to what it called the "essential points of doctrine which have unified the Body of Christ over the years." These points included "agreement that the Bible is God's verbally inerrant, eternal Word," "that Jesus Christ is the Word made flesh," and "that He is man's only hope of salvation." Such affirmations marked EMFJ/SAIJ as part of the broader evangelical movement of the twentieth century. Portraying themselves as David to the LDS Goliath, the group held that one goal was "to see Christian crosses replacing the naked spires and statues of Moroni atop every LDS edifice in the world."[9]

Four years after its founding, things began to change for EMFJ/SAIJ. In January 1979, EMFJ/SAIJ held its first "General Conference," which included "about 25 Ex-Mormons for Jesus and 'gentile' co-workers," the latter of whom had never been Mormons.[10] It was also in 1979 that Ed Decker, a charismatic evangelical who converted out of Mormonism after twenty years of membership, transformed EMFJ/SAIJ at the national level. In 1979, Decker committed himself to full-time leadership of the group, sought nonprofit status for it, and decided to change the group's name to Saints Alive in Jesus.

Decker's rise to power and his centralization of authority fundamentally changed the nature of EMFJ/SAIJ and set it on a trajectory to become a strictly hierarchical group, with Decker at the helm. Quite simply, this process occurred because of a combination of Decker's full-time commitment, his incorporation of the group, his establishment of national-level rules of organization, and his personality. It was after 1979, and particularly with the 1982 production of the film *The God Makers,* which made Decker one of the most well-known and controversial ex-Mormons of record, that the national organization and Decker's personality became increasingly synonymous. The production of the film solidified Decker's claim to leadership and pushed the group toward an emphasis on its second mission. Before exploring the changes Decker made, I will first investigate the initial stated intent of the group in its most democratic form. In its earliest years, the group focused on supporting Mormons who were exiting the LDS Church and providing them with a new and understanding community.

"Ex-Mormons is what we are"[11]

By merging elements of evangelical Christianity, popular psychology, the structure and rhetoric of addiction programs such as Alcoholics Anonymous, and the cult theories of the 1970s and 1980s, the early founders and members of the EMFJ/SAIJ created a unique view of their identity as ex-Mormons. This group, like many evangelical groups in the late twentieth century, embraced popular psychology and the self-help model as important explanatory devices for individual and communal behavior.[12]

Though the experience of being "born again" and converting to evangelical Christianity implies that EMFJ/SAIJ members rejected their Mormon identity, the situation is much more complicated. Early EMFJ/SAIJ members wanted to create a "sacred space" (both psychologically and within their group meetings) in which their new identity and past identity were in constant relation with one another. In her study of people leaving religious groups, Helen Ebaugh writes that individuals who leave groups that are already viewed as 'outsiders' by the religious mainstream find that they "are often caught in 'no man's land' because they lose the strong primary group's association with their fellow deviants and find it hard to be accepted in mainstream society. They are often caught in between the two worlds and find little acceptance from either world."[13] It was precisely on the site of this "no man's land" that local members of EMFJ/SAIJ constructed a world in which *both identities* and *both worlds* mattered. They imagined themselves as crucial players in God's plan—missionizing to the people they understood best, the Mormons, "their people." This initial expectation is evident in the newsletters of several local chapters, and some chapters have maintained this impulse as a central component of their identity.

Perhaps the best explanation of the feelings that some ex-Mormon members had toward their previous religious faith lies in the literature that examines Mormonism as not just a religious tradition but an ethnicity as well. Ethnic studies scholars describe ethnicity as formed out of a complex matrix of communal identity factors. When individuals are asked about their identity, they place themselves within the context of history and community.[14] Because members of the LDS Church faced fierce persecution from critics throughout their early history and because they believed that the blood of Israel flowed through all members' veins, they constructed a tightly knit concept of peoplehood that continues in many ways to the present.[15] Mormons have tended to maintain boundaries between their own community and the outside world by emphasizing that which makes them unique.[16] Though the LDS Church has not been able to preserve the strength of its sense of peoplehood as well in the twentieth and twenty-first centuries as it did in the nineteenth, many complicated strands still bind the individual to the religious community in ways that more culturally mainstream Protestant denominations do not. Regardless of whether or not the terms "ethnicity" or "peoplehood" can be accurately applied to the LDS community of the late twentieth century, what is clear is that Ex-Mormons for Jesus felt and described the bonds in these ways.

Because of the strength of this communal network, those wishing to leave claimed that they were leaving behind much more than their faith and their Sunday morning activities. Many described the transition as one of social and cultural disconnection, of feeling lost. "The rather total social cocoon of Mormonism, when coupled with the repeated mocking of 'orthodox' Christianity in the LDS temple ceremonies," one newsletter reported, "forces feelings of alienation on the departing LDS persons. Even for those who have come out of bondage and into a **right** relationship with the real Jesus Christ."[17] Studies of those who have left the LDS Church show individuals often have an intense identity crisis.[18] Leaders of EMFJ/SAIJ hoped that members might find resolution for that crisis in their new community, identity, and faith. For example, consider a letter reprinted in the February 1990 newsletter from the Southern California chapters. The anonymous author wrote: "I am currently a Mormon who is searching for answers. So far, my studies have led me to have serious doubts about Mormonism, however, I am so fearful and emotionally distraught over leaving the religion that it's sometimes difficult for me to think rationally. I have been a member for 25 years (I am now 34) and I have 4 children who are very involved in LDS activities. All my friends (most of them anyway) are members and my immediate family is too."[19] Early EMFJ/SAIJ newsletters abound with letters like this one, illustrating the kind of ongoing commitment leaving the church required. They claim, in the words of Ed Decker, that the LDS Church was "more than a church for they [controlled] all areas of our lives."[20]

It is for this reason that some EMFJ/SAIJ members felt they had a special divine calling and mission in the world. They alone, they argued, could understand the kind of obstacles people faced when leaving the church: "Christians that have not been Mormons themselves often do not understand the difficulties that leaving Mormonism presents."[21] Thus EMFJ/SAIJ provided a network for people attempting to leave the church: twenty-four-hour hotlines, supportive letter writing, and new social circles. One EMFJ/SAIJ member who helped staff a twenty-four-hour hotline remembered a phone call from a Mormon woman "who left the LDS church a year ago but is still having problems with her Mormon friends." The caller claimed her old friends had a "hateful attitude" toward her.[22] The EMFJ/SAIJ member operating the hotline felt she had provided this woman the companionship she could find nowhere else in her community.

After leaving the LDS faith, ex-Mormons *reduced* their past identity to a cultural and ethnic one, thus constructing for themselves a particular and unique divine calling. That reduction let them construct a religious world in which God required them to go back to save "their people."[23] In effect, their construction of a Mormon ethnic identity enabled the invention of a new mission field on the boundaries of the Mormon faith. Even Ed Decker uses this rhetoric to describe his mission. Likening himself to the biblical Nehemiah, Decker "felt that same brokenness for the Mormon People that [Nehemiah] felt for his people . . . I needed to share the truth with my people the Mormons."[24]

As part of their missionary vision, EMFJ/SAIJ members often likened the struggle of leaving Mormonism to overcoming a drug or alcohol addiction or to cult deprogramming. Designed to be much like twelve-step programs, and part of the "therapeutic culture" of the late twentieth century, some EMFJ/SAIJ groups met monthly.[25] These meetings could include a speaker, who would give an in-depth discussion of one aspect of Mormonism, followed by testimonials given by EMFJ/SAIJ members about how they were able to leave the LDS Church because of the supportive networks that EMFJ/SAIJ friends gave them. A member was provided with steps to follow, much like those of other twelve-step programs; in this case, though, the addiction to be "cured" was one's ties to Mormon culture and theology. Leaders structured these meetings to help members in "recovery from their damaging experience," a recovery that required "sensitive, loving but firm guidance." Similarly, EMFJ/SAIJ pamphlets counseled new members that they might experience "dependency, depression, low self-esteem, confusion and anger."[26] Particularly important to the EMFJ/SAIJ in this addiction model, I believe, is the twelfth step. For Alcoholics Anonymous, this step reads: "Having had a spiritual awakening as a result of these steps, we tried to carry this message to alcoholics. . . ."[27] For the EMFJ/SAIJ it could have easily read: "Having had a spiritual awakening . . . we tried to carry this message to Mormons." Sensing a divine imperative to return in mission to those who were still Mormon, EMFJ/SAIJ members used the addiction model to tie together their sense of identity, their commitment to God, and their sense of divine calling.

Closely related to the concept of addiction was the EMFJ/SAIJ's use of the cult theories that gained wide popularity in the 1970s. "Because of this work," one newsletter author argued, "many were kept out of the clutches of this deceptive cult [Mormonism]."[28] According to these new theories, cults preyed on the most unsuspecting and naïve people they could find. Once found, cult members "brainwashed" or "programmed" the new participant into believing every idea the cult leader taught and carrying out the wishes of that same leader.[29] Applying this model in an LDS context, the EMFJ/SAIJ position was that Mormons had given "unquestioned loyalty to their church."[30] Recovery was said to be particularly difficult because individuals were searching "for the fellowship we experienced as . . . Mormon[s]."[31] Popular narratives in the group promised that the individual coming out of the Mormon "cult," if successful, would finally reach the point of acceptance and adaptation. Members of EMFJ/SAIJ envisioned themselves as crucial to this process because "those who have never been Mormon just don't quite understand what all the big deal is about." What they could not understand, from EMFJ/SAIJ's perspective, was that "the bondage of this cult is very real and very difficult to get free from."[32] It is precisely for this reason that EMFJ/SAIJ members told their personal narratives; in so doing, they hoped to deconstruct the power of the institution that they believed had such powerful sway over them.[33]

Alongside their explanations of the culture they left behind were discussions about the theological reasons EMFJ/SAIJ members left the church. A common theme throughout the newsletters was a feeling of betrayal, the sense that the LDS Church lied to its members and was driven by its efforts to deceive. Members of EMFJ/SAIJ argued that the LDS Church would "misrepresent what they believe in order to induce you to join their organization."[34] They said the deceit lasted until one was "hooked" on the church; then, slowly, one would learn what Mormonism was *really* about.

For members of EMFJ/SAIJ, the ultimate deceiver was Joseph Smith, Jr., the founder of the Mormon faith. It is clear that many of EMFJ/SAIJ's members remembered being taught that Joseph Smith was a perfect person.[35] With this view of a perfect prophet as the basis of their faith, EMFJ/SAIJ members said they became disenchanted when they learned about Joseph Smith's shortcomings as a human being (including, in their view, his polygamy, his revision of divine revelations, his gold digging, etc.). For them Smith was "*too* human."[36] Once convinced of this ultimate deception, they felt they should use that knowledge in their missions to Mormons, because "Joseph Smith is the most vulnerable thing the Mormons have."[37]

Just as frequently, EMFJ/SAIJ newsletters and pamphlets described changes in church revelations, doctrines, and rituals. For them, change implied deception. In one of his stock public lectures, Ed Decker explained that "there isn't a single LDS produced standard work that hasn't undergone hundreds and even thousands of changes, additions, deletions and corrections . . . all of which were done without indications or acknowledgment of the actions taken."[38] In fact, many of the pamphlets created by EMFJ/SAIJ detail the changes to LDS Church documents over the years.[39] All of these were described as deceptions and counterfeits, what Bob Witte called "the $3.00 bill of Christianity."[40]

Despite their feelings of disillusionment and betrayal, ex-Mormon members of the EMFJ/SAIJ retained aspects of their past cultural and religious worldviews. For example, the Mormon structure of testimony is apparent in the testimonies of EMFJ/SAIJ members. The testimonies given on Testimony Sunday in LDS wards around the country tend to follow a certain format. Though laced with individual stories and flair, the testimonies more than likely end with a statement of faith that Joseph Smith was a true prophet, that the Book of Mormon is the word of God, and that the current prophet of the church is a living prophet. Of course, testimony is certainly not foreign to evangelical Christianity. In fact, EMFJ/SAIJ testimonies tend to merge models of addiction testimony, evangelical testimony, and Mormon testimony. In the addiction testimonial model, testifiers discussed their sinful past and asserted that through overcoming the addiction they found salvation.[41] Testimonies within the EMFJ/SAIJ newsletters abound. They will sometimes begin, "As a Mormon, I believed. . . ." Sometimes they end with a statement of what the individual knew was *not true*. Thus, the testimonies served to seal past and present identities together into a seamless narrative and justification for mission work. For example, Ed Decker's personal testimony claimed that "I do not place my eternal life in the hands of any latter-day prophet," that "Joseph Smith was not a prophet of God," and that "[t]he Book of Mormon is a contrived document and not of divine origin."[42] This mirroring of LDS testimonies served both as a familiar method of relating personal spiritual commitment as well as a missionary tactic.

Though EMFJ/SAIJ members believed they had firmly divorced themselves from Mormonism, they still remained—and chose to remain—tied to it in a number of ways. First, the residual structures of Mormon theology and culture appear in their published literature. Second, they clearly believed that coming out of Mormonism required a process of deprogramming and rehabilitation that continued to refer back to past life and identity. And, finally, the EMFJ/SAIJ members felt that they had a positive calling—to witness to Mormons about the evils of Mormonism. These various strands of connection ensured that EMFJ/SAIJ members were continuously tied to their previous religious and cultural identity—in both unconscious and conscious ways. In their words, the burden they felt for Mormons made them responsible for the souls of "their people."

"For Jesus is what we do"

Two goals vied for the spirit and identity of EMFJ/SAIJ in its foundational years. Despite the founders' intentions to be a supportive network for Mormons leaving the faith, EMFJ/SAIJ did not retain most of its ex-Mormon members for very long. Rather, some ex-Mormons used the EMFJ/SAIJ as a supportive community during their passage out of Mormonism, but they did not make lifetime commitments to the group.[43] Because of this pattern, EMFJ/SAIJ's membership and funds tended to come from evangelicals with no previous ties to Mormonism or those who believed a family member or friend had fallen into Mormonism's snares. The composition of the membership is intimately tied to the question of identity: non-Mormons and ex-Mormons relate to Mormonism differently.[44]

Pivotal to EMFJ/SAIJ's conception of identity and mission in more recent years, then, is its immersion in twentieth-century evangelicalism.[45] Because so much financial support came from persons who had never been Mormons and because educating other Christians can be counted as successful in ways missionizing to Mormons can never be, the focus of EMFJ/SAIJ changed. It is for this reason, along with the personality and goals of Ed Decker, that the second goal—to warn other Christians away from Mormonism—became the foremost EMFJ/SAIJ goal. This put EMFJ/SAIJ on a trajectory of aligning itself with traditional anticult movements whose goal was simply to destroy those religious movements that they defined as cults.

Though the two impulses within the movement might be read as parts of one organic whole rather than as separate from one another, it is clear that the two were at times envisioned as entirely separate and potentially contradictory. Note the response in this 1982 letter written by the assistant director of SAIJ, Jim Witham, to a woman who requested that EMFJ/SAIJ officials like Witham and Decker visit her town to warn other Christians about the evils of Mormonism: "We require that our seminars not be an expense to the ministry, since it would not be right for us to spend money donated to minister to Mormons, in teaching the Christian body."[46] This view from the early years of EMFJ/SAIJ clearly distinguished between the two goals and demonstrates an early commitment to "minister to Mormons."

Over time, however, EMFJ/SAIJ began to favor the second goal and interpreted it to mean direct "warfare" with the LDS Church. This shift is directly tied to Ed Decker's rise to power. For this reason, more detailed background information on Decker is appropriate. Born in 1935, Decker converted to Mormonism at the age of twenty after being introduced to the LDS Church by his wife, Phyllis, an inactive Mormon, and Mormon missionaries. Over the next fifteen years, Decker worked in middle management at several large corporations, fathered five children with Phyllis, and considered himself a faithful "Temple" Mormon. After a complicated divorce from his first wife and a second marriage to a woman named Carol, with whom he had more children, Decker began to go through a spiritual crisis in the early 1970s. That changed in 1975, when Decker claimed he found a true faith in Jesus through prayer. Within a few years he had committed his life and career to actively evangelizing and providing evidence of what he described as the fraudulent claims of the LDS Church (and, to a lesser degree, Freemasonry). Since that time Decker has lived primarily in Issaquah, Washington, where EMFJ/SAIJ was and is headquartered. His wife, Carol, worked to financially support the family, with Decker taking only a small salary from EMFJ/SAIJ "when the ministry could afford it."[47]

Perhaps Decker's most prominent contribution to the evangelization movement was the production of the 1982 film *The God Makers*. The film was an attempt to expose what Decker and others found most absurd about the Mormon faith. Possibly the best known part of the film is a ten-minute cartoon claiming to portray the Mormon story of the creation of humanity. The film created quite a controversy when it appeared, drawing in even more viewers. Some Jewish and Protestant communities stepped in to defend the LDS Church from the claims made against it in the film. Other Protestant congregations showed the film to church members and an interested public. Because of the film, Decker received hundreds of letters of support. To this day, Jeremiah Films advertises it as a documentary that recounts the "Heart-breaking accounts of families and lives destroyed by the Mormon church" and "depicts accurate dramatizations of occult Mormon temple rituals . . . secrets so guarded that those who protect the rituals risk death!"[48] The LDS Church responded to the film on November 16, 1983: "In a country which prides itself on religious freedom and religious plurality, fairness and mutual regard should not let that happen. Simple courtesy would dictate a decent respect for that which is sacred to others."[49]

Decker, who was the "doctrine guy" and raised "the bulk of the [money] to do the film," believed that the film worked quite well as a central tool that encouraged Mormons to leave the church: "Thousands upon thousands of people are coming out of Mormonism because of *The God Makers, The Temple of the God Makers,* the books and tracts, the summer mission work, and all of the other ongoing projects." He did, however, know that it was sometimes perceived as anti-Mormon. He wrote, "I'm sorry that *The God Makers* at times seems like an anti-Mormon film, particularly when whoever is ministering with the film [is] there answering questions from an outsider's point of view, and not because they are broken by the shed blood of Jesus Christ." It is clear that Decker considered the question-and-answer period after a showing of the film an important part of the ministry. He would show the film and then "after the lights come on, I usually stand by the podium and share very briefly the power of Jesus Christ drawing people out of darkness. I will also give an altar call at times."[50] In fact, Decker found the film such a strong evangelization tool that *The God Makers* was followed in 1987 with *Temple of the God Makers* and in 1992 with *God Makers II.*

When Decker committed himself full-time to the movement, and especially after the 1982 release of *The God Makers,* his influence shaped the EMFJ/SAIJ, particularly at the national level. On the local level, some members resented that Decker's controlling behavior allowed him to become *the* personality of EMFJ/SAIJ.[51] Written institutional histories of the movement found in Decker's papers express the centralized role Decker played in the organization: "While some were called to plant the seed, Ed Decker was called to distill the loose organization into a mature, tightly functioning organization."[52] In fact, one timeline of "The Chapter" has as the first date January 1975: "Ed Decker finds Jesus." The second date given is 1975: "Bob Witte and Melanie Layton found Ex-Mormons for Jesus (Non-Incorporated)." These documents confirm an attempt on the part of Decker and others at the national level to recast the history of the group to emphasize Decker's centrality.

Where the founders imagined EMFJ/SAIJ as a loosely connected set of chapters within a democratic national organization, Decker's impact has made it "not a 'democracy' in the simple sense. This may seem a bit 'authoritarian' in a sense, but put simply, We have a Vision to walk, and it is open to investigation. Those who want to walk this vision with us are welcome as long as they keep in step." Keeping "in step" included not only a commitment to the goals of the movement as Decker envisioned them, but also a willingness to change other aspects of personal identity. Individuals were not allowed to smoke, drink, or neglect personal hygiene because it might offend potential Mormon converts.[53] Though Decker at times embraced the idea that EMFJ/SAIJ was for Mormons coming out of Mormonism, his leadership skills helped him recognize where the future membership of the group lay.

All of these elements of organizational development may place Decker in the category that religious studies scholars call "career apostates." A particularly important example of the use of the term "career apostate" for this study is Lawrence Foster's analysis of Jerald and Sandra Tanner, founders of Utah Lighthouse Ministries, a publication-oriented endeavor that seeks to expose the historical changes in LDS doctrine and argues that these changes demonstrate that the central messages of Mormonism are lies—after all, they claim, how could God change God's mind? In his analysis of the Tanners, Foster writes of career apostates that "[R]ather than moving on to make a new and more happy life for themselves, career apostates tend to define themselves more in terms of what they are against rather than what they are for." For Foster, they remain reactive, in a "sort of limbo"; they are never satisfied nor can they create a "positive alternative synthesis of their own." From Foster's perspective, the Tanners "have not yet developed a faith which is sufficiently inclusive to encompass the full depth and richness of a mature Christianity."[54]

Studying the role of the apostate has become an important aspect in understanding how people identify themselves in relation to their religious beliefs. In their study of different types of religious leave-takers, sociologists of religion have defined an apostate as "a person [who] exits, either voluntarily or involuntarily, an unconventional or 'new' religious group or movement . . . and then becomes an outspoken, visible critic of the latter."[55] In so doing, the "apostate seeks to polarize the former and present identities" and become a "moral entrepreneur" who desires only to "expose the evils of the suspect group."[56] An apostate is "not primarily committed to the positive contents of his new belief and to the realization of its aims," but rather "lives only for [his or her former faith's] negation."[57] The new faith of the apostate is simply a disguise that allows the apostate to attack her or his past identity.[58]

Such definitions of apostasy are quite rigid and specific. For that reason, they fail to allow for a spectrum of responses from those who leave religious traditions and actively choose to maintain an identity in response to those traditions. The aforementioned standard definition of apostasy implies a lack of maturity on the part of the apostate; thus if the leave-taker then joins the evangelical movement, which so often defines belief and action in either/or terms, it is impossible to be recognized as having a mature faith. "Apostate" is therefore a problematic category.

Decker has committed decades of his life to attempting to dismantle the LDS Church; he may in fact be a "career apostate" according to sociological categories. However, many ex-Mormons within the EMFJ/SAIJ movement do not fit the apostate mold. Therefore, it is necessary to move beyond these definitions to a more nuanced perspective. Members of EMFJ/SAIJ join the group for a variety of reasons. Though they may well have a dualistic worldview, that worldview does not differ in kind from many believers within American evangelicalism. So for scholars of religion to call their faith immature, superficial, or simplistic seems a problematic claim at best. On some levels, EMFJ/SAIJ members serve as examples that these accepted definitions of apostasy are too simplistic and dualistic. This is perhaps most obvious in terms of identity. Local members of EMFJ/SAIJ often maintain some sense of affiliation with their past identities while still constructing a new understanding of that identity and a new ground on which they might view that identity. Lay members of EMFJ/SAIJ do not operate in black and white categories, as the above definitions of "apostate" suggest, but rather choose to operate in the gray worlds of past and future, missionaries and missionized, self and other. The two missions of the EMFJ/SAIJ, often at odds with one another for the soul of the movement, show just how complicated defining the membership can be.

The EMFJ/SAIJ came to find the mission to warn other Christians so important that in the 1980s they increasingly portrayed suburban America as a battlefield between the Christian God and the Mormon cult. Their literature reminded other Christians that "[t]he Mormon missionaries are not going into the poorest regions of India. They are going into virtually every middle-class town in America, and some 80% of their converts are coming from the traditional Christian churches."[59] Their pamphlet titled, "Here they come . . . 30,000 of them," detailed the threat to suburban America that Mormon missionaries supposedly posed: "They are out to get the members of your church—those who will listen to them—those who are non-attenders—members who are weak in doctrine—members who have wealth or civic prestige." Most importantly, "[t]hey are out to gather in your people."[60] Interestingly enough, the "your people" in these documents implies EMFJ/SAIJ connections to evangelical Christians, rather than the "our people" used to identify themselves with Mormons. Thus EMFJ/SAIJ employed these images and language of warfare and danger both to inspire their members to action and to emphasize the immediacy and importance of their religious mission.[61]

Newsletters of EMFJ/SAIJ, often sent unsolicited to Protestant churches in their communities, discussed the various aspects of Mormonism that Christians might encounter. First and foremost, the EMFJ/SAIJ alerted other Christians to the fact that Mormonism would attempt to disguise itself as Christianity. Newsletters in the 1980s claimed that Mormons were attempting to "buddy up" with Protestant churches in their neighborhoods. This was all part of the church's strategy: "With Mormonism's latest ploy to look, act and talk like Christians, many more-than-usual unsuspecting souls are being taken in by their ever evolving deception!"[62] According to the EMFJ/SAIJ, the LDS Church had the most-skilled psychologists and marketers working on packaging the religion. What these masterminds had come up with was ingenious, they said: "Mormons use the same words as Christians, but they are not the same in meaning. Therein lies the trap." The unsuspecting Christian "hears of the joys of the Gospel, the love of Christ, and God's desires for us—and steps into the realm of subtle doublethink."[63]

The EMFJ/SAIJ pamphlets were often sent out in general mailings, but probably most important to the mission was the organized distribution of pamphlets at temple openings. It was—and is—at the temple openings that members looked the most *anti-*, rather than *ex-*, Mormon. Prior to their dedication, new temples are open to the general public for tour. The LDS Church has these openings to make a gesture of goodwill to the community and to dispel myths about the kinds of secret rituals that occur in the temples. In response, EMFJ/SAIJ members seek to be present at every temple opening. In this, as in many aspects of the EMFJ/SAIJ mission, images of warfare prevail. For example, some EMFJ/SAIJ literature told members that "the battle lines have been drawn and the enemy isn't happy."[64] Usually, EMFJ/SAIJ activists stand on the public sidewalk outside the temple carrying picket signs and passing out literature. Newsletter accounts reveal how EMFJ/SAIJ spent months fund-raising and soliciting volunteers for the Portland Temple opening in 1989, allowing them to be on the front lines of the battle.[65]

Likewise, the vision of battle and exposure of underlying intentions was visible in their discussion of the 1989 temple opening in Seattle: "20,000 Mormons will be brought into the Seattle area during the time that the temple tours will be taking place and they're going to be knocking on every door," Decker warned. But the EMFJ/SAIJ mission was not going to be outdone, because "there are going to be four or five thousand Christians running faster than the Mormons, and we're going to leave a package at every door."[66] This aspect of their mission was quite simply a wish for the future. They had no idea how many people they reached. Speaking of their protests at the Las Vegas Temple opening, one newsletter recounted that "Most [visitors] drove away quickly before realizing that they were in possession of 'anti-Mormon' material. Who knows how many searching hearts will be led to pick up those materials at a later time." This is the promise on which EMFJ/SAIJ members rely; their job is to get the word of God into the hands of others, trusting that God will do the rest. In that respect, their hope is not unlike Mormon missionaries' desire to "plant seeds" that will grow in the future.

A survey of EMFJ/ SAIJ national newsletters from 1993 to the present (found at www.saintsalive.com) shows that over the past two decades the emphasis on the second goal has become even more central to EMFJ/SAIJ. The fact that persons at the Issaquah, Washington, headquarters maintain the website, and it is their newsletters that appear there, shows that Decker's hold on the group continues. Decker is still committed to the group full time. This means that the group has embraced the larger evangelical anticult movement and has become committed to its first goal primarily in word only. This is evidenced in its description of the group's aim: "While our major ministry areas deal with Mormonism and Freemasonry, you will find numerous other world religions, cult groups and issues covered."[67] The focus of articles in the newsletters is still the exposure of "fraudulent" beliefs and people in the LDS Church and, to a lesser degree, Freemasonry. Yet numerous articles now appear disparaging other world religions and new religious movements. Take, for example, the February 2009 e-mail newsletter: its features include a call to evangelical ministry and faith, an article claiming that the LDS Church performed a posthumous baptism of serial killer Ted Bundy, and several statements and articles against Islam and Muslim Americans.[68] In this way, Decker's group has become an apologetic movement that defends "orthodox Christianity" from all other religious perspectives. A recurring theme in the past decade has been one of fighting against a godless world. In the September-October 2008 newsletter, Decker wrote: "I do not think that organizations like Saints Alive have much time left before we are closed down for spreading 'hate' against other faiths. . . . In what I now consider our post-Christian society, every orthodox Christian belief is held up to scorn and every anti-Christian action lauded."[69] With that perception as a guide, the EMFJ/SAIJ newsletters portray a group fighting numerous enemies, both secular and religious, for the soul of the nation and the world. Though Mormonism may still be the primary enemy, it is now clearly one among many.

The goal of fighting the Mormon enemy for the souls of Christian America has overcome the attempts to provide Mormons with a supportive community to pass through on their way out of Mormonism. This shift in EMFJ/SAIJ, reflected in its two names, occurred because evangelical groups who had few if any connections to Mormonism supplied the majority of the membership and funding for the organization. Decker, able to perceive each goal's potential, created a hierarchy within the movement and pushed it toward supporting the second goal—to warn other Christians. Changes in the EMFJ/SAIJ's identity and mission have led to an increasingly tense relationship with members of the LDS community. In many ways, Decker's influence situated EMFJ/SAIJ wholly outside the boundaries of the Mormon faith, attacking the institution while claiming to save its believers. And, perhaps for this reason, Decker may fit into the category of "career apostate." However, on a local level, some EMFJ/SAIJ chapters and members continued and continue to construct their religious identity on the boundary of the faith, choosing to maintain an active and complicated relationship to insiderhood. They crossed into outsider status, but created a space on the boundary of the tradition where their mission allowed them to intermingle with insiders. In fact, their sense of religious identity combined insider and outsider status and placed them at the center of what they understand to be a divine plan for Mormons.

NOTES

I am grateful for comments made on earlier drafts of this piece by Richard Bushman, Lawrence Foster, Mel Hammarberg, Eric F. Mason, and Quincy D. Newell.

1. Decker, communication with author, February 2007, in author's possession. See also Ed Decker to Scott De Long (RLDS), February 19, 1980, and "The Chapter" (n.d.), MSS 210, Special Collections of Utah State University Library, Logan, Utah (hereafter Special Collections, Utah State University Library). For more recent discussions of the name of the organization, see www.saintsalive.com/general/getinvol.htm (accessed March 8, 2007).

2. Decker, communication with author, February 2007.

3. January 1976 Newsletter, box 52, fld. 3, MSS 900, J. Willard Marriott Library, University of Utah, Salt Lake City (hereafter Marriott Library, University of Utah). In this essay I rely primarily on newsletters from the various chapters of EMFJ/SAIJ. Though not all chapters have newsletters, some have seen them as a primary form of mission work. Because I believe it is important to capture the goals and beliefs of movement members *in their own words,* I have chosen to use their words without noting all grammatical errors. These EMFJ/SAIJ newsletters tend to use much capitalization, boldfacing, and underlining for emphasis.

4. For ease of reading, I have called the group EMFJ/SAIJ throughout, even though the Saints Alive in Jesus (SAIJ) name was not added until 1979.

5. January 1976 Newsletter, Marriott Library, University of Utah.

6. Ibid.

7. Ibid.

8. February 1990 Newsletter, L. Tom Perry Special Collections, Harold B. Lee Library, Brigham Young University, Provo, Utah (hereafter Perry Special Collections, Lee Library, BYU). An example of the churches listed by the EMFJ/SAIJ in Orange, California, includes various Baptist, Evangelical Free, Foursquare, and Lutheran congregations.

9. Utah Summer Missions Sheet, May 1982, box 52, fld. 5, MSS 900, Marriott Library, University of Utah.

10. January–April 1979 Newsletter; February 1978 Newsletter, box 52, fld. 3, MSS 900, Marriott Library, University of Utah. It is difficult to determine an accurate membership count of either chapters or individual members in EMFJ/SAIJ. The constitution and bylaws of the group state that "The Corporation shall have no membership," and so no records are kept of individual members. Despite uncertainty about membership numbers, there are some things that we can know about the structure of EMFJ/SAIJ. During the early years, three levels existed within the group: First, there was the status of general member, which is "simply a chapter of one person." Second, there were "Fellowship Chapters." That designation referred to groups that, according to headquarters, were meeting regularly. Finally, there were

"Corporate Chapters," groups in existence for a year with "at least one ex-Mormon involved who does not necessarily have to be in a leadership role—yet must certainly be more than a 'token ex.'" Achieving this level enabled a group to have a bank account and nonprofit status. Box 105, fld. 8, MSS 210, Special Collections, Utah State University Library.

11. This and the following subhead title are slogans from a California EMFJ/SAIJ group.

12. David Harrington Watt, *A Transforming Faith: Explorations of Twentieth-Century American Evangelicalism* (New Brunswick, N.J.: Rutgers University Press, 1991).

13. Helen Rose Fuchs Ebaugh, *Becoming an Ex: The Process of Role Exit* (Chicago: University of Chicago Press, 1988), 159.

14. Patricia Nelson Limerick, *Something in the Soil: Legacies and Reckonings in the New West* (New York: Norton, 2000), 241.

15. See Thomas F. O'Dea, *The Mormons* (Chicago: University of Chicago Press, 1957); R. Laurence Moore, *Religious Outsiders and the Making of Americans* (New York: Oxford University Press, 1986); Armand L. Mauss, *The Angel and the Beehive: The Mormon Struggle with Assimilation* (Chicago: University of Illinois Press, 1994); Armand L. Mauss, *All Abraham's Children: Changing Mormon Conceptions of Race and Lineage* (Chicago: University of Illinois Press, 2003).

16. "The distinctive elements of Mormon theology, the receiving of endowments in the temple and the sealing of marriages for time and eternity; the growing emphasis on the Word of Wisdom; the daily practices of the priesthood; the Relief Society; Mutual, Primary, and the round of activities at the Ward Houses; the General Conferences; the missionary experience of young men; the baptizing of the dead; tithing; the creation of the church welfare system and the fasting funds for the poor; Family Home Evenings; large families to take part in those evenings; and, perhaps more than anything, the told and retold stories of Mormon history made it very unlikely that Mormons would lose their distinctive ethnicity and disappear into a homogeneous, mainstream American whole." Limerick, *Something in the Soil,* 249. See also Mauss, *Angel and the Beehive.*

17. November 1984 Newsletter, box 52, fld. 3, MSS 900, Marriott Library, University of Utah.

18. See James W. Ure, *Leaving the Fold: Candid Conversations with Inactive Mormons* (Salt Lake City: Signature Books, 1999); and Leslie Reynolds, *Mormons in Transition* (Salt Lake City: Gratitude Press, 1996). Readers should note that Reynolds's study has the goal of showing how Mormons can best make a transition out of the church.

19. February 1990 Newsletter, Perry Special Collections, Lee Library, BYU.

20. Ed Decker to Richard Christensen, April 1, 1981, box 48, fld. 4, MSS 210, Special Collections, Utah State University Library.

21. March 1990 Newsletter, Perry Special Collections, Lee Library, BYU.

22. February 1990 Newsletter, Perry Special Collections, Lee Library, BYU.

23. For an example of this construction of ethnicity, see Wendy Frazier (an SAIJ office worker) to Marc Beauchamp (n.d.): "We are ex-Mormons going back to our people to tell them the true gospel of Jesus Christ." Box 44, fld. 5, MSS 210, Special Collections, Utah State University Library.

24. Decker, communication with author, April 2009.

25. R. Marie Griffith characterizes the "therapeutic culture" in this way: "The boom of twelve-step groups or recovery groups has often been treated as marking a kind of spiritual shift in American life, in which the boundaries between the public and private have been repeatedly challenged and redrawn." See Griffith, *God's Daughters: Evangelical Women and the Power of Submission* (Berkeley, University of California Press, 2000), 34. See also Eva Moskowitz, *In Therapy We Trust: America's Obsession with Self-Fulfillment* (Baltimore: Johns Hopkins University Press, 2001); Ellen Herman, *The Romance of American Psychology: Political Culture in the Age of Experts* (Berkeley: University of California Press, 1995); and Wendy Simonds, *Women and Self-Help Culture: Reading between the Lines* (New Brunswick, N.J.: Rutgers University Press, 1992). For a history of Alcoholics Anonymous, see George H. Jensen, *Storytelling in Alcoholics Anonymous: A Rhetorical Analysis* (Carbondale: Southern Illinois Press, 2000).

26. July 1990 Newsletter, Perry Special Collections, Lee Library, BYU.

27. *Alcoholics Anonymous: The Story of How Many Thousands of Men and Women Have Recovered from Alcoholism* (New York: Works Publishing, 1951).

28. February 1990 Newsletter, Perry Special Collections, Lee Library, BYU.

29. See Sean McCloud, *Making the American Religious Fringe: Exotics, Subversives, and Journalists, 1955–1993* (Chapel Hill: University of North Carolina Press, 2004); Philip Jenkins, *Mystics and Messiahs: Cults and New Religions in American History* (New York: Oxford University Press, 2000); Harvey Cox, "Deep Structures in the Study of New Religions," in Jacob Needleman and George Baker, eds., *Understanding the New Religions* (New York: Seabury Press, 1978); Anson Shupe and David G. Bromley, "Apostates and Atrocity Stories: Dynamics of Deprogramming," in Bryan Wilson, ed., *The Social Impact of New Religious Movements* (New York: Rose of Sharon Press, 1981); Mark Silk, *Unsecular Media: Making News of Religion in America* (Urbana: University of Illinois Press, 1995); Anson Shupe and David G. Bromley, "The Modern Anti-Cult Movement 1971–1991: A Twenty-Year Retrospective," in Anson Shupe and David Bromley, eds., *Anti-Cult Movement in Cross-Cultural Perspective* (New York: Garland Publishing, 1994).

30. EMFJ members enjoyed the work of Enroth in Ronald Enroth with J. Gordon Melton, *Why the Cults Succeed Where the Church Fails* (Elgin, Ill.: Brethren Press, 1985).

31. Box 14, fld. 1, MSS 210, Special Collections, Utah State University Library.

32. July 1990 Newsletter, Perry Special Collections, Lee Library, BYU.

33. Through analyzing what they call "atrocity tales" (scary stories of what happens within cult boundaries), Shupe and Bromley demonstrate the importance to

apostates of telling their personal narratives to counter the claims of the institutions/groups they have left in "Apostates and Atrocity Stories," 189–91.

34. Ed Decker to Irving Gavin, August 21, 1985, box 56, fld. 2, MSS 210, Special Collections, Utah State University Library.

35. See, for example, Lawrence Foster's discussion of Jerald Tanner in "Career Apostates: Reflections on the Works of Jerald and Sandra Tanner," *Dialogue: A Journal of Mormon Thought* (Summer 1984): 35–60, esp. 41.

36. December 1990 Newsletter, Perry Special Collections, Lee Library, BYU.

37. Ed Decker, "Witnessing to Mormons," May 1982, box 140, tape 13, MSS 210, Special Collections, Utah State University Library.

38. Ed Decker, "Some Unanswered Questions on the Mormon Gospel" (Issaquah, Wash.: Saints Alive in Jesus, n.d.), Perry Special Collections, Lee Library, BYU.

39. Their critiques continue and are aimed at various theological concepts such as Jesus's marriage, God's origins as a human being, the insufficiency of the blood of Christ for salvation, multiple gods, a mother in heaven, and the idea that humans could achieve godhood.

40. Bob Witte, "Mormonism, the $3.00 Bill of Christianity" (Safety Harbor, Fla.: Ex-Mormons for Jesus, n.d.), Perry Special Collections, Lee Library, BYU.

41. Eva Moskowitz, *In Therapy We Trust,* 245–47.

42. Ed Decker, "To Moroni, with Love." See also Decker to Pat Largent, August 31, 1981, box 66, fld. 2, MSS 210; and Decker to Sandra Manness, August 18, 1981, box 69, fld. 1, MSS 210, Special Collections, Utah State University Library.

43. As stated earlier, there is no official count of how many EMFJ/SAIJ members there are and therefore no count of how many are ex-Mormon versus evangelical Christians. However, Decker, the leader of the group for over twenty years, has confirmed that evangelicals far outnumber (in membership and contributions) ex-Mormons and always have. See Decker to Sherry Clark, April 4, 1986, box 48, fld. 4, MSS 210, Special Collections, Utah State University Library. In it, Decker wrote, "Most of our support comes from non-Mormons." See also Decker correspondence with author, February 2007.

44. Ebaugh discusses this distinction in *Becoming an Ex.* She writes: "To be an ex is different from never having been a member of a particular group or role-set. Nonmembers do not carry with them the 'hangover identity' of a previous role and therefore do not face the challenge of incorporating a previous role identity into a current self-concept" (149).

45. For histories of twentieth-century evangelicalism, see Randall Balmer, *Blessed Assurance: A History of Evangelicalism in America* (Boston: Beacon Press, 1999); Heather Hendershot, *Shaking the World for Jesus: Media and Conservative Evangelical Culture* (Chicago: University of Chicago Press, 2004); Susan Friend Harding, *The Book of Jerry Falwell: Fundamentalist Language and Politics* (Princeton: Princeton University Press, 2000); Steve Bruce, *The Rise and Fall of the New Christian Right: Conservative Protestant Politics in America, 1978–1988* (Oxford:

Clarendon Press, 1990); Walter H. Capps, *The New Religious Right: Piety, Patriotism, and Politics* (Columbia: University of South Carolina Press, 1990); R. Marie Griffith, *Born Again Bodies: Flesh and Spirit in American Christianity* (Berkeley: University of California Press, 2004); Clyde Wilcox, *God's Warriors: The Christian Right in Twentieth-Century America* (Baltimore: Johns Hopkins University Press, 1992); and Sara Diamond, *Not by Politics Alone: The Enduring Influence of the Christian Right* (New York: Guiford Press, 1998).

46. Jim Witham to Heidi R. Brennan, March 24, 1982, box 45, fld. 3, MSS 210, Special Collections, Utah State University Library.

47. Decker, communication with author, April 2009.

48. www.jeremiahfilms.com (accessed March 1, 2009).

49. Box 31, fld. 4, MSS 210, Special Collections, Utah State University Library.

50. Decker, communication with author, April 2009; Decker to Sherry Clark, April 4, 1986, box 48, fld. 4, MSS 210, Special Collections, Utah State University Library.

51. See, for example, Dave Roberts to Ed, Carol and Jim, May 29, 1986, box 135, fld. 3, MSS 210, Special Collections, Utah State University Library.

52. "Chapters and Organizations," box 98, fld. 14, MSS 210, Special Collections, Utah State University Library.

53. Ibid.

54. See Foster's analysis in Foster, "Career Apostates," 54, 56, 60.

55. Anson Shupe, "The Role of Apostates in the North American Anticult Movement," in David G. Bromley, ed., *The Politics of Religious Apostasy: The Role of Apostates in the Transformation of Religious Movements* (Westport, Conn.: Praeger, 1998). See also Stuart A. Wright, "Exploring Factors That Shape the Apostate Role," in the same collection; David G. Bromley, ed., *Falling from the Faith: Causes and Consequences of Religious Apostasy* (Newbury Park, Calif.: Sage Publications, 1988); H. Kippenberg, "Apostasy," in Lindsay Jones, ed., *Encyclopedia of Religion* (Detroit: Macmillan Reference, 2005); Elizabeth A. de Wolfe, *Shaking the Faith: Women, Family, and Mary Marshall Dyer's Anti-Shaker Campaign, 1815–1867* (New York: Palgrave Macmillan, 2002); John D. Barbour, *Versions of Deconversion: Autobiography and the Loss of Faith* (Charlottesville: University Press of Virginia, 1994).

56. Wright, "Exploring Factors," 95–97.

57. Max Scheler, *Ressentiment*, trans. William W. Holdheim (New York: Free Press, 1961).

58. David G. Bromley identifies the role of apostate as a particular type of leave-taking from a particular type of institution. He identifies three types of leave-taking: defectors, who negotiate their leaves "with organizational authorities, who grant permission for role relinquishment, control the exit process and facilitate role transition"; whistleblowers, who form "an alliance with an external regulatory [authority]" and offer "personal testimony . . . [their narratives claim they are] motivated by personal conscience"; and apostates, who "undertake a total change of loyalties by allying with one or more elements of an oppositional coalition." These three types

of leave-taking, claims Bromley, coincide with three institutional types: allegiant institutions, which "coincide to a high degree with other organizations in their environments . . . [and] most external organizations are positioned either as neutrals or coalitional allies"; contestant organizations, which have "a moderate level of tension with other organizations in their environments"; and subversive groups, which are "confronted by a broad coalition of opponents and few allies." Bromley argues that apostates arise in opposition to subversive groups; after they leave, they join oppositional organizations, actively seek to destroy their past religious identities and organizations, and draw their spiritual zeal through negative activity. David Bromley, "The Social Construction of Contested Exit Roles: Defectors, Whistleblowers, and Apostates," in Bromley, ed., *Politics of Religious Apostasy,* 21–38.

59. Letter to mailing list, October 1981, box 52, fld. 6, MSS 900, Marriott Library, University of Utah.

60. "Here they come . . . 30,000 of them," Saints Alive, n.d., pamphlet found in box 52, fld. 5, MSS 900, Marriott Library, University of Utah.

61. Military images abound in the anticult movement, though they are not always understood in religious terms, as in the Ex-Mormons for Jesus. For a discussion of military metaphors in the anticult movement, see Wright, "Exploring Factors," 98.

62. December 1990 Newsletter, Perry Special Collections, Lee Library, BYU.

63. J. Edward Decker, Jr., "Mormonism: What should you say when Mormon missionaries show up at your front door? Here's a Christian primer from an ex-Mormon on one of today's fastest-growing cults." Ex-Mormons for Jesus, Issaquah, Wash., April 1979, Perry Special Collections, Lee Library, BYU.

64. November 1989 Newsletter, Perry Special Collections, Lee Library, BYU.

65. See discussion of the 1989 Portland Temple opening in October 1989 Newsletter, Perry Special Collections, Lee Library, BYU.

66. Ed Decker, "Mormon Dilemma," box 135, fld. 41, MSS 210, Special Collections, Utah State University Library.

67. www.saintsalive.com (accessed March 1, 2009).

68. www.injesus.com/index.php?module=message&task=view&MID=PB007FXK&GroupID=KT02UVXT&label=&paging=all (accessed March 1, 2009).

69. September–October 2008 Newsletter, www.saintsalive.com (accessed March 1, 2009).

Part 3
Boundary Crossing in the Academy

7
"But I Say Unto You, Who Is Elias?"

Stevan Davies

Like other essays in this volume, mine originated in the 2005 National Endowment for the Humanities Summer Seminar on Joseph Smith and the origins of Mormonism at Brigham Young University. My approach to writing differed from that of my fellow non-Mormon participants, however, because rather than write from an "etic," or outsider's point of view, I sought to write Mormon theology from an "emic," or insider's perspective, assuming the truth of Mormon "believer history" and the truth of the revelatory claims of the prophet Joseph Smith.

Joseph Smith was a theologian. Critics might say he was a naïve theologian or an unsystematic theologian or an uninformed theologian, but a theologian he was. He created a system of ideas about God and salvation that was satisfying to his people and has been inspirational to the Church of Jesus Christ of Latter-day Saints ever since. It would seem, therefore, that an analysis of Smith's theology, or, by practical necessity, a particular part of his theology, would be a significant aspect of the historical analysis of the man's work. But must one necessarily approach Smith's theological program with an attitude of suspicion? Must one assume that his thinking lacked systematic coherence, that his claims should not, even for the purpose of argument, be considered true, that his naïveté and inventiveness cancel out any profundity? I do not think so.

To approach Smith's thinking with the operating assumption that it is, for the purpose of argument, true, systematic, and profound means that one would work from an insider's perspective, and work as a Mormon theologian would work rather than as a critical historian would, for the sympathetic exegesis of Smith's theological program is the foundation of Mormon theology. The theological enterprise begins from the operating assumption that Smith had a coherent theological vision. To reconstruct that vision in a systematic manner so that Smith's various statements cohere does not in and of itself require one to believe that his vision was in fact true. The coherence of his vision can be constructed by interested skeptics, just as interested skeptics work to construct coherent versions of the theological visions of Jesus and of Paul.

Is there a boundary or barrier to contributions by an outsider to the theology of a particular church? In practice there sometimes is. There may be an assumption that not only historical knowledge and intellectual competence are at issue in the creation of a theological essay, but also a level of sincere intentionality coupled with membership in the church and acceptance of the truth of its central propositions. But this is not necessarily a reasonable assumption. Can one, for example, be an atheist and a Roman Catholic theologian? I do not see why not. How would one distinguish a theological essay by an atheist adopting Roman Catholic assumptions for the purpose of argument, from a theological essay by a faithful Catholic Christian who accepts those assumptions as revealed truth? I do not think it would be possible to do so. Scholars within the field of religious studies generally find sympathetic understanding to be crucial. Chris Partridge defends the phenomenological approach to the study of religion, writing that scholars "need to interpolate the phenomena into their own lives. That is to say, they need to try and understand empathetically (*Einfuhlung*) the religion from *within*."[1] I try to do that here.

One does not need to be a Mormon to work from the assumption that Smith spoke truthfully and systematically and profoundly. The assumption that Smith spoke the truth about God does not entail any commitment to the proposition that he did so in fact, or even to the proposition that there is a God about which any statement at all can be truthfully made. An assumption is only a working hypothesis that may lead to interesting results. If those results then make a contribution to the theological understanding of the LDS Church, so much the better.

New Testament scholars like myself who are not believing Christians regularly work to make sense of Paul's ideas, making the assumption, which might be unfounded, that while there may be apparent contradictions and evident variations in Paul's points of view over time, there is nevertheless a coherent system of thought to be found. We also work to construct a system of thought from the scattered remnants of Jesus's discourse that can be judged to be authentically his. Similarly, scholars may work to find coherent systematic theological constructions behind the remains of Joseph Smith's discourse and writing.

It is often the case with religious founders that their full coherence must be constructed by others rather than be discovered in the plain sense of their texts; such persons very rarely wrote books of systematic theology. Any historical scholar of Moses, Muhammad, Jesus, or Paul knows that the Torah, Hadith, Gospels, and the Epistles that go under Paul's name are not coherent systematic texts and are, to a significant degree, not representative of the ideas of the persons they supposedly do represent. As regards Joseph Smith, we have considerably better sources with fewer interpolations of the ideas of others than we do from the four founders mentioned above, but even so, Smith's ideas changed radically over time, at least in how those ideas were expressed, and when we have transcriptions of his discourses made on-the-spot by eyewitnesses, those transcriptions vary considerably. Accordingly, the coherence of what Smith taught theologically must be constructed on his behalf, just as the teachings of Moses, Muhammad, Jesus, and Paul must be constructed.

My theological essay begins by addressing a specific question: who was the Elias who appeared to Joseph Smith and Oliver Cowdery in the Kirtland, Ohio, Temple on April 3, 1836? More generally, it concerns the nature of Elias in Latter-day Saint tradition, for without a clear understanding of the meaning of the term "Elias," its meaning in the Kirtland vision must remain obscure. I will argue that Elias is best understood to be a spirit person in some ways analogous to the spirit person known as the Holy Ghost, and that the human person filled with the Spirit of Elias whom Smith and Cowdery saw in Kirtland was John the Baptist. In my discussion of scripture I will make use of the interpretive stance of the Latter-day Saints insofar as I understand it, making no claim that this is or should be the understanding of other Christian churches or of historical-critical biblical study.

The Origin of the Problem

The nature of Elias has been a puzzle to the Latter-day Saints from at least the time when an essayist (probably John Taylor) in Nauvoo's *Times and*

Seasons (March 1, 1843) wrote, "There are few subjects that have puzzled the children of men more than the solution of this one question, Who is Elias?" It continues to be a topic of much interest, as indicated by the publication in 2006 in *Dialogue: A Journal of Mormon Thought* of Samuel Brown's essay entitled, "The Prophet Elias Puzzle."[2] In the classic book *Mormon Doctrine*, Elder Bruce R. McConkie devotes six columns to his discussion of Elias, but only two and a half to Elijah, two to Moses, and two to John the Baptist.[3] Jesus himself (in Matthew 17:13 in the Joseph Smith Translation [henceforth JST]) asks the rhetorical question, "But I say unto you, who is Elias?"[4] That is the question this essay attempts to answer.

Smith describes the Kirtland Temple vision as follows:

> We saw the Lord standing upon the breastwork of the pulpit, before us; and under his feet was a paved work of pure gold, in color like amber. . . . [T]he heavens were again opened unto us; and Moses appeared before us, and committed unto us the keys of the gathering of Israel from the four parts of the earth, and the leading of the ten tribes from the land of the north. After this, Elias appeared, and committed the dispensation of the gospel of Abraham, saying that in us and our seed all generations after us should be blessed. After this vision had closed, another great and glorious vision burst upon us; for Elijah the prophet, who was taken to heaven without tasting death, stood before us. (transcribed by Warren Cowdery, Doctrine and Covenants 110:2, 11–13)

Smith and Cowdery see Jesus Christ, then Moses, then Elias and Elijah the prophet, and they apprehend the latter as two entirely different persons. But "Elias" is the Greek transcription of the Hebrew name "Elijah." Accordingly, "Elias" appears in the Greek New Testament, and subsequently in the King James translation, in reference to the same person called "Elijah" in the Hebrew Old Testament. Some have accused Smith of making the trivial mistake of misreading the King James Bible by thinking that Elias and Elijah are the names of two separate people, and announcing the presence of both at Kirtland Temple.[5]

If it ever was the case that Smith simply failed to realize that the words Elijah and Elias are the same, but in different alphabets, certainly by 1836 he had discussed biblical matters with enough educated Christian ministers (e.g., Sidney Rigdon) that such a simple mistake could not persist. We know, for example, that Smith's diary entry for November 6, 1835, tells of a man who came to visit him who "seems to have forgotten the saying that fell from the lips of St. James, that Elias was a man of like passions like unto us, yet he had such power with God that He in answer to his prayer, shut the heavens that they gave no rain for the space of three years and six months, and again in answer to his prayer the heavens gave forth rain and the earth brought forth fruit."[6] This reference to the prophet Elijah (see 1 Kings 17:1–18:45) would be unmistakable to a man like Smith who had been deeply concerned with these scriptures his whole life; the simplest reflection would have revealed to him that Elias is Elijah in James 5:17–18 and elsewhere. To say that Elias in Doctrine and Covenants 110 is some sort of mistake is no solution to the problem, so a different solution to the problem must be proposed.

At present there are several theories about who Elias was at Kirtland. Bruce R. McConkie gives his thoughts in a 1980 essay, "This Final Glorious Gospel Dispensation": "After Moses, came Elias. We know not who he was in mortality. There were many prophets who bore that name and title. One was Noah. Apparently this Elias lived in the day of Abraham, and may even have been Abraham himself."[7] He suggests in *Mormon Doctrine* that Elias of Kirtland was an unknown individual: "We have no information, at this time, as to the mortal life or ministry of Elias. Apparently he lived in the days of Abraham, but whether he was Abraham, or Melchizedek, or some other prophet, we do not know."[8] Joseph Fielding Smith wrote in reference to Elias of Kirtland that "Joseph Smith revealed that Gabriel was Noah; Luke declared that it was the angel Gabriel who appeared to Zacharias and Mary; and the Lord has declared that Elias appeared to Zacharias and Joseph Smith. Therefore, Elias is Noah."[9] B. H. Roberts suggested that Elias might have been either Shem or Melchizedek.[10] Frankly, I do not think those answers are very satisfactory. The hypotheses that some personage otherwise unknown to us must have been Elias, or that Noah, who otherwise had played no major role in Smith's life, must have been Elias, go beyond necessity. It is simpler and more natural to understand that John the Baptist was Elias for Smith in 1829 and also in 1836. This identification fits the circumstances and is consistent with all of our evidence, including evidence that points to John the Baptist as one intimately connected with the gospel of Abraham. During the course of the present essay I will attempt to show that this is the case.

Joseph Smith's Discourse on Elias and Elijah

On the occasion of King Follett's funeral, March 10, 1844, four weeks before he gave the memorial address known as the "King Follett Discourse," Smith gave a talk that Wilford Woodruff entitled, "Joseph Discourses on Elias–Elijah–Messiah." The latter is preserved in six partial transcriptions, the most extensive of which is that of Woodruff.[11] In this address, Smith engages the problem of who Elias was and makes careful distinctions between the powers and responsibilities of Elias, Elijah, and the Messiah.[12]

Smith's discussion of Elias, Elijah, and the Messiah begins with his experience of Elias at the Susquehanna River near Harmony (now Oakland), Pennsylvania. He saw, he says, an angel who laid hands on his head and ordained him to the priesthood of Aaron. This, he was told, was "a preparatory work, or a going before, which was the spirit of Elias, for the spirit of Elias was a going before to prepare the way for the greater, which was the case with John the Baptist."[13] James Burgess's record of the discourse tells us that Smith quoted the angel in regard to the preparatory gospel: "This," said the angel, "is the spirit of Elias."[14] Franklin Richards's record notes that Smith said, "Jesus said of John, 'this is Elias which was for to come if you will receive me, otherwise he cannot do the work of an Elias.'"[15] He means that since the work of Elias is preparatory, anyone who fails to receive that which was being prepared for has failed to benefit from the work of Elias.

Smith makes it quite clear that the role of Elias, which he calls "the doctrine of Elias" and "the keys and power of Elias," is to be sent by God into the world to prepare for a greater work. It is a limited role; Smith uses the case of John the Baptist as the classic case, for John was to preach and to baptize to prepare for the greater work of Christ, who would come to baptize with fire and the Holy Ghost.[16]

These elements are so clear in Smith's mind that he has to take issue with a passage in the New Testament. Acts 19:1–6 reads in the King James Version (KJV):

> And it came to pass, that, while Apollos was at Corinth, Paul having passed through the upper coasts came to Ephesus: and finding certain disciples, He said unto them, Have ye received the Holy Ghost since ye believed? And they said unto him, We have not so much as heard whether there be any Holy Ghost. And he said unto them, Unto what then were ye baptized? And they said, Unto John's baptism. Then said Paul, John verily baptized with the baptism of repentance, saying unto the people, that they should believe on him which should come after him, that is, on Christ Jesus. When they heard this, they were baptized in the name of the Lord Jesus. And when Paul had laid his hands upon them, the Holy Ghost came on them; and they spake with tongues, and prophesied.

Smith argues that they could not possibly have received John's baptism because, if they had, they would have heard him speak of the Holy Ghost. Since they had not, they "have been duped by some designing knave who has come in the name of John. An imposture."[17]

When he speaks of Elias in his discourse, Smith never once refers to Elias as a unique historical person; Elias is always spirit or spirit and power. The spirit of Elias permits some to "do the work of an Elias." Others through the spirit of Elias receive Elias as a personal identity, as was the case of John the Baptist. Every person said to be Elias in Latter-day Saint tradition has another personal identity as well; there is no known person "Elias" apart from individuals who have received the spirit of Elias.

When Smith turns his attention to Elijah in the same discourse, he does speak of the spirit and power of Elijah, but more than once he refers to Elijah as a unique historical human person. Smith quotes Malachi 4:5: "I will send you Elijah the prophet before the coming of the great and dreadful day of the Lord," and he notes that before any destruction in the last days, "Elijah should first come." He asks the rhetorical question, "Elijah! What would you do if you were here? Would you confine your work to the living alone? No!" Elijah is a particular historical individual to Smith, and that is very clear in the discourse under discussion.

In addition to using the term "Elijah" for a historical prophet, Smith uses it to denote a particular variety of spirit and power. Six times he refers to the "power of Elijah," and he uses the phrase the "spirit and power of Elijah" five additional times, saying, for example, that "Elias is a fore runner to prepare the way, and the spirit and power of Elijah is to come after holding the keys of power, building the Temple to the Cap stone, placing the seals of the Melchezedeck [*sic*] priesthood up on the house of Israel and making all things ready." Although Smith can speak of the "spirit of Elijah," he is much more prone to speak of the "power of Elijah," or "the spirit and power of Elijah." Indeed, he only uses the phrase "spirit of Elijah" four times, two of which occur in the following enigmatic statement: "This spirit of Elijah was manifest in the days of the apostles, in delivering certain ones to the buffetings of Satan, that they might be saved in the day of the Lord Jesus. They were sealed by the spirit of Elijah unto the damnation of hell until the day of the Lord, or revelation of Jesus Christ." Overall, Smith appears to be contrasting Elias, of whom he almost always speaks in terms of "spirit" but occasionally also in terms of "power," with Elijah who is usually spoken of in terms of "power" but also occasionally also in terms of "spirit."

Smith uses the phrase "spirit and power of Elias" twice, and "power of Elias" three times. But he chooses to use "spirit of Elias" thirteen separate times throughout his discourse. Not once does he even hint that Elias ever was a unique embodied historical person.

Elias Is a Personage of Spirit

Our question must now shift from "Who is Elias?" to "What is Elias?" I think we should look principally at Smith's repeated emphasis on the "spirit of Elias" and take it seriously to the point of taking it literally. When Smith thinks of Elias he thinks of spirit. One can make the clearest sense of the Elias problem by focusing on the reiterated phrase "spirit of Elias" and concluding that it is the case that Elias is, literally, a spirit person, as I will explain in some detail below.

One can understand something of the nature of the spirit of Elias by analogy to the spirit called the Holy Ghost. Smith thought of the Holy Ghost as a spirit person who has a variety of important functions, including revelation, sanctification, teaching, and a role as comforter. The Holy Ghost is the third member of the Godhead, a spirit person, and Smith revealed that "the Holy Ghost has not a body of flesh and bones, but is a personage of Spirit. Were it not so, the Holy Ghost could not dwell in us" (Doctrine and Covenants 130:22). He may some day receive a human body, but this has not yet happened. On June 16, 1844, Smith said, "But the Holy Ghost is yet a Spiritual body and waiting to take to himself a body as the Savior did or as God did or the Gods before them took bodies."[18] Furthermore, he said that "the Holy Ghost is now in a state of probation which if he should perform in righteousness he may pass through the same or a similar course of things that the Son has."[19]

We can understand the puzzle of Elias if we think somewhat the same way about the spirit of Elias as about the Holy Ghost. Both are spirit persons with important purposes who come to individuals and convey to them particular competencies. Neither has yet been an embodied person, but they can and do dwell in people of the past, present, and future. We can speculate that the spirit of Elias, like the Holy Ghost, will someday take a body, but this has not yet happened. In LDS teaching there are unnumbered spirits in heaven with God who will someday receive bodies, and if God should choose to assign some of them special roles because of their special merits, this is nothing to cause astonishment.

In his discourse on "Elias, Elijah, and Messiah," Smith says that "What I want to impress upon your minds is the difference of power in the different parts of the Priesthood, so that when any man comes among you, saying, 'I have the spirit of Elias,' you can know whether he be true or false; for any man that comes, having the spirit and power of Elias, he will not transcend his bounds." Smith assumes that there could be any number of individuals who truly do "have the spirit of Elias," and so the question is not whether such a condition could exist but how to test the truthfulness of such a claim. Men can and will, according to Smith, come claiming to have the spirit of Elias. If we regard Elias as a spirit in some ways analogous to the Holy Ghost, then Smith's statement is easily comprehensible. Any number of people can claim truthfully to have received the Holy Ghost, and some will falsely claim to have received it; the same appears to be true for the spirit of Elias.

We hear of an example of a person coming in the spirit of Elias when Smith discusses the apostle Phillip: "In the case of Phillip when he went down to Samaria, when he was under the Spirit of Elias, he baptized both men and women. When Peter and John heard of it, they went down and laid hands upon them, and they received the Holy Ghost. This shows the distinction between the two powers." This shows the distinction to be sure, but it also shows the generic connection between one who is under the spirit of Elias and people who are under the spirit called the Holy Ghost.

Note particularly the phrase "when he was under the spirit of Elias." This presumably would be the case for any one of those men who "comes among you, saying, 'I have the spirit of Elias,'" and who speaks truthfully. Phrasing like this makes it difficult to avoid the conclusion that the spirit of Elias is indeed a spirit, one that people can "receive," "have," and "be under." If Elias were only a descriptive category for a type of person, then no one could speak truthfully by saying, "I have the spirit of Elias." If Elias were just a word for a person carrying out a particular function, Smith would not have spoken of Phillip going to Samaria "under the Spirit of Elias."

Elias and Spirit Identification

Several times as Smith translated the gospels, he identified persons who are Elias. In the Gospel of John, Jesus is revealed to be Elias: "John answered them, saying; I baptize with water, but there standeth one among you, whom ye know not; *He it is of whom I bear record. He is that prophet, even Elias,* who, coming after me, is preferred before me, whose shoe's latchet I am not worthy to unloose *or whose place I am not able to fill; for he shall baptize, not only with water, but with fire, and with the Holy Ghost*" (John 1:27–28 JST; the italicized portions were restored by Smith). Here Elias is Jesus Christ, whose superiority to John the Baptist is clearly indicated.

In the Gospel of Mark, however, Elias is John the Baptist himself: "And there appeared unto them Elias with Moses *or in other words, John the Baptist and Moses:* and they were talking with Jesus" (Mark 9:3 JST). And Jesus says in Matthew's gospel that "Elias truly shall first come, and restore all things, *as the prophets have written. And again* I say unto you that Elias has come already, *concerning whom it is written, Behold, I will send my messenger, and he shall prepare the way before me;* and they knew him not, and have done unto him, whatsoever they listed. Likewise shall also the Son of Man suffer of them. *But I say unto you, Who is Elias? Behold, this is Elias, whom I send to prepare the way before me.* Then the disciples understood that he spake unto them of John the Baptist, *and also of another who should come and restore all things, as it is written by the prophets*" (Matthew 17:10–14 JST). In this passage Elias is John who prepares the way. It might be suggested that the other Elias who will come and restore all things is Christ in his second coming. However, W. Jeffrey Marsh writes in *Ensign* about Matthew 17:14 (JST) that "Joseph Smith, it seems from our perspective now, was this other prophet, to whom Peter, James and John themselves appeared in 1829, restoring the authority and keys of the Melchizedek Priesthood which they held (see Doctrine and Covenants 128:20)."[20] It seems clear that by receiving the spirit of Elias, some exceptional people are entitled to the identity of Elias.

To say that John the Baptist and others are Elias is to say that they may be under the spirit of Elias and thus have an Elias identity. The adoption of identity due to the reception of a divine spirit can be called spirit identification. Other cases of spirit identification are found in scripture. For example, those Christians who have received the Spirit of the Son can be identified with the Son and be called Sons of God. Paul writes: "And because ye are sons, God hath sent forth the Spirit of his Son into your hearts, crying, Abba, Father. Wherefore thou art no more a servant, but a son; and if a son, then an heir of God through Christ" (Galatians 4:6–7). Also, "For as many as are led by the Spirit of God, they are the sons of God. For ye have not received the spirit of bondage again to fear; but ye have received the Spirit of adoption, whereby we cry, Abba, Father" (Romans 8:14–15). Because they have received the Spirit of the Son, Christians are entitled to be known as Sons of God. Similarly, Christians who have received the Spirit of Elias are entitled to come claiming, "I have the spirit of Elias," and some are entitled even to be identified as Elias.

John the Baptist had the spirit of Elias to the degree that he could be identified as Elias, and because John and Elias are so closely linked in Christian tradition, it is necessary to consider their relationship in some detail. In the Gospel of Luke we read that the angel Gabriel appeared to Zacharias, father-to-be of John the Baptist, and told him that his son John would be "filled with the Holy Ghost, even from his mother's womb. And many of the children of Israel shall he turn to the Lord their God. And he shall go before him in the spirit and power of Elias, to turn the hearts of the fathers to the children, and the disobedient to the wisdom of the just; to make ready a people prepared for the Lord" (Luke 1:15–17). When John has the "spirit and power of Elias" within him in this special way, he can be said to be Elias himself, and in Matthew's Gospel we hear Jesus say in regard to John the Baptist that "For all the prophets and the law prophesied until John. And if ye will receive it, this is Elias, which was for to come" (Matthew 11:13–14).

John's status as Elias was prophesied by Gabriel, who himself also is Elias according to the following revelation: "John the son of Zacharias, which Zacharias as he (Elias) visited and gave promise that he should have a son, and his name should be John, and he should be filled with the spirit of Elias" (Doctrine and Covenants 27:7–8). Gabriel, who also is Noah (*History of the Church* 3:386), was the individual who appeared to Zacharias. To say that Gabriel/Noah is also Elias means that the spirit and power of Elias operate within Gabriel/Noah. If Noah has the spirit of Elias within him, that spirit permits the identity of the human being to be transferred to the spirit's identity for certain purposes. Accordingly, in Luke's account, Gabriel comes to Zacharias, and in Smith's revelation, Elias comes to Zacharias. This is not a contradiction but a case of looking at the same thing from two different perspectives, one of which is spirit identification. Here Gabriel is Elias as forerunner to John the Baptist who, in turn, is Elias as forerunner to Jesus.

According to John 1:20–22 (JST), "And this is the record of John, when the Jews sent priests and Levites from Jerusalem, to ask him; Who art thou? And he confessed, and denied not *that he was Elias;* but confessed, *saying;* I am not the Christ. And they asked him, saying; *How then art thou Elias? And he said, I am not that Elias who was to restore all things. And they asked him, saying,* Art thou that prophet? And he answered, No." John the Baptist here does not deny that he is Elias; he denies that he is Elias in the particular sense of being "that Elias who was to restore all things." Significantly, passages in the Joseph Smith Translation of the gospels show both Jesus (Matthew 17:13–14) and John the Baptist (John 1:21–28) carefully discussing Elias in terms of the personal identity of individuals. Elias is a spirit who, like the Spirit of the Son whom Paul discusses, conveys both powers and identity to a few selected persons. If it should seem odd that Jesus Christ is given the identity Elias through the spirit of Elias, as stipulated in John 1:28 (JST), one should remember that Jesus Christ is empowered by the Holy Ghost as well, beginning at his baptism (Matthew 3:16–17), and subsequently, in Matthew 4:8 (JST): "*And* again, *Jesus was in the Spirit, and it* taketh him up into an exceeding high mountain, and sheweth him all the kingdoms of the world, and the glory of them." As Jesus Christ received the Holy Spirit, so evidently he received the spirit of Elias and an Elias identity, or so we read in John 1:28 (JST).

The Diverse Gifts of Elias

We do know that the restoration of all things is the central element in one of Elias's roles. John, the author of Revelation, also is Elias as a restorer, for we read in Doctrine and Covenants 77:14: "Q. What are we to understand by the little book which was eaten by John, as mentioned in the 10th chapter of Revelation? A. We are to understand that it was a mission, and an ordinance, for him to gather the tribes of Israel; behold, this is Elias, who, as it is written, must come and restore all things." So Jesus Christ, John the Revelator, and quite probably Smith himself were all three identified with the Elias who would come and restore all things. Curiously, as Smith spells it out carefully in his "Discourse on Elias, Elijah, and Messiah," the role of Elias is largely to be a forerunner to those who have powers of restoration while also being those who perform the restoration.

The spirit of Elias has two separate sets of powers. Sometimes Smith speaks of one set of powers—to be a forerunner and to baptize for repentance—appropriate to John the Baptist. Sometimes Smith speaks of another set of powers given through the spirit of Elias that enables divine restoration.

Bruce R. McConkie points out that Elias has a supremely important restoration role, for it is he who "restored the marriage discipline of Abraham, the way was prepared for the planting in the hearts of the children of the promises made to the fathers. (D&C 2:2.) These are the promises of eternal life through the priesthood and the gospel and celestial marriage."[21] "This is," McConkie writes, "the great commission, given of God to Abraham our father, whereby the seed of Abraham has power to gain eternal blessings forever through eternal marriage; that is, Elias restored the marriage discipline that had eternal efficacy, virtue, and force in the days of Abraham, Isaac, and Jacob."[22] Similarly, Robert L. Millett writes of Elias in his essay, "The Ancient Covenant Restored": "This heavenly messenger restored the keys necessary to establish the Abrahamic covenant, making the Prophet Joseph Smith and the faithful Saints who receive celestial marriage heirs to the blessings and promises made to the fathers (see Doctrine and Covenants 27:10). Elias thus restored the patriarchal order, the power by which eternal families are organized through the new and everlasting covenant of marriage."[23] Through this restoration, "Every person married in the temple for time and for all eternity has sealed upon him, conditioned upon his faithfulness, all of the blessings of the ancient patriarchs, including the crowning promise and assurance of eternal increase, which means, literally, a posterity as numerous as the dust particles of the earth."[24] Elias appeared in the Kirtland Temple to restore the marriage discipline of Abraham and the patriarchal order.

The Gifts of the Spirit

To understand how the spirit of Elias might sometimes confer forerunner power and sometimes restoration power, we should think of the gifts of the Holy Ghost as discussed in 1 Corinthians 12. We can infer from that chapter that there are Corinthian Christians who believe that a diversity of supernatural empowerments means that a variety of spirits must be giving those empowerments. This, Paul writes, is not the case: "For to one is given by the Spirit the word of wisdom; to another the word of knowledge by the same Spirit; To another faith by the same Spirit; to another the gifts of healing by the same Spirit; To another the working of miracles; to another prophecy; to another discerning of spirits; to another divers kinds of tongues; to another the interpretation of tongues: But all these worketh that one and the selfsame Spirit, dividing to every man severally as he will" (1 Corinthians 12:8–11). Similarly, it may be argued, while the spirit of Elias comes to various people in connection with the Aaronic priesthood with a power of preparation, and the spirit of Elias comes to John the Baptist especially to be the forerunner both to Jesus Christ at the Jordan and to Smith at the Susquehanna, none of those people is given the gift of restoration that Elias gives to Jesus and Smith. As with the Holy Spirit in Corinth, it might erroneously be supposed that since there are at least two quite distinct "gifts" of the spirit of Elias, there must be two spirits of Elias, but in fact there is but one spirit of Elias that dispenses two quite different sets of powers.

Understood in terms of the spirit of Elias, passages in Doctrine and Covenants 27 become clearer. Jesus Christ says that he will drink the fruit of the vine with Moroni "(6) And also with Elias, to whom I have committed the keys of bringing to pass the restoration of all things spoken by the mouth of all the holy prophets since the world began, concerning the last days; (7) And also John the son of Zacharias, which Zacharias he (Elias) visited and gave promise that he should have a son, and his name should be John, and he should be filled with the spirit of Elias; (8) Which John I have sent unto you, my servants, Joseph Smith, Jun., and Oliver Cowdery, to ordain you unto the first priesthood which you have received, that you might be called and ordained even as Aaron."

In verse 6, Jesus is speaking of Elias as spirit, one of whose powers is to give the key of the restoration of all things spoken by the prophets. This key is given to Jesus Christ and probably to Smith and, accordingly, both of them can be called Elias in terms of restoration. But here the passage does not refer either to its speaker, Jesus, or to the one hearing, Smith, but to the spirit of Elias per se. To the spirit Elias, the powers and keys of the restoration of all things are entrusted and that spirit, in turn, confers them on Jesus and on Smith. During his lifetime Jesus received the keys from Elias, who was John the Baptist, but then, evidently, Jesus committed the keys to Elias again so that Elias, again in the form of John the Baptist, might confer them on Joseph Smith on May 15, 1829. In verse 7, Jesus is speaking of the spirit and power of Elias in reference to being precursor and forerunner, and those particular functions are the ones Smith discusses at length in his discourse of March 10, 1844. Elias comes as Gabriel (who is Noah) to Zacharias and reveals to him that his son John will be filled with the spirit of Elias. It is reasonable to surmise that Zacharias saw the physical form of Noah when the angel Gabriel spoke this to him, by analogy to the fact that Smith saw the physical form of John the Baptist when he heard an angel speak to him near the Susquehanna. In any event, we read in verse 8 that John the Baptist will be filled with the spirit of Elias, and it is he who ordains Smith and Cowdery into the first priesthood; the phrase "which John" specifically refers back to the phrase "filled with the Spirit of Elias," and that status permits John to be named Elias when Smith describes his and Cowdery's experience of May 1829.

How Joseph Smith Chose to Describe Visions

Smith describes the restoration of the priesthood of Aaron thusly: "The messenger who visited us on this occasion, and conferred this Priesthood upon us, said that his name was John, the same that is called John the Baptist in the New Testament, and that he acted under the direction of Peter, James and John who held the keys of the Priesthood of Melchizedek, which Priesthood he said would in due time be conferred on us, and that I should be called the first Elder of the Church, and he (Oliver Cowdery) the second. It was on the 15th day of May, 1829, that we were ordained under the hand of this messenger and baptized."[25] This account has become the standard version of Smith's experience, one that has an important place in Latter-day Saint preaching and Latter-day Saint visual arts. However, Smith did not publicly mention the presence of John the Baptist in Harmony for some time after the event, and the statements quoted above were *not* included in the earliest accounts of it. As Richard Bushman puts it,

> Joseph did not tell anyone about John the Baptist at first. Summarizing the key events in his religious life in an 1830 statement, he mentioned translation but said nothing about the restoration of priesthood or the visit of an angel. The first compilation of revelations in 1833 also omitted an account of John the Baptist. David Whitmer later told an interviewer he had heard nothing of John the Baptist until four years after the Church's organization. Not until writing his 1832 history did Joseph include "reception of the holy Priesthood by the ministering of angels to administer the letter of the Gospel" among the cardinal events of his history, a glancing reference at best. . . . Cowdery was the first to recount the story of John's appearance, not Joseph himself. In an 1834 Church newspaper, Cowdery exulted in his fresh memory of the experience. . . . When Joseph described John's visit, he was much more plainspoken [than Cowdery had been]. Moreover, he inserted the story into a history composed in 1838 but not published until 1842. It circulated without fanfare, more like a refurbished memory than a triumphant announcement.[26]

Smith's reluctance to make specific reference to John the Baptist in discussing his experience of Elias is also evident in his discourse on "Elias, Elijah, and Messiah." He begins by saying, "It is the Spirit of Elias that I wish first to speak of," and immediately he began to discuss his own experience of Elias on the banks of the Susquehanna River on May 15, 1829. Smith said, "I saw an angel, and he laid his hands upon my head and ordained me to a

Priest after the order of Aaron." James Burgess records the words this way: Smith spoke of "the vision of his ordination to the priesthood of Aaron," and Smith recalled the words he heard as follows: "'This,' said the angel, 'is the spirit of Elias.'"[27]

Here, while John is mentioned, it is in a historical reference to Jesus's time rather than a reference to Smith's own experience. When recording this same part of the discourse, Franklin Richards gives us the same statement, but in a wonderful phrasing. Smith told his audience that the Spirit of Elias was "the power which John the babtist [*sic*] was clothed with when he came bounding out of the wilderness saying 'repent ye, for the kingdom of heaven is come.'"[28]

For the purpose of the present argument, it is important to note even in this account from 1844, when Smith discusses his experience on the banks of the Susquehanna, he does not refer to the personage he encountered as "John the Baptist," even though by that year it was firmly established in his record that the angel that appeared was John. It was evidently of greater significance to Smith that an angel appeared bearing the spirit of Elias than that this personage had the unique identity of John the Baptist. Similarly, although the restoration of the Melchizedek priesthood by James, Peter, and John occurred in the summer of 1829, it is not until much later that we hear their names in connection with that event (in Doctrine and Covenants 128:20, which is Smith's epistle of September 6, 1842). It seems clear that Smith found the personal identities of heavenly personages of less significance, or just of less interest, than he found their roles in the divine scheme. Instead of individuals' names, he reports their status as messengers of God, as angels, or sometimes as recipients of the Spirit of Elias.

Now, I think, we are able to understand what Smith and Cowdery saw when (in the Kirtland Temple) "Elias appeared, and committed the dispensation of the gospel of Abraham, saying that in us and our seed all generations after us should be blessed." They saw the person to whom they already connected the spirit of Elias, the human form in which the spirit of Elias had already appeared to them. They saw the spirit of Elias, which is what Elias is, and saw him in the human form of John the Baptist.

Since Smith and Cowdery had known John the Baptist as Elias with the power of a forerunner ever since they were the two recipients of the Aaronic priesthood in 1829, it is *prima facie* likely that they knew John the Baptist as

Elias in the Kirtland vision as well. Since they had met before, they recognized him immediately, but as was their custom, they did not refer to him by his given name but by the spirit that empowered him.

Others might find it of surpassing importance that particular historical persons were encountered in a vision, but that is not how Smith or Cowdery responded to visions. They were much more interested in the category of messenger with whom they interacted. If Elias in the Kirtland vision had a human identity in addition to being an embodiment of the spirit of Elias, Smith would not have been particularly interested in reporting it. He did not do so with the personal identities of James, Peter, and John until well over a decade after they appeared to him at the Susquehanna between Harmony, Pennsylvania, and Coleville, New York. In the 1844 discourse about Elias presently under discussion, he never bothers to specify that the angel who conveyed the Spirit of Elias to him fifteen years earlier was John the Baptist.

Since Smith can be shown to have been more interested in the types, powers, and roles of the supernatural beings who came to him than he was in their personal identities, if the embodied person who appeared in Kirtland was John the Baptist, we would expect him to describe that person as Elias in preference to describing him as John the Baptist. And that, indeed, seems to have been what happened.

John the Baptist and the Gospel of Abraham

But is it reasonable to associate John the Baptist with the gospel of Abraham, and the restoration of the marriage discipline of Abraham, the delivery of which was the main purpose of Elias's presence in Kirtland? As Smith records the vision, Elias "committed the dispensation of the gospel of Abraham, saying that in us and our seed all generations after us should be blessed." The answer is "yes"; there is unquestionably a close connection between John the Baptist acting centuries after Abraham's time and the covenant between God and Abraham himself.

We read in Luke's gospel that at the circumcision of his newborn son John, Zacharias was filled with the Holy Ghost and prophesied, telling people in general and John specifically that they should "remember his holy covenant; the oath which he sware to our father Abraham, that he would grant unto us, that we being delivered out of the hand of our enemies might serve him without fear, in holiness and righteousness before him, all the days of our life. And thou, child, shalt be called the prophet of the Highest: for thou shalt go before the face of the Lord to prepare his ways" (Luke 1:67–76). Here the Holy Ghost connects John's mission with the oath, the holy covenant between God and father Abraham, well in advance of John's active mission to be Elias for Jesus.

As Smith and Cowdery met the angel who was the resurrected and glorified John the Baptist by the Susquehanna River and knew him as Elias the forerunner, so they also met the angel who was John in the temple at Kirtland and knew him to be Elias who "committed the dispensation of the gospel of Abraham." As Jesus Christ met John the Baptist by the Jordan River and knew him as Elias the forerunner, so Jesus also knew John the Baptist in reference to "The oath which he swore to our father Abraham," which is, of course, the covenant and gospel of Abraham. The New Testament tells us that the individual who signified the Abrahamic covenant is none other than John the Baptist, for Jesus himself said that "the law and the prophets testify of me; yea, and all the prophets who have written, even until John, have foretold of these days. Since that time, the kingdom of God is preached, and every man who seeketh truth presseth into it" (Luke 16:17–18 JST; cf. the different wording and verification in the KJV). Abraham signifies the beginning of the covenant and John the Baptist, who is Elias, signifies its conclusion and transition into the Kingdom of God. McConkie suggests that John the Baptist may have been present at the transfiguration "as the last legal administrator under the Old Covenant, to symbolize that the law was fulfilled and all old things were done away, thus contrasting his position with that of Peter, James, and John who were then becoming the first legal administrators of the New Kingdom."[29] John, accordingly, represents the "gospel of Abraham" at its transition at the time of Jesus Christ, and similarly the same John, who is Elias, may have had a similar function in the time of Smith, as revealed in the Kirtland Temple vision.

Conclusions and Implications

In *Mormon Doctrine,* Bruce McConkie writes that there is, on the one hand, an Elias who does preparatory work and has to do only with the

Aaronic priesthood, and separately another "Elias of the Restoration," evident in Christ, in Noah, and in John the Revelator. This brings him to ask: "[T]here are three different revelations which name Elias as being *three different persons*. What are we to conclude?"[30] Elder McConkie concludes that since various messengers have brought the restoration, each with a specific endowment from on high, "*Elias is a composite personage. The expression must be understood to be a name and a title for those whose mission it was to commit keys and powers to men in this final dispensation.*"[31] But if we understand that Smith's reiteration of the phrase "spirit of Elias" means literally what it says and reveals that Elias is a spirit, then the otherwise unattested notion of "a composite personage" should be laid aside. Further, Elder McConkie's conclusion that certain people sometimes have a particular terminology applied to them, a "name and title," and that is what there is to Elias does not seem to be a sufficient explanation for the complex vision Smith had of the role and nature of Elias. Smith's "Discourse on Elias, Elijah, and Messiah" indicates that the phrase "Spirit of Elias" is the most appropriate for that personage, and to say that this spirit is merely a name or a title is not in accordance with Smith's usage.

If Elias is spirit, then Elias can convey a variety of gifts and keys and powers to men as the Holy Spirit, analogously, conveys a variety of gifts. We do not need to hypothesize two separate Eliases, one of preparation and one of restoration, but rather understand that the same spirit conveys both kinds of empowerment, but to different people. In 1 Corinthians 12, Paul insists that a diversity of gifts does not imply a diversity of Spirits; nor does a diversity of empowerments through Elias imply a diversity of Eliases. There is one Spirit but there are many gifts.

In "The Prophet Elias Puzzle," Samuel Brown writes about the roles of Elijah and Elias.[32] He concludes that "Even if the name Elias had been rejected for its philological ambivalence, another would have been chosen to serve as the prefatory prophet, a way to preserve and highlight Elijah as the guiding angel of the Mormon conquest of death."[33] He notes that Elias had a preparatory function associated with the Aaronic priesthood, but he argues that Smith's conception of Elijah is the greater and more marvelous new religious idea, one that "drew the Church of the Latter-day Saints from antebellum Protestantism beyond the second coming into the creation of a new world beyond death."[34] He does well to distinguish Elias from Elijah, but he does not offer a comprehensive solution to the Elias problem, however much we can learn from him about the important role of Elijah in early Mormonism.

I have argued that we should understand Elias to be a spirit person analogous to but different from the Holy Ghost. This solution to the Elias problem has several implications. Since the spirit of Elias is closely bound up with the restored Aaronic priesthood, the LDS Church could consider that the young men receiving this priesthood are receiving the spirit of Elias, which would be somewhat analogous to the fact that people who receive baptism may receive the gift of the Holy Ghost. Thus, all of those who are Aaronic priests would be understood to have the spirit of Elias and so be spiritually bound together with those who came as Elias before them. Smith seems to have referred to those priests when he said, "What I want to impress upon your minds is the difference of power in the different parts of the Priesthood, so that when any man comes among you, saying, 'I have the spirit of Elias,' you can know whether he be true or false." He certainly did believe that some persons who had a part of the priesthood were entitled to come saying, truthfully, "I have the spirit of Elias," and the implication certainly is that such men would continue to appear.

The identification of John the Baptist as Elias in the Kirtland vision allows us to see some very significant parallels between that event and the transfiguration. At the transfiguration four people were present, two of whom went by the same Greek name and so some confusion has resulted. We read that Elias, who is John the Baptist, was present: "And there appeared unto them Elias with Moses *or in other words, John the Baptist and Moses:* and they were talking with Jesus" (Mark 9:3 JST). In Matthew 17:1–9, we read that Elias who is Elijah was present. That both were present is stipulated in the Latter-day Saints' *Bible Dictionary* as follows: "The curious wording of JST Mark 9:3 does not imply that the Elias at the Transfiguration was John the Baptist, but that in addition to Elijah the prophet, John the Baptist was present."[35] It is not at all difficult to see how some confusion between Elijah and Elias (John the Baptist) will occur in Greek texts where both individuals are denominated "Elias." We have, therefore, at the transfiguration, Jesus Christ, Moses, Elijah, and Elias who is John the Baptist, along with James, Peter and John as witnesses who received the Melchizedek priesthood. At Kirtland eighteen hundred years later, in the summer of 1829, Jesus Christ, Moses, Elijah, and Elias who is John the Baptist are present, with Smith and Cowdery as witnesses, who themselves received the Melchizedek priesthood from James, Peter, and John, the men present at the transfiguration. It is hard to imagine that such a complete parallel is sheer accident. If Elias at Kirtland had been someone other than John the Baptist, an unknown prophet of Abraham's time perhaps, or an appearance of Noah, or of Shem, or of Abraham himself, the parallel would be incomplete.

John the Baptist, who had received the spirit of Elias, appeared on May 15, 1829, to Smith and Cowdery on the banks of the Susquehanna to restore the Aaronic priesthood, and they called him Elias. John the Baptist, who had received the spirit of Elias, appeared again on April 3, 1836, to Smith and Cowdery in the temple at Kirtland to restore the Gospel of Abraham. It is he who is called Elias.

NOTES

1. Chris Partridge, "The Academic Study of Religions: Contemporary Issues and Approaches," *Evangel* 18, no. 2 (Summer 2000): 43 (referring to Gerardus van der Leeuw, *Religion in Essence and Manifestation,* 1933). Italics in original.

2. Samuel Brown, "The Prophet Elias Puzzle," *Dialogue: A Journal of Mormon Thought* 39, no. 3 (2006): 1–17.

3. Bruce R. McConkie, *Mormon Doctrine* (Salt Lake City: Bookcraft, 1966).

4. Biblical quotations not marked JST are from the King James Version (KJV). Normally, differences between the JST and KJV renderings are indicated in italic type, but in some cases the wording and/or versification in the two versions is so different as to make this impractical.

5. For example, see Keith Piper's "Errors of Mormonism," section 14, at www.gospeloutreach.net/mormerr.html.

6. November 6, 1835, "Joseph Smith Teachings: Section Two 1834–1837," W. V. Smith, ed., and the Book of Abraham Project, www.boap.org/LDS/Parallel/1843/27Aug43.html (accessed March 2, 2009).

7. Bruce R. McConkie, "The Final Glorious Gospel Dispensation," *Ensign* 10 (April 1980): 23.

8. McConkie, *Mormon Doctrine,* 221.

9. Joseph Fielding Smith, *Answers to Gospel Questions,* vol. 3 (Salt Lake City: Deseret Book Company, 1960), 140–41. Elder John A. Widtsoe makes a similar argument in *Evidences and Recollections* (Salt Lake City: Bookcraft, 1960), 372. In reference to the appearance of Elias in the Kirtland Temple, Widtsoe writes, "Elias as a person is none other than Noah, the second great progenitor of mankind."

10. B. H. Roberts, *The Truth, the Way, the Life* (Provo, Utah: BYU Studies, 1994), 436–37.

11. "Sermon delivered at Nauvoo temple grounds on March 10, 1844." Sources: Wilford Woodruff journal, James Burgess notebook, Franklin D. Richards "Scriptural Items," Joseph Smith diary (Willard Richards), Thomas Bullock diary and the

John S. Fullmer papers, W. V. Smith, ed., and the Book of Abraham Project, www.boap.org/LDS/Parallel/1844/10Mar44.html (accessed March 2, 2009). Unless specified otherwise, I will be using Wilford Woodruff's transcription in what follows.

12. Ibid.

13. Ibid.

14. Ibid.

15. Ibid.

16. Ibid.

17. Ibid., per Franklin Richards's transcription.

18. "Sermond [*sic*] delivered at Nauvoo temple grounds on Sunday June 16, 1844." Sources: Thomas Bullock report, McIntire Minute Book, and the George Laub journal, W. V. Smith, ed., and the Book of Abraham Project, www.boap.org/LDS/Parallel/1844/16Jun44.html (accessed March 2, 2009).

19. "Sermon delivered at Nauvoo temple grounds on Sunday August 27, 1843." Sources: Joseph Smith diary (Willard Richards), Franklin D. Richards "Scriptural Items," William Clayton diary, James Burgess notebook and the Levi Richards diary, W. V. Smith, ed., and the Book of Abraham Project, www.boap.org/LDS/Parallel/1843/27Aug43.html (accessed March 2, 2009).

20. W. Jeffrey Marsh, "A Mission Long Foreknown," *Ensign* 30 (January 2001): 33.

21. Bruce R. McConkie, *A New Witness for the Articles of Faith* (Salt Lake City: Deseret Book Company, 1985), 322.

22. Ibid., 508.

23. Robert L. Millett, "The Ancient Covenant Restored," *Ensign* 28 (March 1998) paragraph 23, http://lds.org/ensign/1998/03/the-ancient-covenant-restored?lang=eng (accessed March 2, 2009).

24. Bruce R. McConkie, *The Millennial Messiah: The Second Coming of the Son of Man* (Salt Lake City: Shadow Mountain, 1982), 264.

25. *History of the Church* 1:40, The Book of Abraham Project, www.boap.org/LDS/History/HTMLHistory/v1c5history.html (accessed March 3, 2009).

26. Richard L. Bushman, *Joseph Smith: Rough Stone Rolling* (New York: Knopf, 2005), 75.

27. "Sermon delivered at Nauvoo temple grounds on March 10, 1844."

28. Ibid.

29. Bruce R. McConkie, *Doctrinal New Testament Commentary,* 3 vols. (Salt Lake City: Bookcraft, 1965), 1:404.

30. McConkie, *Mormon Doctrine,* 221 (italics in original).

31. Ibid. (italics in original). McConkie cites Joseph Fielding Smith's *Doctrines of Salvation,* vol. 1, 170–74.

32. Brown, "Prophet Elias Puzzle."

33. Ibid., 11.

34. Ibid.

35. Robert J. Matthews, ed., *Bible Dictionary* s.v. "Elias," http://scriptures.lds.org/bd/e/30 (accessed March3, 2009).

8

The Saints and the Scrolls

LDS ENGAGEMENT WITH MAINSTREAM DEAD SEA SCROLLS SCHOLARSHIP AND ITS IMPLICATIONS

Eric F. Mason

In August 1999, Daniel Peterson of Brigham Young University (BYU) delivered a campus devotional address in which he attributed to Weston Fields, a non-Mormon and managing director of the Dead Sea Scrolls Foundation, the declaration that Provo, Utah, "along with Jerusalem itself and the University of Notre Dame—[is] one of the three most active centers for [Dead Sea] scroll research in the world."[1]

No doubt such praise would come as a surprise to many people—including many biblical scholars who do not specialize in study of the Dead Sea Scrolls (DSS)—unaware of BYU's contributions in the 1990s to scrolls scholarship. But while some might quibble about the exclusion of the University of Oxford from this short list, anyone knowledgeable about research on the scrolls who heard the quotation that day could affirm its validity.

In the 1990s BYU burst into the consciousness of Dead Sea Scrolls scholars in dramatic and untraditional ways. A number of factors, however, would seem to have made this ascent extremely unlikely. As an institution of the Church of Jesus Christ of Latter-day Saints, BYU traditionally has not been a university immersed in the mainstream world of historical-critical biblical scholarship. Though the LDS Church leaders had, in the early twentieth century, encouraged Church Educational System teachers to study "cutting-edge historical and literary approaches to biblical scholarship," particularly at the University of Chicago Divinity School, such openness had fallen out of favor by the 1930s. The impact of church leaders' concern for the detrimental effects of modernism on Mormon piety was particularly felt in subsequent decades at BYU.[2]

It is certainly true that numerous prominent biblical and scrolls scholars have visited BYU or contributed to LDS publications.[3] Also, many BYU professors attend meetings of the Society of Biblical Literature (and the American Academy of Religion). Since 2005 the national SBL Annual Meeting has included thematic sections on "Latter-day Saints and the Bible," and it is now common for BYU-affiliated and other LDS scholars to present papers at SBL in a wide variety of program sections.[4] While several BYU professors in religious education have Ph.D. degrees from elite graduate programs in biblical or ancient Near Eastern studies, others have studied chiefly (or exclusively) at BYU. Similarly, many BYU professors are prolific writers; though some have published in "mainstream" biblical or religious studies publications (and the trend is increasing), most have contributed to LDS journals and books.[5] (Similar comments, of course, could also be made about many scholars in other conservative religious traditions.) Professors of Asian and Near Eastern languages and history have considerable freedom to teach mainstream textual criticism and other similar methods, as do professors in the interdisciplinary Ancient Near Eastern Studies program. Those in religious education (encompassing the fields of ancient scripture and church history and doctrine), however, are expected to emphasize faith formation and personal application more than academic biblical studies methodologies.[6]

This activity in scrolls scholarship seems further unlikely because BYU lacks a graduate program in Hebrew, biblical studies, or even the Book of Mormon.[7] While extremely puzzling to outsiders, the lack of research-oriented graduate education in ancient scriptures at BYU is consistent with the LDS practice of lay leadership in local congregations and the church's aversion to systematized theology.[8] Furthermore, in recent decades LDS Church authorities have again determined that it is preferable and beneficial—both to BYU and to the individuals—for promising students to undertake their graduate studies at outstanding non-LDS graduate schools instead of staying within the church confines for doctoral study at BYU.[9] For faculty members working on the Dead Sea Scrolls, this policy means their teaching load is more similar to that at small teaching-oriented colleges than at large research universities, and they have no graduate students in the discipline available to assist in their projects.

Despite these obstacles, BYU gained prominence in study of the Dead Sea Scrolls. Some, including Elder James E. Faust, an LDS Church official in the First Presidency, have explained this successful involvement as the fulfillment of divine prophecy (Doctrine and Covenants 105:31–32, a triumphal passage about widespread recognition of Mormonism's divine role).[10] Others reckon it as the fortuitous convergence of happenstance, high-tech inclinations, and generous LDS philanthropists. Clearly, the latter two factors played a significant role. As explained below, "official" BYU participation in Dead Sea Scrolls scholarship began in the technical realm but made possible numerous other endeavors, both in scrolls research and other scholarly arenas. At a minimum, these developments paralleled the renewed emphasis on broader engagement by BYU faculty and LDS graduate students with academic biblical studies, and in some cases direct links can be traced. At the same time, these endeavors charted a very different course for study of the scrolls by Mormons than had earlier been the norm.

Many aspects of the story of BYU's involvement in scrolls scholarship have been much publicized by the university, but to non-Mormons this information remains largely unknown, even among biblical scholars. The intent here is not to discuss every way in which LDS scholars have been involved in Dead Sea Scrolls research, but rather to focus on significant involvements—especially on an institutional level—relevant for understanding Mormon interest in and impetus toward such study, as well as the significance and ramifications of these endeavors.

The Legacy of Hugh Nibley

Hugh Nibley could rightly be called the father of Mormon studies of the Dead Sea Scrolls. Nibley, who died in 2005 at the age of ninety-four, had been a towering figure at BYU since the 1940s, and his reputation approaches mythic proportions among many Mormons.[11] Nibley published frequently in LDS circles, but earlier in his career he also placed occasional articles in journals such as *Revue de Qumrân*, the only journal (until the appearance of *Dead Sea Discoveries* in 1994) specifically devoted to study of the scrolls.[12] In recent years Nibley's essays and books have been reprinted by the Foundation for Ancient Research and Mormon Studies (FARMS) and the LDS Church–owned Deseret Book Company in a series titled "The

Collected Works of Hugh Nibley" (nineteen volumes published between 1986 and 2010).

Nibley claimed proficiency in numerous ancient and modern languages, and his academic interests ranged widely. His name is synonymous, however, with efforts to substantiate the antiquity and authenticity of the Book of Mormon through comparative study of texts from the ancient Near East, and he frequently expressed chagrin that most mainstream scholars summarily dismissed those claims. In Nibley's essays, one was likely to encounter citations from virtually *any* ancient literary corpus, presented as confirmations of the validity of various elements of the Mormon scriptures.

Nibley's work has had relatively little influence outside of Mormon circles. Terryl Givens notes his transition by the 1960s from someone engaging the broader scholarly world in favor of increasing attention to Mormon apologetics: "as his work shifted increasingly to LDS-published apologetics, the church's best hope to engage other intellectuals in refereed forums about Mormon positions ceded the field and turned to address the choir."[13] Among Mormons, however, his influence has been demonstrable. The late Truman Madsen, a younger colleague of Nibley on the BYU faculty and himself revered at the university, credited Nibley with the creative interpretation of a revelation reported by Joseph Smith that fostered Mormon interest in manuscript discoveries of the mid-twentieth century, including the Dead Sea Scrolls.[14]

Certainly Mormon interest in discovered texts had long been present. Just as Latter-day Saints esteem the Book of Mormon as an ancient record divinely hidden and later miraculously revealed, so 1 Nephi 13:39–40 mentions yet-to-be-disclosed "other books," or "last records . . . [that] shall establish the truth of the first." Similarly, in March 1833 Smith was in the midst of his project of retranslating the Christian Bible, but he was unsure whether to include the books of the Apocrypha in his edition. Smith claimed the following brief revelation, preserved in Doctrine and Covenants 91:

> [1]Verily, thus saith the Lord unto you concerning the Apocrypha—There are many things contained therein that are true, and it is mostly translated correctly;
> [2]There are many things contained therein that are not true, which are interpolations by the hands of men.

[3]Verily, I say unto you, that it is not needful that the Apocrypha should be translated.
[4]Therefore, whoso readeth it, let him understand, for the Spirit manifesteth truth;
[5]And whoso is enlightened by the Spirit shall obtain benefit therefrom;
[6]And whoso receiveth not by the Spirit, cannot be benefited. Therefore it is not needful that it should be translated. Amen.

On the surface this revelation deals only with about a dozen books whose worthiness for retention in the Christian canon had been debated at various times since the early centuries of Christianity. According to Smith, those with spiritual discernment can read with benefit the existing translation of these texts (presumably the King James Version [KJV], copies of which normally included these books in the 1800s), and he did not need to duplicate this work. But for Nibley, the key element here was the declaration that "extracanonical" texts contain elements of truth. Thus, Mormons should *expect* to find truth in newly discovered religious texts.[15] No doubt this impulse was even stronger for Nibley and his fellow LDS believers when previously unknown texts—including one inscribed on a scroll made of copper, reminiscent of Mormonism's golden plates—turned up in caves near a salty lake. Indeed, he thought support for the Mormon understanding of the gospel could be uncovered in numerous places, even when this truth would not be recognized by the possessors of the texts:

> For years the evidence of the Egyptians, Greeks, Babylonians, and so on has been brought into court as a powerful refutation of the Bible's claims to originality and inspiration. Their voices do indeed refute the claim of conventional Christianity to the absolute originality and exclusive inspiration of the Bible, but the Bible itself never made such claims. What the outside texts prove is the antiquity and universality of the gospel and its central position in the whole history of civilization. . . . But what are we to make of pagans possessing the gospel, and that from the most ancient times? We did not say that they had it but only that their records testify to it. If we examine those records we soon discover that all that their authors possess are mere fragments which they do not pretend to understand.[16]

Thus, for Nibley *any* ancient text should be examined to ascertain what truth it contains.

Nibley's approach and work inspired the formation of the Foundation for Ancient Research and Mormon Studies (FARMS). Nibley deeply impacted a cadre of young BYU alumni, including John W. (Jack) Welch.[17] Welch received an M.A. in classics as a graduate student at BYU and studied Greek philosophy at the University of Oxford before enrolling in law school at Duke University. Even during his law studies he maintained his interest in ancient texts, however, and developed a friendship with biblical scholar James H. Charlesworth, then on the Duke faculty. In 1975 Welch and several of his former BYU classmates organized a colloquium in honor of Nibley's sixty-fifth birthday. He and his peers were dispersed geographically and engaged in various careers, but they were active in the LDS Church, frequently had opportunities to address church audiences at "firesides" on subjects like those Nibley championed, and kept in close contact with each other. Their need for an organized forum for the coordination of research and distribution of resources became apparent. Welch, by this time a tax lawyer in Los Angeles specializing in nonprofit organizations, founded FARMS in 1979, and shortly thereafter he was invited to join the BYU law school faculty. After discussions with the BYU administration, he also relocated FARMS to the BYU campus, but still as an institute independent of the university. This "scholars' cooperative" (to borrow a phrase from BYU's Peterson) included several members of the BYU faculty. Though projects in the first decade of FARMS were limited to subjects directly related to the Mormon scriptures, in the late 1980s the institute nurtured the careers of several young scholars who later would contribute to DSS research, including Donald Parry, Dana Pike, Stephen Ricks, and David Rolph Seely.

If Nibley is recognized as the father of Mormon study of the Dead Sea Scrolls, his progeny took very different paths. Sensational and fanciful interpretations of the scrolls certainly are not the exclusive prerogatives of Mormons, but such ideas find a ready home in a church whose members *expect* on scriptural grounds to find new sacred texts that confirm their faith. Nibley's eclectic approach, seeking confirmation of the antiquity of Mormon tenets from disparate sources, was not without critics.[18] Yet this aspect of his legacy was extended by self-publishing pamphleteers and cassette-tape-circuit speakers.[19] On the other hand, FARMS, the organization whose very existence is indebted to Nibley's apologetic zeal, became instrumental in BYU's production of sober scrolls scholarship that avoided such a tenor.

BYU Enters Dead Sea Scrolls Scholarship

The late 1980s and early 1990s were tumultuous days for Dead Sea Scrolls scholarship, as unrest developed in the academic world over the slow pace of their publication. Significant arguments ensued over wider access to the scrolls and the legal rights of scholars working on the texts; the chair of the international team of translators was accused of making anti-Semitic remarks; and conspiracy theories accusing Christian religious groups of silencing revelations from the scrolls that might challenge theological tenets abounded. In response to these and other issues, the translation team was dramatically reorganized, resulting in a large, diverse group headed by the Israeli scholar Emanuel Tov.[20]

Meanwhile, BYU was busy establishing itself as a significant presence in Jerusalem. After conducting a Jerusalem study program for two decades in various rented facilities, BYU opened its lavish Jerusalem Center for Near Eastern Studies in 1988 on Mount Scopus near Hebrew University, Tov's institution.[21] According to Madsen, a former director of the center, BYU's intent was to establish a campus to facilitate both international opportunities for its students and scholarship programs for advanced research. Ties quickly were developed with the W. F. Albright Institute of Archaeological Research, and BYU students participated in some Albright-sponsored excavations. In addition, BYU hoped its center would be a meeting place for Jews, Christians, and Muslims; later its location near Hebrew University and in the Palestinian sector of the city would pay great dividends.

Madsen was director of the Jerusalem Center in the 1991–92 academic year when Fields invited him to join the advisory board of the Dead Sea Scrolls Foundation, which had been formed to help finance publication of the scrolls in the Discoveries in the Judaean Desert (DJD) series (Oxford University Press).[22] Madsen accepted the invitation after finding Fields forthcoming. Fields acknowledged that the invitation was prompted both by Madsen's scholarly credentials and his ties to potential Mormon donors, and soon Madsen was suggesting ways BYU scholars could participate in scrolls scholarship while also providing names of philanthropically minded LDS Church members.

Madsen discerned interest in a computerized edition of the scrolls texts, and he and William Hamblin, another BYU professor at the Jerusalem Center, began contacting leaders of FARMS about the possibility of utilizing their computer technology for such a project. Accessibility of the Qumran texts—even among scholars on the international team—had long been a major issue: texts were unavailable for study (often for decades) until they were published by their official editor, and this system created an impediment to comparative study of the manuscripts even among those scholars on the official publication team. As such, an electronic concordance of the entire corpus was quite desirable. James Rosenvall and Monte Shelley of BYU earlier had developed WordCruncher, a software program that allowed for quick, sophisticated searches of a text database, and had successfully employed the search engine with the texts of the Mormon scriptures. Though FARMS had intended eventually to incorporate electronic editions of other texts deemed relevant to interpretation of the Book of Mormon, this plan had not yet been realized. Furthermore, WordCruncher at this time lacked the capabilities of handling ancient Semitic alphabets and their right-to-left orientation, issues not faced with the English-language Mormon texts.

Leaders of FARMS eagerly embraced this opportunity, though the fledgling project faced several hurdles. The most basic of these was convincing Tov that the project was viable, and BYU's Noel Reynolds inferred that Tov was not impressed after the original demonstration in fall 1992.[23] (Tov, however, does not recall such skepticism and remembers instead an initial enthusiasm about the project, which launched "many years of fruitful cooperation.") Fields remained optimistic about the project's potential, and FARMS technicians continued to make technical advances with the software. Meanwhile, Ricks, a BYU professor of Hebrew language and by this time chair of the FARMS board of directors, helped organize a conference in northern California that included scrolls scholars Joseph Fitzmyer and Norman Golb, giving BYU more exposure in the academic community.[24] Also, Parry, a FARMS board member, recent Ph.D. graduate of the University of Utah, and faculty member at BYU, began working on the project. According to Reynolds, "Parry quickly emerged as the technical director responsible for compiling the texts that would be included in the database and for working with the software team to bring texts and program together."[25]

A subsequent meeting with Tov in early spring 1993 proved more decisive. Reynolds perceived that Tov and Fields had investigated other database possibilities and determined that the FARMS/BYU proposal was most promising. Tov asked probing questions but also seemed ready to champion the project. According to Reynolds, "It was clear that there were enormous sensitivities in the community of Dead Sea Scrolls scholars and institutions, and FARMS needed [Tov's] guidance to steer around the lethal reefs in these waters. His interest and support, however, moved the Provo project to a new level."[26]

With Tov's implicit support of the project now gained, the next steps were the delicate negotiations for rights to reproduce photographs and transcriptions of the manuscripts, as the parameters of the project included digitized images of the manuscript fragments linked to scholarly transcriptions of the nonbiblical texts. Gaining permission to include photographs of the scrolls was the easier of the two tasks. The Ancient Biblical Manuscript Center (ABMC) in Claremont, California, was one of the few institutions in the world that served as a depository of photographs of the DSS, and FARMS arranged to finance and perform digital scanning (under the direction of Steven Booras) from negatives of the Palestine Archaeological Museum and other relevant photos of the scrolls held by ABMC. The groups arranged for FARMS to give AMBC digital files in exchange for the opportunity to use these images in the FARMS database, with the caveat that FARMS also must obtain permission from the copyright holder of the photos, the Israel Antiquities Authority.[27]

The task of gaining rights to the transcriptions was much trickier. This was an era of great controversy over the intellectual property rights to scholars' work on critical editions of ancient texts. Reynolds notes that Tov was extremely concerned with this issue: "[Tov] did not know FARMS, BYU, or Mormons well. He did not know if we could be trusted not to take short cuts. Everyone else seemed willing to do that. Why should he think the Mormons would be different? Reynolds explained repeatedly that FARMS would not include any transcriptions in its collection for which it had not been able to acquire permission. For cases where permissions were not forthcoming, interim transcriptions would be prepared."[28]

Reynolds briefly raises two issues here that demand more attention. First, the success of the FARMS database would hinge on the nature of the transcriptions used. Acquisition of the rights to reproduce the transcriptions published in the DJD series would be crucial for scholarly acceptance of the project; a digital product based on nonstandard editions would have limited appeal to scholars. Though ultimately agreements to use the DJD transcriptions were reached, negotiations with Oxford University Press for these rights were difficult and lengthy.[29]

Second, Reynolds raises the question of whether Tov and other scrolls scholars hesitated to deal with BYU and FARMS because of their Mormon identity. Knowledgeable persons at BYU differ on this question. No Mormons at the time had official connections with the Dead Sea Scrolls, so there was no precedent for LDS involvement in the enterprise. (In fact, only in recent years, under the direction of Tov's predecessor John Strugnell, had the network been expanded even to include Jewish scholars, as the original team had been dominated by Roman Catholics and mainline Protestants in residence at American and European archaeological institutions in the late 1940s and early 1950s when the scrolls first came to light.) One BYU faculty member sensed an initial awkwardness in his working relationship with a veteran scrolls scholar because of the latter's previous negative encounter with Mormonism, but this situation was very quickly resolved. In fairness, most at BYU report no personal difficulties of *any* sort arising from their LDS identity and instead felt warmly embraced, especially by Tov and Fields.

Indeed, some argue that LDS identity was instead a *positive* factor. The previous absence of Mormons from international scrolls scholarship meant they were not entangled in the earlier controversies. Also, the presence of the Jerusalem Center was a tangible expression of BYU's commitment to Jerusalem and Middle East studies.[30] Though estimates for the precise amount differ, clearly contributions from LDS donors funded a significant part of the publication expenses for the DJD series.[31] *If* LDS identity had been an initial impediment, it quickly dissipated. Tov accepted an invitation to lecture on the scrolls at BYU, and in 1994 Parry and Seely were invited to join the expanding international publication team. Shortly thereafter invitations also were extended to Dana Pike and Andrew Skinner.

These four BYU scholars share deep Mormon roots, and each has a Ph.D. degree in Hebrew language or cognate studies relevant to scrolls research.

Also, while all but Skinner completed their undergraduate studies at BYU, each also earned his Ph.D. elsewhere, often mentored by prominent scrolls scholars. Parry received his Ph.D. in Hebrew language at the University of Utah but had significant study at Hebrew University in Jerusalem. His first scrolls assignment was to coedit the 1–2 Samuel manuscripts with Harvard's Frank Moore Cross for the DJD edition (volume 17), but his subsequent focus has been on Isaiah scrolls. Seely's doctoral advisor at the University of Michigan was David Noel Freedman, who published an important manuscript outside the DJD series. Seely joined Moshe Weinfield to publish 4Q434–438 (4QBarkhi Nafshi^{a-e}) in DJD 29, and the two collaborated on an additional project (see below). Pike and Skinner coedited DJD 33, a volume of unidentified text fragments from Qumran cave 4, but neither dedicated his subsequent career to scrolls study. Pike earned his Ph.D. at the University of Pennsylvania, where he had taken a course under Tov while the latter was a visiting professor; Skinner studied the scrolls with Cross and Strugnell in his Th.M. program at Harvard Divinity School before receiving his Ph.D. from the University of Denver.[32]

Rising Stock in the 1990s

The mid-to-late 1990s were heady days for BYU in the world of scrolls scholarship. The database project was progressing, and beginning in 1993, FARMS publicized the project at the annual national meeting of the Society of Biblical Literature. Reynolds recalls Fields's report that BYU's activities were the talk of the international scrolls committee a year later: "[Fields] said, 'Noel, I just wanted you to know what happened here today. Two years ago none of these people knew where BYU was or what a Mormon was. Today, half our time was spent discussing the FARMS/BYU projects and the great things the Mormons are doing for Dead Sea Scrolls studies. Provo has suddenly become an international center of Dead Sea Scrolls study.'"[33]

Numerous other scrolls-related activities for BYU soon followed. In February 1994, Tov was warmly received when he visited the BYU campus in Provo to present a lecture sponsored by FARMS. On April 30, 1995, FARMS hosted a major scrolls conference at the BYU Jerusalem Center and gave the first public presentation of the scrolls database.[34] Invitations for the conference were extended to all scrolls scholars in Israel, and papers were delivered by a variety of scholars on a number of topics. The program, however, clearly emphasized the emerging scholarship at BYU; Parry, Pike, and Seely discussed texts they were preparing for DJD editions, and other presentations concerned scientific studies of the scrolls being executed by BYU faculty members. Presentations from this conference were published in 1996 in a volume included in the major series devoted to Qumran topics, Studies on the Texts of the Desert of Judah (or STDJ, published by Brill).[35]

A much more ambitious three-day international conference was held in Provo on July 15–17, 1996. Unlike the earlier Jerusalem conference, the Provo conference was co-organized by Parry and the chief editor of the biblical scrolls from Qumran, Eugene Ulrich of the University of Notre Dame. While reports of BYU work on the scrolls again were included in the program, the speakers list was a veritable "who's who" of scrolls scholars. A massive volume of forty-three papers resulted in 1999, again published in the STDJ series. Scheduled between these conferences, on March 23, 1996, was a one-day event in Provo addressing the scrolls from an LDS perspective. All the presenters were BYU faculty members (and LDS Church members), except for Florentino García Martínez of the University of Groningen. These presentations were revised for publication in 1997 as the popular-level book *LDS Perspectives on the Dead Sea Scrolls.*

Two video documentaries from this period also reached popular audiences and spread the word on research at BYU. The first, titled *Dead Sea Scrolls: Unraveling the Mystery,* was a fifty-minute film coproduced by the Discovery Channel, KBYU Television, and Scandinature Films USA and released in 1998.[36] As one might expect from a program designed for a secular cable outlet like the Discovery Channel, the emphasis was historical and scientific. Research at BYU received significant attention, but the scholars providing expert commentary on the subject tended to be eminent non-LDS scholars.

The following year another documentary appeared, this time coproduced by the same parties, less the Discovery Channel. Like its namesake book, the video *LDS Perspectives on the Dead Sea Scrolls* was intended for a Mormon audience.[37] Though it shared numerous elements with the earlier video—and often included the same visuals and expert commentary—the tone of this documentary was much more sectarian. Numerous persons related to BYU and FARMS now entered the ranks of the "talking heads," addressing possible connections between the Qumran community and Mormonism.

As noted above, great attention was given in the BYU-affiliated conferences and documentaries to scientific work being undertaken on the scrolls by BYU faculty members. Two major projects were discussed—DNA analysis of the Qumran scrolls and synthetic aperture radar (SAR).

Scientists reported the first successful attempt to obtain DNA sequences from an extinct animal in 1984, and the following year, others reported success cloning DNA from an ancient Egyptian mummy.[38] Later, Scott Woodward, a BYU geneticist, would be part of a scientific team at the forefront of applying such technology to study of the scrolls. His work on analysis of mitochondrial DNA from ancient animal and human materials took him to Israel, where he lectured on his work on Egyptian royal mummies. There, Woodward met a scrolls scholar who asked if his technique could be applied to parchment fragments, as otherwise decisions about which fragments came from a particular manuscript chiefly were made on the basis of paleographic analysis. Upon his return to BYU, Woodward experimented with old deerskins before requesting scrolls fragments from Jerusalem. According to Reynolds, "Woodward's subsequent work in Israel [in 1994–95] proved that scroll fragments can be identified through DNA analysis according to species, to individual animals, and to closely related animals (same herds). He also has been able to show how many pages of a parchment scroll were ordinarily derived from a single hide."[39] In addition, Woodward and his colleagues proposed that other questions about the scrolls could be addressed through such DNA research, including which species of animals provided the skins for various scrolls (which might indicate how sacred certain texts were considered at Qumran) and whether various scrolls were written on parchments from differing geographical areas (which could help distinguish between scrolls written at Qumran and those brought there from elsewhere).[40]

The other major scrolls-related scientific endeavor at BYU concerned synthetic aperture radar (SAR), "an imaging system operating at microwave radio frequencies and usually flown aboard an aircraft or spacecraft [that] works by sending microwave energy pulses toward the ground and processing the return echoes to produce an image."[41] Electrical engineers David Arnold and David Long represented BYU in this project, which Reynolds described as follows: "Using expensive spy technology from the Gulf War, these two professors developed means whereby microwaves can be used inexpensively to locate ruins, objects, or cavities that are underground but near to the surface while flying over in an airplane. . . . In August and October 1996 experimental aerial surveys were conducted at Qumran and other sites in Israel and Palestine using both SAR and multispectral scanning. It may help settle the question of whether there are other caves at Qumran or in the larger Dead Sea area that might contain additional scrolls."[42]

In their major article three years later, the scientists stated that their "main purpose was not to identify possible cave locations but rather to look at the global traffic patterns and human disturbances" with the goal of "developing a regional picture of life in the area surrounding Qumran."[43] They also reported being encouraged by their results (despite the fact that their imaging was blurred because of excessive turbulence acting against their aircraft) and having received a grant from NASA to design and build superior imaging equipment.[44]

Of all of its scrolls-related projects, some people at BYU were most proud of hosting a major exhibit of manuscripts and artifacts from Qumran and Masada. Simultaneous exhibits, titled *Qumran and the Dead Sea Scrolls* and *The Story of Masada: Discoveries from the Excavation*, were on display at BYU's Museum of Art on March 13–September 18, 1997. The Masada exhibit included four original scrolls from the permanent collection of the Institute of Archaeology at the Hebrew University of Jerusalem and was cosponsored by various agencies in Israel and at BYU (including FARMS).[45] The Qumran exhibit, sponsored by FARMS and marking the fiftieth anniversary of the discovery of the first scrolls, included five original scrolls, three replica scrolls, and photographs of seven scrolls.[46]

In addition, the BYU exhibit was groundbreaking in that it also included four Qumran manuscripts on loan from the Hashemite Kingdom of Jordan. Three of these four scrolls had never previously been on public display, and none had left Jordan since 1967.[47] Fields and his wife personally transported these scrolls from Amman to Provo.[48] Not mentioned in Fields's account, however, is that Jordan required no contractual paperwork for the loan, even though no international insurer contacted (including Lloyd's of London) would underwrite a policy covering the transportation of these scrolls. Welch asserts that Jordan allowed BYU to exhibit the scrolls because the LDS Church, BYU, and FARMS had earned the trust of the administration.[49] Others at BYU surmise that the presence of BYU's Jerusalem Center in the Palestinian section of the city and BYU's longstanding nursing program in Jordan were positive factors.

This unlikely decade of scrolls activity climaxed in 1999 with the official release of the database program that began BYU's ascent to international prominence in Dead Sea Scrolls scholarship.[50] Titled *The Dead Sea Scrolls Electronic Reference Library CD-ROM, 2*, the program provided for the first time a computerized collection of transcriptions and translations—now in addition to the manuscript photos—of the nonbiblical scrolls with sophisticated search capabilities. Beyond its tremendous research value to scrolls scholars, however, it also served as an important symbol and milestone of what had been accomplished at BYU in only a few short years. This was the project that had introduced BYU to the world of scrolls scholarship, and by the time it was released as a commercial product, BYU scholars had secured their place in this corner of the academic world in numerous ways.

The Next Chapter

The inclusion of four faculty members on the international translation team, two very successful scholarly conferences and another aimed at the LDS Church audience, new scientific endeavors to study the scrolls, and a triumphant museum exhibit—not to mention the software program that initiated official LDS involvement with the scrolls—both established and solidified BYU's reputation in scrolls scholarship as a major player in the 1990s. The university also established a level of participation and anticipation that would be extremely difficult to maintain.

Individual BYU scholars, especially Parry, continue to publish on the scrolls and undertake new projects. One major project was Parry's six-volume work, *The Dead Sea Scrolls Reader* (edited with Tov).[51] This publication was significant for two reasons—it was the first print edition to organize translations of all of the nonbiblical scrolls by genre, and it formed the textual basis for the revised edition of the database, now titled *The Dead Sea Scrolls Electronic Reference Library CD-ROM Volume 3*. Released in 2006, advances in this new version included incorporation of recently identified texts, revised and corrected transcriptions and translations, and superior photographs for many manuscripts, along with more sophisticated lexical and grammatical search capabilities.[52] Work now is well underway (led by Parry, Tov, Ulrich, and Skinner) on a similar resource for the biblical scrolls, tentatively scheduled for release in late 2012.

Beyond the production of the database itself, involvement with scrolls scholarship has had significant impact on FARMS, which officially became an institute of BYU in 1997 at the persistent request of the university and later the LDS Church leadership. The first release of the database in 1999 bore the name of FARMS, but the 2006 edition is officially a product of BYU's Center for the Preservation of Ancient Religious Texts (CPART).[53] In fact, the success of the scrolls database led to other opportunities and initiatives concerning digitization of ancient religious texts—in turn leading to more scholarly outlets for BYU faculty members—and the university deemed it prudent to reconfigure the organizational chart in regard to FARMS. Thus the scrolls projects have had significant impact on BYU as an institution.

In March 2001, FARMS became one of three subsidiaries of the Institute for the Study and Preservation of Ancient Religious Texts (ISPART), which in turn was renamed The Neal A. Maxwell Institute for Religious Scholarship in 2006.[54] The reorganization was needed so as not to imply that scholarship on topics like the scrolls was being conducted for LDS apologetic purposes, as the FARMS name and legacy implied. With the change, FARMS became responsible only for projects that directly relate to interpretation of the Mormon scriptures and apologetics.[55] Projects concerning other ancient texts, such as digitizing numerous ancient texts including the Freer gospels, ancient Syriac manuscripts held by various libraries (including the Vatican Library and the Pontifical Oriental Institute), documentary papyri from Petra, and the Herculaneum papyri, often through multispectral imaging, are assigned to a second subsidiary, CPART.[56] A third subsidiary of the Maxwell Institute, the Middle Eastern Texts Initiative (METI), publishes scholarly translations of Arabic texts (both Islamic and Christian) and the medical works of the medieval Jewish philosopher Moses Maimonides.[57]

Less successful, though, were the scientific endeavors that received so much attention in the 1990s. Woodward's last published report on the DNA analysis appeared in 2001, and scrolls scholars at BYU are unaware of any official conclusion to this project.[58] As for the SAR project at Qumran, it never progressed; the turbulence-marred flight reported in the congress volume articles and broadcast in the two BYU-related video documentaries turned out to be the only attempt. Admittedly, in this case political tensions in the late 1990s and early 2000s impacted this decision. Though no further work was undertaken at Qumran, the broader project remained active; SARs can now be deployed on small unmanned drones, and two-dimensional topography maps are now possible using interferometric systems.[59]

The dissolution of plans for a scrolls exhibit at the LDS Church History Museum in conjunction with the 2002 Winter Olympics in Salt Lake City was particularly disappointing for many at BYU. It would have been the most significant Dead Sea Scrolls exhibit ever in the United States, with artifacts coming from Israel, Jordan, France, and Norway along with portions of the Leningrad Codex (the primary manuscript basis for editions and translations of the Hebrew Bible) from Russia. Advanced plans for the entire exhibit were scuttled in the wake of the terrorist attacks of September 11, 2001, when insurers balked and cancellation clauses in certain museum contracts were invoked.

Assessment

How did BYU become a center of Dead Sea Scrolls scholarship? Whether the fulfillment of prophecy or simply good fortune, several factors were in place when the opportunity arose. For over a decade, FARMS had been pursuing apologetic research in the tradition of Nibley, and the organization had begun utilizing computers for the study of Mormon scriptures. Young scholars with strong Hebrew language skills were associated with FARMS and were on the BYU faculty. Stirred both by passages in the LDS scriptures and by Nibley, Mormons were already attuned to the idea of recovering lost religious texts. Finally, generous Mormon philanthropists were eager to contribute to causes that advanced their faith, church, and BYU. Leaders at BYU effectively invested the considerable financial resources of their donors in projects that raised the academic profile of the university and provided scholarly opportunities for select faculty members. Projects undertaken by FARMS and now the various divisions of the Maxwell Institute broadened the influence and horizons of BYU significantly.

It is more difficult to explain what motivated this explosion of work on the scrolls. As noted above, Nibley had pioneered such study among Mormons, but for apologetic purposes, seeking to find religious truth in these recovered texts. Other LDS scholars with apologetic motivations make similar claims, but the definition of the "truth" being sought in other texts may appear to an outsider to be anything that agrees with or even resembles something in the Mormon scriptures.

Perhaps surprisingly to some, though, BYU scholars on the international scrolls translation team consistently *downplay* the role of apologetics in their work. Instead, their cited motivations for scrolls work tend to be much more academic and intellectual than apologetic. While LDS scholars admit certain narrative parallels (for example, at Qumran and in the Book of Mormon, faithful Jews disgruntled with corruption in the temple withdrew to the wilderness), they see these as superficial and lacking theological significance. They deny the presence of distinctly Mormon practices at Qumran, refusing, for example, to equate the Qumran washings with Mormon baptisms. By taking such an approach, these scholars depart from the kinds of positions Nibley championed.

Admittedly, these scholars write books and articles intended for two distinct audiences, the academic community on one hand and faithful Mormons on the other. Nothing hints of their Mormonism in their professional writing beyond the listing of their institutional affiliation. Theoretically this is also expected of scholars of any other (or no) religious commitment in this particular academic subdiscipline, though persons of Jewish and more traditional Christian affiliations freely consider things like interpretation of Hebrew scriptures in the scrolls and similarities between Qumran practices and ideas with those described in early Christian and rabbinic Jewish literature. Indeed, those sorts of questions are de rigueur for contemporary study of the scrolls. But LDS scholars never refer to parallels between Qumran and Book of Mormon texts in their scholarly scrolls publications, even though a key tenet of LDS faith is that the Book of Mormon is translated from an ancient text. To do so almost certainly would result in ostracism from the scholarly guild, yet this need not imply that LDS scholars working on the scrolls do so at the expense of their personal faith commitments.

LDS scholars do sometimes include comparisons with Mormon texts in their writings intended for a popular LDS audience, but these are very restrained. The essays in the book *LDS Perspectives on the Dead Sea Scrolls,* for example, bear hardly any resemblance to the use of the scrolls in Nibley's writings or those of his apologetic successors. Also, one notices disjunctions in the opinions expressed by LDS scrolls scholars and other BYU persons with interest—but not academic expertise—in the scrolls in the video documentary of the same name; consecutive speakers occasionally contradict one another on the proposed parallels between Qumran and Mormonism. Parry decided to write (with Stephen Ricks) a popular-level book after seeing a certain photocopied chart claiming to correlate doctrines of the LDS Church with those espoused in the scrolls.[60] Scrolls scholars at BYU report often spending as much or more time refuting such speculations in their firesides as they do talking about what one may actually draw from the manuscripts.

One might legitimately ask, then, which group may really claim the legacy of Nibley, the BYU scrolls scholars or the popular writers and speakers? For this observer, the verdict is mixed. The scholars are the heirs of Nibley's intellectual curiosity and commitment to study of ancient languages. The sensationalists, though, produce writings much more in line with Nibley's own apologetic objectives.[61]

Because BYU scrolls scholars have chosen to approach their academic endeavors without apologetic goals, however, involvement in this arena has opened numerous other opportunities to transcend traditional religious boundaries and engage mainstream biblical and religious scholarship in important ways. As noted above, success with the scrolls projects led to opportunities for CPART to expand its work into numerous other areas, and these technological projects also opened doors for LDS textual scholars to join the ranks of the international scrolls publication team. It now is commonplace for BYU faculty members to participate in international scrolls conferences and publications, and this successful work in scrolls textual projects has made possible a further step that will be the most significant and unprecedented contribution by an LDS scholar to mainstream biblical scholarship—coauthorship of a volume in a mainstream biblical commentary series.[62] Whether this will be an anomaly or portends greater scholarly interchange between Mormons and others on *canonical* texts remains to be seen.

NOTES

The author wishes to thank the following current and former faculty and staff members at Brigham Young University and the Foundation for Ancient Research and Mormon Studies who graciously consented to personal interviews in connection with this study: Steven Booras, Truman Madsen, Donald Parry, Daniel Peterson,

Dana Pike, Stephen Ricks, James Rosenvall, David Rolph Seely, Andrew Skinner, and John Welch. In addition, Noel Reynolds, David Long, Emanuel Tov, and several of the aforementioned BYU scholars provided valuable information by e-mail correspondence. The author expresses appreciation to Richard Bushman and Grant Underwood, directors of the 2005 NEH Summer Seminar on "Joseph Smith and the Origins of Mormonism: Bicentennial Perspectives" and Richard Lloyd Anderson (BYU) for their input on the shape of this project and for their help facilitating several of the aforementioned interviews. Special thanks are due to Parry, Pike, and Reynolds for their very helpful comments on various drafts of this paper.

Much information received in these interviews has been incorporated below, but in most cases the specific personal source has not been cited. Whenever possible, however, information relating to a particular person has been provided by that individual.

1. This statement is cited by Terryl L. Givens, *By the Hand of Mormon: The American Scripture That Launched a New World Religion* (New York: Oxford University Press, 2002), 151, who credits it to Peterson, "Ancient Documents and Latter-day Saints Scholarship" (Provo, Utah: Foundation for Ancient Research and Mormon Studies, 1999). Peterson quoted Fields in a devotional address delivered to the BYU community. Though less effusive, see also brief comments in Weston W. Fields, *The Dead Sea Scrolls: A Short History* (Leiden: Brill, 2006), 73, 120. This volume was a prelude to a fuller historical project, of which the first volume (covering the years 1947–60) has appeared: *The Dead Sea Scrolls, A Full History,* vol. 1 (Leiden, Brill, 2009).

2. Terryl L. Givens, *People of Paradox: A History of Mormon Culture* (New York: Oxford University Press, 2007), 204–10. Despite this tension, Givens notes that scientific—including evolutionary—studies have flourished at BYU.

3. Examples include Frank Moore Cross, David Noel Freedman, Florentino García Martínez, and James H. Charlesworth.

4. See below on the current trend for LDS graduate students to study outside BYU.

5. Examples of publications by LDS scholars in non-LDS venues through the late 1990s were listed (and lamented) in Carl Mosser and Paul Owen, "Mormon Scholarship, Apologetics, and Evangelical Lament: Losing the Battle and Not Knowing It?" *Trinity Journal* 19, no. 2 (1998): 179–205. (See also the more recent list of LDS scholars from outstanding graduate programs in Givens, *People of Paradox,* 233.) Mosser and Owen wrote for apologetic purposes, seeking to spur evangelical Christians to take seriously the academic sophistication of Mormon scholarship; they also observed that evangelical scholars occasionally appeal unwittingly to scholarship written by LDS persons, whether from books primarily intended for LDS readers or in "mainstream" publications like articles from *The Anchor Bible Dictionary,*

6 vols., David Noel Freedman, ed. (New York: Doubleday, 1992) or editions of three ancient texts in James H. Charlesworth, ed., *The Old Testament Pseudepigrapha*, 2 vols., Anchor Bible Reference Library (New York: Doubleday, 1983–85).

6. Study of ancient scriptures at BYU encompasses the texts of the Protestant Christian Bible (Old and New Testaments, but not books considered apocryphal by Protestants or deuterocanonical by Roman Catholics; on the latter, see below) and the uniquely Mormon scriptures, including the Book of Mormon, a narrative set chiefly in the ancient Americas spanning several centuries; Doctrine and Covenants, canonized revelations received by Joseph Smith and subsequent LDS Church leaders; and the Pearl of Great Price, a brief anthology of excerpts from Smith's other writings. All references to and quotations of uniquely Mormon scriptures are taken from the 1981 edition of the Book of Mormon, Doctrine and Covenants, and Pearl of Great Price, published by the Church of Jesus Christ of Latter-day Saints. Though Joseph Smith produced a translation and expansion of the Christian Bible and excerpts from it appear in the Pearl of Great Price, the LDS Church instead uses the Authorized (King James) Version as its official biblical text.

7. An M.A. in religious education is offered for teachers already employed in LDS seminaries and institutes and for military chaplains, and coursework for these programs includes seminars on biblical and historical topics. See www.byu.edu/gradstudies/catalog/department.php?program=141. An M.A. program in ancient Near Eastern studies was disbanded in recent years.

8. Givens observes that the distaste for theology can be traced as far back as Brigham Young and aptly describes the mood as follows: "Theology, after all, is what happens when revelation fails, in the Mormon view" (*People of Paradox*, 196).

9. See, for example, the array of outstanding graduate programs represented by recipients of the Nibley Fellowship, sponsored by the Neal A. Maxwell Institute for Religious Scholarship (htttp://maxwellinstitute.byu.edu/publications/insights/?vol=31&num=2&id=963). See below for discussion of both Nibley and the Maxwell Institute.

10. Noel B. Reynolds, "From the Caves of Qumran to CD-ROM," *Brigham Young Magazine* 50, no. 4 (November 1996): 44–52, esp. 49. The article is available online at http://magazine.byu.edu/?act=view&a=454.

11. A tribute to Nibley is available at the Foundation for Ancient Research and Mormon Studies website (http://farms.byu.edu/publications/nibleyobituary.php). Hagiographical comments about Nibley are common. He completed his Ph.D. dissertation at the University of California in a mere three *weeks*, and the Harvard New Testament scholar George MacRae is reputed to have quipped after hearing Nibley speak that "it is obscene for a man to know that much." On the former, see John W. Welch, "Foreword," in Hugh W. Nibley, *Old Testament and Related Studies*, John W. Welch, Gary P. Gillum, and Don E. Norton, eds., *The Collected Works of Hugh Nibley* 1 (Provo, Utah: Deseret Book and the Foundation for Ancient Research and Mormon Studies, 1986), vi–x, esp. viii; on the latter, see Truman G. Madsen, "Fore-

word to the First Edition," in Hugh W. Nibley, *Nibley on the Timely and the Timeless,* 2d ed., Religious Studies Center Monograph Series 1 (Provo, Utah: Religious Studies Center [BYU], 2004), xix–xxvii, esp. xxi.

12. Hugh W. Nibley, "Qumran and the Companions of the Cave," *Revue de Qumrân* 5 (1965): 177–98.

13. Givens, *People of Paradox,* 229–30.

14. Personal interview with Truman Madsen, July 21, 2005.

15. Interestingly, Donald W. Parry and Stephen D. Ricks cite this same text but in a more nuanced way: "Latter-day Saints will recognize many truths in the scrolls. Even so, the scrolls should be approached with the same caution that the Lord revealed concerning those who read the Apocrypha." See *The Dead Sea Scrolls: Questions & Responses for Latter-day Saints* (Provo, Utah: FARMS, 2000), xi.

16. Hugh W. Nibley, "The Expanding Gospel," in *Nibley on the Timely and the Timeless,* 23–52, esp. 43–44.

17. The following information concerning Welch and the origins of FARMS is based on a personal interview with Welch on July 18, 2005.

18. A classic critique from a fellow Mormon is found in Kent P. Jackson's review of *The Collected Works of Hugh Nibley,* vol. 1, *Old Testament and Related Studies,* in *Brigham Young University Studies* 28, no. 4 (1988): 114–19. Jackson notes Nibley's positive contributions but critiques his methodology in the essays of this volume, particularly in taking materials from ancient texts and modern scholars out of context in order to substantiate his own arguments.

19. Note the measured but critical words of Parry and Ricks in the preface to *Dead Sea Scrolls:* "We have also tried to avoid the sensationalism and gratuitous comparisons between Latter-day Saints and the Qumran people that have marred many publications and public presentations on the scrolls" (xii). For more explicit intra-Mormon critique of popular, sensational books on the scrolls, see S. Kent Brown, "The Dead Sea Scrolls: A Mormon Perspective," *Brigham Young University Studies* 23 (1983): 49–66. See also a very sober treatment from the early days of scrolls research, Lewis M. Rogers, "The Dead Sea Scrolls—Qumran Calmly Revisited," *Brigham Young University Studies* 2 (1960): 109–28.

20. These issues are discussed in numerous publications. See, for example, James C. VanderKam, *The Dead Sea Scrolls Today,* 2d ed. (Grand Rapids: Eerdmans, 2010), 227–47; Adam S. van der Woude, "Fifty Years of Qumran Research," in Peter W. Flint and James C. VanderKam, eds., *The Dead Sea Scrolls after Fifty Years: A Comprehensive Assessment,* 2 vols. (Leiden: Brill, 1998–99), 1:1–45; and Fields, *Dead Sea Scrolls,* 68–73.

21. For photographs and further information about the center, see http://ce.byu.edu/jc.

22. The following discussion of the history of BYU's engagement with DSS scholarship is dependent on Reynolds, "From the Caves," 44–52. Reynolds, a BYU political philosopher, was president of FARMS during this era, and his is considered by many at BYU to be the definitive account of the period. His account is supple-

mented—and occasionally challenged—by materials obtained in oral interviews and elsewhere. Though often downplayed in his own chronicle, Reynolds's personal contributions to the events were vital. Tov considers him "the driving force" behind much of what is discussed here, and he describes Reynolds as someone who "displayed much enthusiasm, interest, [and] a sincere wish to improve scholarship" and who possessed "great organizational talents and leadership." Likewise, Tov notes that Reynolds's successor, Kristian Heal, "was equally good in organizing the work and the team." E-mail communication, August 5, 2011.

23. Reynolds notes that a limited version of the revised WordCruncher software (capable of linking text and photographs but still unable to display text right to left) was demonstrated for Tov in the unfinished bomb shelter—appropriately cave-like—below BYU's Jerusalem facility. Reynolds ("From the Caves," 46) described the results in this manner: "Not visibly impressed, Tov mumbled a polite thank-you and departed. It did not seem a promising start."

24. Reynolds, "From the Caves," 47, incorrectly identifies these scholars as Joseph Fitzmeyer and Nathan Golb.

25. Ibid., 47.

26. Ibid., 47.

27. An interesting factor not mentioned in Reynolds's account of the negotiations with ABMC is that Welch, the founder of FARMS, had ties to several key persons or parties significant to ABMC from his years as a lawyer in Los Angeles in the late 1970s.

28. Reynolds, "From the Caves," 47–48.

29. See Reynolds, "From the Caves," 52, for further discussion of the negotiations with Oxford University Press and with Brill, the Dutch press that ultimately published the database. Reynolds ("From the Caves," 48) mentions that alternate arrangements for obtaining texts had been reached with Stephen J. Pfann, an assistant of Tov, who was compiling, under Tov's editorship, a database of all the scroll fragments and photographs, as well as concordances to the individual DJD volumes.

30. Madsen noted in an interview, however, that the construction of the Jerusalem Center at first was highly criticized by members of Jerusalem's Orthodox Jewish community and by numerous Christians on grounds similar to the aforementioned stereotypes. The center also later bore fruit for relations with Jordan, as noted below.

31. Fields states in an interview included in *LDS Perspectives on the Dead Sea Scrolls*, VHS (KBYU Television, 1999) that one LDS donor underwrote a full quarter of the publication costs for the DJD series (presumably for the thirty volumes appearing since the early 1990s), while the sum of all LDS contributions covered one-third of the expenses. Others suggest those estimates may be too high but still credit the LDS funding as "substantial."

32. Space does not allow for inclusion here of the full bibliographic data of these DJD volumes, but see the complete list of DJD publications at http://orion.mscc.huji.ac.il/resources/djd.shtml. Terrence L. Szink of BYU also contributed an ap-

pendix to DJD 33, but he is not an official member of the international publication team.

33. Reynolds, "From the Caves," 49.

34. Conference presentations on the FARMS database were published as Donald W. Parry and Steven W. Booras, "The Dead Sea Scrolls CD-ROM Database Project," in *Current Research and Technological Developments on the Dead Sea Scrolls: Conference on the Texts from the Judean Desert, Jerusalem, 30 April 1995,* Donald W. Parry and Stephen D. Ricks, eds., Studies on the Texts of the Desert of Judah 20 (Leiden: Brill, 1996), 239–50; and Donald W. Parry, David V. Arnold, David G. Long, and Scott R. Woodward, "New Technological Advances: DNA, Electronic Databases, Imaging Radar," in *The Provo International Conference on the Dead Sea Scrolls: Technological Innovations, New Texts, and Reformulated Issues,* Donald W. Parry and Eugene Ulrich, eds., Studies on the Texts of the Desert of Judah 30 (Leiden: Brill, 1999), 496–515, esp. 507–10. See also Donald W. Parry, Steven W. Booras, and E. Jan Wilson, "The FARMS-BYU Dead Sea Scrolls Electronic Database," in *LDS Perspectives on the Dead Sea Scrolls,* Donald W. Parry and Dana M. Pike, eds. (Provo, Utah: Foundation for Ancient Research and Mormon Studies at Brigham Young University, 1997), 207–13.

35. Bibliographic information for volumes resulting from this and the two subsequent conferences is cited in the previous note.

36. *The Dead Sea Scrolls: Unraveling the Mystery,* VHS (KBYU/Scandinature, 1998). Presumably this is the video identified as *The Dead Sea Scrolls: Voices of the Desert* in a review by prominent scrolls scholar Lawrence Schiffman. Schiffman wrote that it was "well-balanced and properly discusses the Jewishness of the material and its use for the understanding of the background of Christianity," though he also noted an "overemphasis on science and technology . . . which is partly due to the role of BYU in these areas and partly the result of the program's placement with Discovery." See Lawrence H. Schiffman, "Inverting Reality: The Dead Sea Scrolls in the Popular Media," *Dead Sea Discoveries* 12 (2005): 24–37, esp. 35.

37. See http://farms.byu.edu/multimedia/index.php?cat=DSS to view this video.

38. These advances and subsequent developments are surveyed in Scott R. Woodward, Gila Kahila, Patricia Smith, Charles Greenblatt, Joe Zias, and Magen Broshi, "Analysis of Parchment Fragments from the Judean Desert Using DNA Techniques," in *Current Research,* 215–38, esp. 217–20. Essentially the same article subsequently was republished twice over the next two years as Scott R. Woodward, "Putting the Pieces Together: DNA and the Dead Sea Scrolls," in *LDS Perspectives,* 191–205; and as pp. 497–507 within a longer article discussing several different projects, Donald W. Parry, David V. Arnold, David G. Long, and Scott R. Woodward, "New Technological Advances: DNA, Electronic Databases, Imaging Radar," in *The Dead Sea Scrolls after Fifty Years,* 1:496–513. No new reports of continued activity are included in these two subsequent versions, though a brief two-page update appeared as Scott R. Woodward, Blake C. Ballif, Lori C. Wood, Gila K. Bargal, and Magen Broshi, "Putting the Pieces Together: DNA and the Dead Sea Scrolls," in *Provo International Con-*

ference, 30–31. (Though sharing the same title, this latter article differs significantly from the longer treatment in *LDS Perspectives.*) See discussion of the final report below.

39. Reynolds, "From the Caves," 50.

40. Woodward, et al., "Analysis of Parchment Fragments," 220–27. Also implied, however, are difficulties with this approach, since one scroll could consist of skins from several animals and patches most likely would derive from yet other skins.

41. Gayle F. Miner, David V. Arnold, David G. Long, Douglas G. Thompson, Thomas W. Karlinsey, Perry J. Hardin, and Elaine M. Alger, "Archaeological Applications of Synthetic Aperture Radar (SAR)," in *Provo International Conference,* 32–43, esp. 33. A briefer account had appeared the previous year in "New Technological Advances," 510–14. Interestingly, no chapter was devoted to this project in *LDS Perspectives.*

42. Reynolds, "From the Caves," 50.

43. Miner et al., "Archaeological Applications," 39, 43.

44. Ibid., 43. It appears that no subsequent studies at Qumran were undertaken, however.

45. Numerous issues related to Masada were addressed in a volume of essays published in conjunction with the exhibit. See John F. Hall and John W. Welch, eds., *Masada and the World of the New Testament* (Provo, Utah: BYU Studies, 1997). Later, the LDS Church was a sponsor of a major scrolls exhibit at the Field Museum of Natural History in Chicago, March 10–June 11, 2000. See the undated pamphlet "Brigham Young University and the Dead Sea Scrolls." A smaller version of the Provo show (less the original manuscripts) formed the core of a traveling exhibit in the United Kingdom and Europe in 2004–05. See http://lds.org/ldsorg/v/index.jsp?locale=0&sourceId=15219150dfcad010VgnVCM1000004d82620a____&vgnextoid=7cecc8fe9c88d010VgnVCM1000004d82620aRCRD.

46. M. Gerald Bradford, "Introduction," in M. G. Bradford, ed., *Ancient Scrolls from the Dead Sea* (Provo, Utah: Foundation for Ancient Research and Mormon Studies, 1997), 1–3. This volume is an attractive catalog of the scrolls, replicas, and photographs at both the Qumran and Masada exhibits, but it was published *after* the exhibit closed, as evidenced by reflection on the number of visitors attracted to the exhibits (almost 150,000; see Bradford, "Introduction," 3). One text of particular interest to Latter-day Saints was 5/6Ḥev 44. This papyrus manuscript, inscribed with a business transaction mentioning "Alma son of Judah," dates to 134 C.E. (during the second Jewish revolt against Rome, led by Simon Bar Kokhba in 132–135 C.E.) and was found in 1961 in Naḥal Ḥever. According to David K. Geilman, "The name Alma in this Hebrew document is the oldest known occurrence of the name outside of the Book of Mormon." See David K. Geilman, "5/6Ḥev 44 Bar Kokhba," in *Ancient Scrolls,* 39. John W. Welch, "Two Windows on the Ancient World," in *Ancient Scrolls,* 13–14, notes that unfortunately this manuscript was not on display at BYU, as the wrong text was shipped from Jerusalem.

47. Weston Fields, "BYU Entrusted with Jordanian Scrolls," in *Ancient Scrolls,* 15.

48. For an account, see Fields, "BYU Entrusted," 15.

49. Welch, "Two Windows," 14.

50. Emanuel Tov and the Foundation for Ancient Research and Mormon Studies, *The Dead Sea Scrolls Electronic Reference Library CD-ROM, 2, Including the Dead Sea Scrolls Database, Edited by Emanuel Tov* (Leiden: Brill, 1999). The FARMS database was designated volume 2 because it appeared following an earlier Brill CD-ROM set that contained only images of the scrolls, Timothy H. Lim in consultation with Philip S. Alexander, *The Dead Sea Scrolls Electronic Reference Library CD-ROM, 1* (3 CD-ROMs; Oxford: Oxford University Press/Leiden: Brill, 1997). This arrangement was a condition of the compromise reached with Oxford University Press, which was primarily responsible for the Lim collection; for brief discussion, see Reynolds, "From the Caves," 52.

51. Donald W. Parry and Emanuel Tov, eds., *The Dead Sea Scrolls Reader,* 6 vols. (Leiden: Brill, 2003–2004). The contents largely were drawn from the database compiled for the 1999 database, with key additions and revisions. See the discussion in the "General Introduction" of the first volume (vii–xv).

52. The author expresses appreciation to Parry and Rosenvall for an advance demonstration of several of the new features of the database on July 21, 2005, and to Booras for additional information on the database on July 27, 2005.

53. In private correspondence, Reynolds, a former president of FARMS, stated that the Dead Sea Scrolls database program technically was under the auspices of CPART since the mid-1990s; it commonly was associated with FARMS because CPART at the time was a subsidiary of FARMS.

54. For a brief history, see http://maxwellinstitute.byu.edu/about/introduction.php.

55. Further information on the new iteration of FARMS is available at http://farms.byu.edu/about/farms.php.

56. See the CPART website (http://cpart.byu.edu) for descriptions of these projects.

57. See the METI website at http://meti.byu.edu for more information.

58. Gila Kahila Bar-Gal, Charles Greenblatt, Scott R. Woodward, Magen Broshi, and Patricia Smith, "The Genetic Signature of the Dead Sea Scrolls," in David Goodblatt, Avital Pinnick, and Daniel R. Schwartz, eds., *Historical Perspectives: From the Hasmoneans to Bar Kokhba in Light of the Dead Sea Scrolls, Proceedings of the Fourth International Symposium of the Orion Center, 27–31 January 1999,* Studies on the Texts of the Desert of Judah 37 (Leiden: Brill, 2001), 165–72. The *Temple Scroll* was found to be written on goat skins, while other fragments were of ibex.

59. The author expresses appreciation to David Long for providing this update by e-mail correspondence, July 26, 2005.

60. See note 16 above. The authors note that the format of the book is borrowed from Joseph A. Fitzmyer, *Responses to 101 Questions on the Dead Sea Scrolls* (Mahwah, N.J.: Paulist, 1992).

61. This comparison is limited only to the issue of the Dead Sea Scrolls, as FARMS certainly has many other programs that are explicitly apologetic.

62. Seely joined Moshe Weinfeld, with whom he published scrolls texts in the DJD series, as coauthor of a forthcoming volume on Deuteronomy in the Anchor Yale Bible commentary series. Formerly called the Anchor Bible series and published by Doubleday, the series was acquired by Yale University Press in 2007. Seely's graduate school mentor, David Noel Freedman, served as general editor of the series until his death in April 2008. This is a decades-old standard series, with numerous contributions by Jewish, Protestant, and Catholic scholars. Weinfeld, who died in April 2009, earlier published *Deuteronomy 1–11,* Anchor Bible (New York: Doubleday, 1991).

9
The Commencement of Mormon Studies

Richard Lyman Bushman

The papers in this volume, as Quincy D. Newell explains in the introduction, grew out of a National Endowment for the Humanities seminar on Joseph Smith held at Brigham Young University in the summer of 2005. The seminar was a product of its moment, the bicentennial of Joseph Smith's birth on December 23, 1805, coupled with the NEH's ongoing interest in seminars for college teachers. Along with scores of others, Grant Underwood and I submitted an application and were pleased to be included among the thirty-two funded that year. Doubtless the NEH saw the suitability of sponsoring a seminar on so significant a figure as Joseph Smith on the two hundredth anniversary of his birth.

This seminar, however, required more than a commemorative occasion to bring it about. Before accepting our proposal, the NEH had to satisfy itself on a number of counts: Should a federal agency fund a seminar on the founder of Mormonism held at the church-sponsored university, Brigham Young? Could free inquiry be pursued under watchful Mormon eyes? The seminar participants themselves might well have wondered if the readings and discussion would be impartial, or would they be partisan and protective? For its part, the university considered whether BYU should welcome investigations of Mormonism's much beloved founder by scholars of diverse backgrounds. Would their studies demean the Mormon prophet?

The trust that brought participants, federal money, and BYU approval together was the outgrowth of a long and complicated historiography and more than a half century of laborious effort to bridge the gap between Latter-day Saint and secular historians. Fifty years earlier, the seminar's necessary elements could never have coalesced. Until the second half of the twentieth century, Mormon and non-Mormon historians would have been incapable of cooperating in a seminar on Joseph Smith. Until then, a gulf separated Mormon accounts of their history and the story told by non-Mormon authors. In virtually all non-Mormon accounts, Joseph Smith appeared as a scoundrel—fanatical, devious, lustful—a caricature of a man. In 1903 the distinguished historian of American philosophy, I. Woodbridge Riley, posed what he called "the final question" about Joseph Smith in his Yale dissertation on the founder of Mormonism: "Was He Demented or Merely Degenerate?" Riley, an advocate of the epileptic theory of revelation—the idea that revelations were the side effect of a seizure—left the final diagnosis of Smith's dementia to the psychologists but concluded that his "psychic coordination had disappeared, and his genetic inheritance had degraded his mind and his character." "Heredity had passed down those abnormal tendencies which mark the degenerate."[1] As late as 1932, a University of Chicago Press book by George Bartholomew Arbaugh posed a similar question about Joseph Smith: "Was he only a fraud, or are we to regard him as a mixture of fraud, chance, and mental defectiveness?"[2]

Mormon scholars could not reverse this pattern. William Linn's *The Story of the Mormons: From the Date of Their Origin to the Year 1901*, the most widely used history of the Mormons for decades, assumed that any history favorable to the church was *prima facie* worthless. Of the Mormon Orson Whitney's four-volume *History of Utah*, Linn wrote: "Bishop Whitney's history presents the pro-Mormon view of the church throughout. It is therefore wholly untrustworthy." In Linn's eyes, the eminent Western historian Hubert Howe Bancroft's *History of Utah* was similarly tainted, even though he was not a Latter-day Saint. "While Bancroft's work professes to be written from a secular standpoint," Linn remarked, "it is really a church production having been confided to Mormon hands." Linn based his judgment on a comment by a church official that the church had provided materials from its archive for Bancroft's use.[3]

Mormons meanwhile presented their prophet as the paragon of virtue, continuously under inspiration from heaven, the exact opposite of the person depicted in the secular histories. Mormons practiced what Brad Gregory, an early modern historian at Notre Dame, has termed "confessional history," with the aim of creating a useable history for believers. As Gregory puts it: "Even at its best, confessional history often privileges and seeks sympathetically to understand a given tradition at the expense of explaining others in reductionist terms."[4] In that spirit, George Q. Cannon, a nineteenth-century church leader, wrote of Joseph Smith that his "lofty soul comprehended the grandeur of his mission upon earth; and with divine fortitude he fulfilled the destiny which God had ordained for him before the world was."[5] An enthusiastic biographer, John Henry Evans, writing in the 1930s, said of Smith's reputation: "Such, then, is the impression—an impression of greatness—which Joseph Smith appears to have made upon both the stranger and the disciple. It is the impression of men who knew him personally, and had met him." As for all the non-Mormon accounts of the Prophet, Evans dismissed them in a sentence. "The views of those who did not know him—and hundreds of these have been published in books and magazines—are purposely omitted here as without historical value."[6] Each side created its own history and shunned the antagonists' accounts.

For nearly a century, Mormon historiography featured these two disparate and non-communicating traditions of historical writing. The two survived not just because of the predilections and prejudices of the authors, but because of their respective audiences. Non-Mormons wrote for a critical and suspicious public who thought of Mormons as dupes or deluded fanatics—a primitive and dangerous people. The authors spoke in extreme terms because they were confident that their audience would agree. On their side, Mormons wrote for their own people, faithful believers in Joseph Smith. Their work appeared in Mormon periodicals or was published by Mormon presses. In the late 1860s and 1870s, the church began publishing magazines with titles like *The Juvenile Instructor* and *The Contributor,* and in the 1890s the church started to sponsor lesson manuals for use in church classes.[7] All served to keep Latter-day Saints in the faith. A large proportion of the work by the church's most eminent scholars and intellectuals was written for these periodicals and manuals. *The Life of the Prophet Joseph Smith,* by George Q. Cannon, a member of the First Presidency, was published by the *Juvenile Instructor.*[8] His edited series, "History of the Church," appeared in the *Juvenile Instructor* from January 1871 to February 1874. The monthly periodical *The Historical Record,* which the Danish immigrant Andrew Jensen filled with documents, local histories, biographies, and chronologies beginning in 1886, was intended for Mormon readers.[9] Although not lesson-manual copy, Whitney's *History of Utah* was sponsored by a publisher of "mug shot" histories who hoped to sell the volumes to the people featured in the book.[10] Mormons produced histories for consumption by other Mormons. It was history designed to confirm belief and support the institution, rather than to inform scholars or the general public.[11]

On the infrequent occasions when Mormons wrote for a broader audience, their work took on a different cast. The mercurial Edward Tullidge, who published laudatory accounts of Joseph Smith and Brigham Young for Utah consumption, wrote three articles for the New York *Galaxy* in 1866 and 1867 that his editors thought impartial and sophisticated.[12] Forty years later, an even more prolific Mormon historian, Brigham H. Roberts, received an invitation from *Americana,* a monthly publication of the American Historical Society, to write a Mormon history. From 1909 to 1915 he produced a chapter each month based on his extensive knowledge of Mormon sources. In 1930 a reworked and augmented version of these chapters appeared as the six-volume *Comprehensive History of the Church of Jesus Christ of Latter-day Saints: Century One,* a work Roberts accurately if immodestly called "the masterpiece of historical writings in the first century of the church's history."[13]

Roberts frankly admitted his partiality as a Mormon in writing the history. By the time he wrote the *Comprehensive History,* he was a General Authority of the church. His mother had converted to Mormonism when Roberts was a child and left him and his sister in England while she migrated to Utah with two younger children. Left in the care of an English Mormon family much given to drink, Roberts received no schooling though he passionately desired to read. In 1866, when he was nine, the church arranged for his migration to Utah, where he rejoined his mother but was still very much on his own to make a living. Working in mining camps, he learned such rough manners he was at one time disciplined by a bishop of the church. But driven by ambition, he read voraciously—Plato, Aristotle, Jonathan Edwards, Shakespeare, Emerson, Josephus, Spinoza, filling the margins and flyleaves of each book with notes—and qualified for a year of training to become a teacher. After serving a mission, he found a place as an associate editor of the *Salt Lake Herald* and began to write. On a second mission, to England this time, he served as editor of the *Millennial Star* and wrote a book on the first principles of the Gospel. Upon his return he was called as a General Authority of the church.[14]

Although an official of the church, writing to the non-Mormon readers of *Americana,* Roberts knew he could not idealize the early leaders. "They are treated as men of like passions with their fellow men." Their "earthliness, with their human limitations, was plainly manifested on many occasions." At certain points he omitted familiar Mormon miracle stories as "wholly apocryphal." Roberts acknowledged that Joseph Smith was prone to "give way to reckless denunciation" and had a tendency to "autocracy."[15] As evidence of his fairness, Roberts related the reaction of a Scottish clerk in the church president's office. On reading one of Roberts's chapters in *Americana,* the man exclaimed: "The frankness of it. The frankness o' it. How dare you do it, mon?"[16]

Roberts wrote to a broad national audience from deep inside Mormonism, and his work in its combination of partiality and balance bore the marks of his position as a church authority. Fawn McKay Brodie had moved beyond her faith before she wrote *No Man Knows My History* (1945). Brodie, born in 1915, began life in the heart of Mormonism and grew up as a faithful Mormon girl. The McKays were aristocracy in Utah—her uncle was president of the church—but her father, Thomas McKay, struggled on the poor side of the family. He was a political appointee, never very well off. Brodie's mother, Fawn Brimhall, entertained doubts about Mormonism even after her husband became Swiss-German mission president.

Brodie, who skipped three grades in elementary and high school, was in her mid-teens when she went to Weber College for two years. She first encountered skepticism about Mormonism at the University of Utah, where she completed her B.A. degree. After graduation, she taught English at Weber College and then studied at the University of Chicago for an M.A. in English. There she met Bernard Brodie, romantic, dashing, and well informed. They had a whirlwind romance and, against her family's wishes, married within six weeks. By then, Fawn Brodie's alienation from Mormonism was complete. Her biography of Joseph Smith was her farewell to Mormonism; she went on to a career as a biographer and historian, ending up on the history faculty at the University of California at Los Angeles.[17]

Although it came close, *No Man Knows My History* failed as the first entry in what has been labeled the New Mormon History. While the central aim of the New Mormon historians was to reach both Mormon and non-Mormon readers, Brodie did not speak to Mormons. She wrote for a general audience, not her own people. Her Joseph Smith was a pious fraud who made up his prophethood as he went along, a depiction sure to offend Mormons. Outraged by her work, most could not appreciate her success in portraying a Joseph Smith as a believable human being, not the caricature of the earlier biographies. Non-Mormons thought the book a favorable portrait of a colorful, engaging, exotic personality.

Among the Mormons who wrote for a wider public, Brodie and Roberts stood at opposing ends of the faith-to-disbelief spectrum, he the General Authority, she the agnostic dissenter. In the middle, Juanita Brooks, a Mormon housewife with deep roots in southern Utah, matched their accomplishments with an analysis of the most shameful episode in Mormon history, the Mountain Meadows Massacre. Brooks, with a Columbia M.A. in English, served as dean of women at Dixie College in St. George, Utah, until she married Will Brooks, a sheriff. She raised nine children and served as St. George Relief Society president for seven years while laboring on her historical studies. She dealt with an episode that darkened the memories of her neighbors, many of whom had ancestors at the massacre who had helped slaughter over a hundred defenseless migrants at Mountain Meadows in 1857. Brooks followed the evidence where it led and in 1950, at age fifty-two, produced a work of balanced scholarship that holds up a half century later.[18] The "frankness of it" was more than her Mormon neighbors could bear. Many of them never forgave her. Brooks was the quintessential amateur, a lover of her subject, whose native capacities and irrepressible ambition enabled her to write professional-level history.[19]

In a sense, Roberts, Brodie, and Brooks were all amateurs. Roberts was basically an autodidact. He began with nothing and fought his way to literacy and learning by dint of his feisty nature and hunger for knowledge.[20] He studied at the University of Deseret for a year to become a schoolteacher and taught briefly, but nothing more.[21] Brodie and Brooks had master's degrees in English. None received professional historical training.

Utah Mormons did attend graduate schools in the first decades of the twentieth century. More than a score earned doctoral degrees in history or related social sciences. A few gained positions in Utah universities, but none produced much writing on Mormon history. Ephraim Ericksen's study, *The Psychological and Ethical Aspects of Mormon Group Life* (1922), and Lowry Nelson's *The Mormon Village: A Pattern and Technique of Land Settlement* (1930) stand out as useful doctoral studies that eventually made their way into print, but most of the dissertations remained in university archives.[22] None of the degreed scholars took the lead in writing Mormon history.[23] That task was left to the amateurs, Roberts, Brodie, and Brooks.

That division of labor changed after World War II when increasing numbers of young Mormons went off to graduate school in history to seek their fortunes in the academic world. The prewar trickle turned into a stream. These students did not think of themselves as emissaries of the church. They worked for degrees to get academic jobs; they meant to be professionals. Some detached themselves from their Mormonism, but others held on to their faith, and many chose to write their dissertations on Mormon topics.

The work they produced differed from the historical writing for church periodicals. Doctoral candidates had to write for their graduate school fellows and teachers as well as their friends and fellow believers back home. That double audience affected their writing, as earlier writing for the general public had affected Tullidge and Roberts. Secular academic culture required Ph.D. candidates to find a new voice. Many later told stories of overcoming their advisers' doubts. Leonard Arrington, one of the first of this generation, took his Ph.D. at the University of North Carolina in economic history in 1952. At Arrington's defense of his dissertation on the Utah economy, his adviser, Milton S. Heath, "remarked that he and the other committee members respected my faith but were gratified that it had not affected my work."[24]

This generation wrote across the divide that had long separated Mormon writings from the world at large. They were helped by a rapprochement from the other side. In 1957 Thomas F. O'Dea, a Harvard-trained sociologist and a Catholic, wrote a broad study of Mormon history and culture that stunned Mormon readers with its objectivity and sympathetic insight. O'Dea's *The Mormons* presented a Mormonism that Mormons themselves could recognize.[25] He laid out a middle ground where it seemed possible Mormons and non-Mormons might converse.

After 1952, when Arrington finished his degree at North Carolina, the volume of work by graduate-school-trained Mormon scholars mushroomed.[26] These scholars took the lead in telling the Mormon story as the prewar-trained historians had not. By 1969 this cadre had produced enough scholarship for their work to be perceived as a movement, which the American Jewish historian Moses Rischin labeled "the New Mormon History." Much of the movement's vitality and productivity has to be credited to Leonard Arrington, who fostered and organized the work of generations of scholars. In 1965 he joined forces with other newly minted Ph.D.s to organize the

Mormon History Association. Eighty scholars turned up for the organizational meeting at the American Historical Association convention in 1965. By 1972 membership in the MHA had climbed to three hundred and a journal was contemplated.[27]

The governing impulse of the New Mormon historians was to write for both sides of the divided audience. They respected Roberts for having made the first attempt in his *Comprehensive History* and appreciated Brodie. Brodie, however, could not serve as a model, for while she softened the edges of the usual non-Mormon portrayal of Joseph Smith, she omitted believing Mormons from her intended readers. Besides presenting Smith as a fraud, she demeaned Mormon belief. New Mormon historians wrote for both Mormons and non-Mormons, as she had not. To help bridge the gap, they admitted mistakes in policy and flaws in character; they moderated the miraculous and the providential; they wrote down-to-earth academic prose like most other historians; and they stripped away the polemical and the idealistic. But throughout, their underlying respect for Mormonism was clear.

Partially in response, Mormon history by non-Mormons adopted a similarly moderate tone. The polemical indictments of the earlier years gave way to dispassionate writing in the spirit of the New Mormon History. Even critical writing was respectful. As a sign of the new fraternization, the Mormon History Association happily absorbed writers of all persuasions. The new generation of professionals created a wide arena where historians writing from many perspectives could converse without rancor. Although believing Mormons dominated the MHA, historians who explicitly questioned fundamental Mormon beliefs found a place at its meetings. Professional history offered a way of speaking and a mode of relating that made civil, academic discourse possible.

This work found an outlet in a series of independent periodicals that sprang up almost immediately after the organization of the Mormon History Association. Mormon writing a half century earlier had been confined almost entirely to officially sponsored periodicals, manuals, and books. The New Mormon historians were not dependent on church approval or church sponsorship to put their work before the public. Before the MHA founded the *Journal of Mormon History* in 1974, *Dialogue: A Journal of Mormon Thought,* an independent journal willing to deal with controversial material, served as an informal publishing arm of the association.[28] Readers of *Dialogue,* though largely Mormon, wanted the balanced, objective historical analysis stripped of the favoritism of the older confessional history that MHA writers provided.

As the ultimate mark of the movement's growing influence, church authorities appointed Arrington as church historian in 1972.[29] For a few years the New Mormon History reigned in the church historian's office. Then approval was withdrawn. Church authorities released Arrington and replaced him with a General Authority, going back to an older practice. Arrington's staff of historians moved to Brigham Young University. Although deeply disappointed by this setback, Arrington had made his mark. In 2001, the church instituted a project to publish Joseph Smith's papers according to the highest standards of documentary editing, a project Arrington had initiated. Nothing was to be held back. Every misspelled word, every internal conflict, every controversial incident was to go into the public record. The stated aim was to produce volumes that scholars of all persuasions could accept. The National Historic Public Records Commission validated the high scholarly standards of the project, an impossibility a half century earlier when mistrust of Mormon objectivity almost automatically disqualified Mormon historical work. Arrington, who did not survive to see this day, would have considered the Smith Papers project a shining example of the New Mormon History at its best. More significant still, in 2008, three church historians under an official mandate published an unflinching account of the horrors at Mountain Meadows. The church seemed ready to face up to even the most troublesome episodes in its past.[30]

All this history informed the NEH seminar on Joseph Smith in 2005. A habit of discourse practiced in countless conferences and in hundreds of books provided the confidence that a seminar at BYU, in the heart of Mormondom, involving scholars of all persuasions, would work. The seminar leaders knew by long experience how to cope with critiques and historical puzzles of every kind. The participants were accomplished academics who knew how to pursue historical questions objectively. Above all, the habit of scholarly talk had built up trust. The parties on both sides knew they could count on speech habits practiced in academic conferences and exemplified in publications for half a century. Personal commitments—perhaps even animosities and zeal—were subordinated to the canons of academic discourse.

Viewed in a longer perspective, the seminar can be seen as marking a significant reorganization of Mormon culture. For the first half of the twentieth century, far the larger part of Mormon intellectual and artistic expression had occurred in the realm controlled by the official church—in church magazines and manuals or in publications of highly sympathetic Utah presses. Almost from the beginning, the New Mormon historians moved away from Utah presses to professional journals and national presses. They wrote for an audience that the Utah presses did not reach, seeking, not unimportantly, to demonstrate to tenure and promotion committees that their work met objective professional standards. For two decades, the University of Illinois Press was the preferred outlet, a distinguished scholarly press publishing for a general academic market.[31] Gradually other publishing houses, notably Oxford University Press, discovered that Mormon scholarship had arrived at maturity and Mormon books had a market. These developments reshaped the structure of Mormon culture. The combination of outside press interest in Mormon work and the emergence of independent Mormon journals created a Mormon cultural realm outside the control of church officials. From 1965 to 1978, three independent Mormon periodicals, *Sunstone, Dialogue,* and *Exponent II* began to publish work on all aspects of Mormon culture. In the next quarter century Mormon writers turned out fiction in increasing quantities. Mormon artists developed a clientele for their paintings outside of church patronage. Signature Press, funded by a Mormon, accepted manuscripts both friendly to and critical of the church. Scores of Mormon blogs published Mormon chat on every subject. A vibrant cultural life, thoroughly Mormon but independent and unofficial, flourished outside the jurisdiction of the official church.

Perhaps recognizing that the regulation and sponsorship of Mormon culture was slipping out of official hands, various countermeasures were taken. A revived *BYU Studies,* a scholarly quarterly begun in 1959 under the sponsorship of Brigham Young University, offered an alternative to *Sunstone* and *Dialogue.* Offended by the negative tone of some pieces, the church officially advised BYU faculty and Institute teachers not to publish in these two journals. Work begun in Arrington's church history office was also regulated. Because of objections to a few passages in the original 1976 edition of *Story of the Latter-day Saints,* a book authored under Arrington's sponsorship, sales were suspended until a second edition was published in 1992.[32] Some had a lingering hope that the church could regulate the cultural productions of faithful scholars, or at least draw a line between their work and more critical studies. The impulse was to return to the previous era when pro and con histories were clearly distinguishable, when one knew one's friends and enemies. The irenic works of the New Mormon historians blurred the boundaries.

Ultimately the effort to regulate work in the independent realm receded. The energy of the New Mormon historians and the growing body of like-minded colleagues in related disciplines thwarted every attempt at control. Journals and presses were ready to publish the new work, and professional ambitions drove the growing band of scholars into print. The independent realm grew ever larger, with increasing numbers of scholars and writers making entries. By the turn of the twenty-first century, it was evident that this cultural fluorescence could not be contained. Gradually the benefits to the church became evident. All this independent work brought the Mormon story before a wider public than ever before. Strengthening the trend, a small but influential group of independent scholars led by Jan Shipps, professor of religious studies at Indiana University–Purdue University Indianapolis, won the confidence of church leaders, who came to recognize that independent voices carried more authority with the general public than officially sponsored work.

By the time the proposal for an NEH seminar on Joseph Smith came to the BYU leadership, the practice of Mormon scholarship operating in neutral space had been well established. Entertaining scholars of many persuasions and pursuing free and open inquiry into Mormon subjects had become widely acceptable. Should the seminar participants write critically about Joseph Smith, that would be no surprise. It would be considered part of the give-and-take in the realm of free inquiry. Church officials recognized that academic rules prevailed in the independent realm. Space had been opened for the seminar to convene.

The seminar, then, came at the end of changes that took place over more than half a century. It was an outgrowth of the New Mormon History and of the maturation of Mormon culture generally. But besides emerging from this past, the seminar gestured toward a still-undefined future. That future was hinted at in the great monument to the New Mormon History, the massive, 1,152-page bibliography, *Studies in Mormon History, 1830–1997*, published by the University of Illinois Press in 2000. The thousands of books and articles listed in part I of the bibliography were a tribute to the army of historians who had labored on Mormon history for half a century. The body of work constituted a collective feat that even the ever-optimistic Arrington could not have foreseen in 1952. The detailed indexing was an even greater tribute to the importance of this scholarship in the Mormon historical community. In part II, the contents of the bibliographical entries in part I were broken down into thousands of subjects: folkways; food and eating habits; Ford, Thomas; forgeries; forts, pioneer. The immense labor that went into part II (notably by the historian James Allen) was a sign of the compilers' conviction that Mormon history deserved painstaking bibliographical analysis. The scholarship had to be made accessible.[33]

The final section of *Studies in Mormon History*, part III, a nonhistorical component, however, pointed to the limits of the New Mormon History and at the same time to the future of Mormon studies. "A Topical Guide to Published Social Science Literature on the Mormons" listed by general topics the work on Mormonism by sociologists, economists, anthropologists, and political scientists. The historian-authors had not originally contemplated a social science section. It was added to the volume through the good offices of Armand Mauss, an eminent Mormon sociologist who had long been assembling social science bibliographies. The section reminded historians that they were not the only workers in the field of Mormon studies. Scholarly work on Mormonism had overflowed the bounds of the New Mormon History.

Although the editors made space for sociological studies, *Studies in Mormon History* could not recognize the immense amount of work going on in still other disciplines. The volume of that work exceeded the capacity of any single bibliographical volume. It was the work of other cohorts of Latter-day Saint students who had entered graduate school in the years when history graduate students were inventing the New Mormon History. Like the historians, these young scholars generated dissertations, articles, and books, and eventually scholarly organizations. In 1978 Mormon sociologists organized the Society for the Sociological Study of Mormon Life, soon after renamed the Mormon Social Science Association.[34] The Association of Mormon Letters was organized two years earlier. It exists to promote "the production and study of Mormon literature" and now publishes a thrice-yearly journal *Irreantum,* holds annual meetings, bestows awards, and sponsors an online discussion group.[35] The pace picked up again in the first decade of the new century. In 2003 participants at a conference on Mormon thought at Yale formed the Society for Mormon Philosophy and Theology "to promote disciplined reflection on Latter-day Saint beliefs." The Society holds annual meetings and sponsors a journal, *Element*.[36] The Association of Mormon Scholars in the Humanities held its first annual conference in 2007.[37] Latter-day Saint filmmakers have an extensive website and hold an annual festival.[38] From a broader perspective, the New Mormon History now constitutes but one section of the much larger field of Mormon studies.

Ironically, Mormons in religious studies other than theology and the philosophy of religion have yet to form an organization. Religious studies was among the last of the relevant scholarly fields to attract Mormon students. Despite their own strong religious commitments, Mormons had not felt at home among scholars who systematically studied religion. Forty years ago, Latter-day Saints rarely enrolled in divinity schools where religion as an academic field was taught. For the most part, religious denominations ran the divinity schools to train students for their respective ministries. With its lay ministry, Mormonism had no need for graduates with divinity school degrees. Young Mormons who wanted careers in religion worked for the church's seminaries and institutes, which offered classes for high school and college students and required no advanced training in religion.[39]

In recent years, however, changes in the study of religion have made graduate work in religion more suitable for Mormons. Religion has moved out of the divinity schools into the colleges. A 1963 Supreme Court decision, *Abington School District* v. *Schempp*, ruled that religion could be taught in public schools. Separation of church and state did not prohibit instructors from teaching about religion so long as they did not inculcate faith.[40] In the wake of that decision, religious studies departments have sprung up all over the country. Their proliferation has created a market for faculty, and graduate programs in religious studies have multiplied to supply the need.

Mormons have been swept up in this transformation. Mormons can be found in major religious studies programs all over the country: Harvard, Yale, the Graduate Theological Union, Chicago, Duke, Indiana, University of California Santa Barbara, North Carolina, and Claremont's School of Religion. In 2007 and 2009 conferences for Latter-day Saints in religious studies on the general theme of "Faith and Knowledge" each attracted more than forty participants. For the first time, Latter-day Saints are being exposed to disciplined and critical thinking about religion and devising dissertation topics as did the graduate students who preceded them in other fields.

Like their predecessors, these students will incorporate the methods of their academic study into work on Mormonism. They are certain to produce a scholarly literature like every other cohort of Mormon graduate students. Going beyond the study of history, sociology, and literature, they will work in philosophy, theology, ethics, ritual studies, and comparative religion. The current work of Mormon graduate students at one institution, for example, foreshadows the forms this work will take: comparisons of Joseph Smith and Paul as two charismatic leaders building up a new religious movement; investigations of the Mormon theology of revelations; studies of the ethics and theology of Mormonism's eternal family doctrine.[41] To the work already done by historians, literary critics, social scientists, and philosophers, they will add the perspective of religious studies.[42]

In the coming decades, the New Mormon History will no longer dominate Mormon scholarship as it once did. In time it will be seen as the type of scholarly work that happened to play a leading role in the second half of the twentieth century. In the future, Mormon studies will be understood as the product of many disciplines and will include many expressive forms. Work on Mormonism will come from all the humanities, the social sciences, and the arts. Together they will constitute a new wave of Mormon studies.

In the massive bibliography that this vast literature will someday require, the essays in this volume will surely have an entry. Participants in the 2005 Joseph Smith seminar came from economics, New Testament and Hebrew Bible studies, religious history, literature, film studies, anthropology, education, and theology. In the spirit of new wave Mormon studies, they went at Joseph Smith and Mormonism with the tools of many trades. Their work shows that the meaning of Joseph Smith can best be illuminated by light from many angles. They benefited from the habits of civility and objectivity instilled by the New Mormon History over half a century ago, and they worked in the independent realm formed by their predecessors. But the seminar's work went beyond the limits of the New Mormon History. Shaped by a variety of disciplines, the seminar members followed their own instincts toward what most interested them in Joseph Smith. As it grew out of the past, the seminar also looked to the future. It was like a school's commencement ceremony, both a culmination and a beginning.

NOTES

1. I. Woodbridge Riley, *The Founder of Mormonism: A Psychological Study of Joseph Smith, Jr.* (New York: Dodd, Mead, 1903), xix, 328.

2. George Bartholomew Arbaugh, *Revelation in Mormonism: Its Character and Changing Forms* (Chicago: University of Chicago Press, 1932), 227.

3. William Alexander Linn, *The Story of the Mormons: From the Date of Their Origin to the Year 1901* (New York: Macmillan, 1902), ix, viii; Orson F. Whitney, *History of Utah*, 3 vols. (Salt Lake City: George Q. Cannon and Sons, 1892–1904); Hubert Howe Bancroft, *History of Utah, 1540–1887* (San Francisco: History Company, 1890).

4. Brad S. Gregory, "On the Other Confessional History: On Secular Bias in the Study of Religion," *History and Theory* 45 (December 2006): 132–49.

5. George Q. Cannon, *Life of Joseph Smith, the Prophet* (1888; repr. Salt Lake City: n.p., 2008), 19.

6. John Henry Evans, *Joseph Smith, an American Prophet* (1933; Salt Lake City: Deseret Book Company, 1989), 7.

7. An account of the first Sunday School manual in the 1890s is found in John R. Talmage, *The Talmage Story: Life of James E. Talmage—Educator, Scientist, Apostle* (Salt Lake City: Bookcraft, 1972), 154–55.

8. Cannon, *Life of Joseph Smith.*

9. Davis Bitton and Leonard J. Arrington, *Mormons and Their Historians* (Salt Lake City: University of Utah Press, 1988), 45.

10. Ibid., 61–62.

11. One such work, "written primarily for the young men and women of the Church," was John Henry Evans, *One Hundred Years of Mormonism: A History of the Church of Jesus Christ of Latter-day Saints from 1805 to 1905* (Salt Lake City: Deseret News, 1905), quote, p. iv. A half century later the church published *History of the Church for Children: Teacher's Manual* (Salt Lake City: Deseret Sunday School Board, 1960). On pages xi–xii this volume lists the histories on which it was based. The classic confessional history is Joseph Fielding Smith, *Essentials in Church History: A History of the Church from the Birth of Joseph Smith to the Present Time, with Introductory Chapters on the Antiquity of the Gospel and the "Falling Away"* (Salt Lake City, 1922).

12. Bitton and Arrington, *Mormons*, 32–33, 36–38.

13. B. H. Roberts, *The Autobiography of B. H. Roberts*, ed. Gary James Bergera (Salt Lake City: Signature Books, 1990), 229.

14. Truman G. Madsen, *Defender of the Faith: The B. H. Roberts Story* (Salt Lake City: Bookcraft, 1980), 67–68, 83–90, 161–62, 180.

15. Bitton and Arrington, *Mormons*, 76–77, 80–82.

16. Roberts, *Autobiography*, 229.

17. Newell Bringhurst, *Fawn McKay Brodie: A Biographer's Life* (Norman: University of Oklahoma Press, 1999); and Newell G. Bringhurst, ed., *Reconsidering* No Man Knows My History: *Fawn M. Brodie and Joseph Smith in Retrospect* (Logan: Utah State University Press, 1996).

18. Juanita Brooks, *Mountain Meadows Massacre, Utah, 1857* (Stanford, Calif.: Stanford University Press, 1950).

19. Bitton and Arrington, *Mormons,* 121–23; Levi S. Peterson, *Juanita Brooks: Mormon Woman Historian* (Salt Lake City: University of Utah Press, 1988).

20. Roberts, *Autobiography,* 55–58.

21. Bitton and Arrington, *Mormons,* 71.

22. Nels Anderson, an eminent sociologist best known for *The Hobo: The Sociology of the Homeless Man* (Chicago: University of Chicago Press, 1923), had Mormon roots and wrote a significant book on the Mormons: *Desert Saints: The Mormon Frontier in Utah* (Chicago: University of Chicago Press, 1942).

23. Bitton and Arrington, *Mormons,* 97, 106. Another general account of this period's historiography can be found in Ronald W. Walker, David J. Whittaker, and James B. Allen, *Mormon History* (Urbana: University of Illinois Press, 2001), chap. 2.

24. Leonard J. Arrington, *Adventures of a Church Historian* (Chicago: University of Illinois Press, 1998), 32.

25. Thomas F. O'Dea, *The Mormons* (Chicago: University of Chicago Press, 1957).

26. I am following here the argument in Bitton and Arrington, *Mormons,* 126–46.

27. By 1989, 450 Ph.D. dissertations on Mormon topics had been submitted. Walker, Whittaker, and Allen, *Mormon History,* 92.

28. Ibid., 89. The first issue of *Dialogue* appeared in 1966.

29. Arrington, *Adventures of a Church Historian,* 58–60, 79.

30. Ronald W. Walker, Richard E. Turley, and Glen M. Leonard, *Massacre at Mountain Meadows* (New York: Oxford University Press, 2008). The postwar period in Mormon historiography is analyzed in Walker, Whittaker, and Allen, *Mormon History,* chap 3.

31. The University of Illinois Press had published forty-five Mormon titles by the end of the century. Walker, Whittaker, and Allen, *Mormon History,* 91.

32. James B. Allen and Glen M. Leonard, *Story of the Latter-day Saints,* 2d ed., rev. (Salt Lake City: Deseret Book Company, 1992).

33. The guide is now online and updated annually: http://mormonhistory.byu.edu.

34. "News Letter: Society for the Sociological Study of Mormon Life," 1, no. 1 (April 6, 1979), www.mormonsocialscience.org/files/1979-1-SSSML-text.pdf.

35. http://mormonletters.org/About.aspx.

36. www.smpt.org/index.html.

37. www.mormonscholars.org.

38. www.ldsfilm.com and www.ldsfilmfestival.org.

39. Truman Madsen, Kathryn Shirts, and Philip Barlow, all of whom studied at Harvard Divinity School, were exceptions.

40. *Abington School District* v. *Schempp,* 374 U.S. 203 (1963).

41. These topics are being pursued by Alonzo Huntsman, Paul Miller, and Deidre Green in the School of Religion at Claremont Graduate University.

42. Jan Shipps in *Mormonism: The Story of a New Religious Tradition* (Urbana: University of Illinois Press, 1985) exemplified what can be done when Mormonism is viewed via the methods and governing questions of religious studies. Terryl Givens has led the way in the study of Mormon culture using the tools of a literary historian.

Contributors

Richard Lyman Bushman is Gouverneur Morris Professor of History Emeritus at Columbia University in New York City and, more recently, visiting Howard W. Hunter Chair of Mormon Studies at Claremont Graduate University in California. Educated at Harvard College, he earned an M.A. in history and a Ph.D. in the history of American civilization from Harvard University. His first book, *From Puritan to Yankee: Character and the Social Order in Connecticut, 1690–1765* (Harvard University Press, 1967), was awarded the Bancroft Prize. He has also published *Joseph Smith and the Beginnings of Mormonism* (University of Illinois Press, 1984); *King and People in Provincial Massachusetts* (University of North Carolina Press, 1985); *The Refinement of America: Persons, Houses, Cities* (Random House, 1992); and *Joseph Smith: Rough Stone Rolling* (Alfred Knopf, 2005).

Stevan Davies is professor of religious studies at Misericordia University in Dallas, Pennsylvania. He has written several books on the New Testament apocrypha and on Christian origins, including *The Infancy Gospels of Jesus* (Skylight Paths Press, 2009); *The Secret Book of John Annotated and Explained* (Skylight Paths Press, 2005); *The Gospel of Thomas and Christian Wisdom* (new edition, Bardic Press, 2004); and *Jesus the Healer: Possession, Trance, and the Origins of Christianity* (Continuum Press, 1995). His latest project is a textbook entitled *The New Testament: An Analytical Approach* (Polebridge Press, 2011).

D. William Faupel is director of the library and professor of history of Christianity at Wesley Theological Seminary in Washington, D.C. He did his doctoral studies in the history of Christian thought at the University of Birmingham in England. He is the author of *The Everlasting Gospel: The Significance of Eschatology in the Development of Pentecostal Thought* (Sheffield Academic Press, 1996).

David Charles Gore is associate professor in the Department of Communication at the University of Minnesota Duluth. His research addresses the intersections of rhetoric and religion and rhetoric and economics, with a special interest in Mormonism and the writings of the Scottish moralist Adam Smith. His work has been published in *Philosophy & Rhetoric*, *Communication & Critical/Cultural Studies*, and *Dialogue: A Journal of Mormon Thought* as well as in other scholarly journals and books.

Eric F. Mason is professor and chair of the Department of Biblical and Theological Studies at Judson University (Elgin, Illinois). He is the author of *'You Are a Priest Forever': Second Temple Jewish Messianism and the Priestly Christology of the Epistle to the Hebrews* (Brill, 2008), general editor of *A Teacher for All Generations: Essays in Honor of James C. VanderKam* (2 vols.; Brill, 2012), and coeditor of *Reading the Epistle to the Hebrews: A Resource for Students* (Society of Biblical Literature and Brill, 2011) and *Theology in the Service of the Church: Essays Presented to Fisher H. Humphreys* (Mercer University Press, 2008). Current projects include writing an introductory commentary on Hebrews and editing volumes on 1–2 Peter and Jude, faith and faithfulness in Hebrews and the Catholic Epistles, and the Dead Sea Scrolls.

John Matzko is chair, Division of Social Science, Bob Jones University, Greenville, South Carolina, and the author of *Reconstructing Fort Union* (University of Nebraska Press, 2001). He is currently writing the first scholarly biography of evangelist Bob Jones, founder of BJU.

Quincy D. Newell is associate professor of religious studies at the University of Wyoming. Her research focuses on religion in the American West, with special attention to interracial and interreligious encounters. Her first book, *Constructing Lives at Mission San Francisco: Native Californians and Hispanic Colonists, 1776–1821*, was published by the University of New Mexico Press in 2009. Her next book, tentatively entitled *Marginal Mormons*, analyzes the religious experiences of nineteenth-century African American and Native American Mormons.

Sara M. Patterson is associate professor of theological studies at Hanover College in Indiana where she teaches courses in American religious history and the history of Christianity. Her current research focuses on sacred space and religious memory in the American West. She coedited *Race, Religion, and Region: Landscapes of Encounter in the American West* (University of Arizona Press, 2006) with Fay Botham, and her work has appeared in several scholarly journals, including *Gender and History, The Journal of Mormon History,* and *Restoration Quarterly.*

Jan Shipps is professor emerita of history and religious studies at Indiana University–Purdue University, Indianapolis, and an Andrew W. Mellon Emeritus Faculty Fellow. Although she has never been a Mormon, Shipps is a recognized authority on the Latter-day Saints and is regularly consulted by members of the media seeking informed commentary on Mormonism. She has authored and edited numerous books and articles, including *Mormonism: The Story of a New Religious Tradition* (University of Illinois Press, 1985) and the prize-winning *Sojourner in the Promised Land: Forty Years among the Mormons* (University of Illinois Press, 2000). A popular lecturer and seminar leader, Shipps is currently working on a study of Mormonism since World War II.

Grant Underwood is professor of history at Brigham Young University. He has published extensively in Mormon history and currently serves as co-chair of the Mormon Studies Consultation of the American Academy of Religion and as a member of the board of directors of the Mormon History Association.

Index

CPSIA information can be obtained at www.ICGtesting.com
Printed in the USA
LVOW042341300113

317803LV00002B/6/P

9 780806 143132